THE DRAMA
AND THE SYMBOLS

THE DRAMA
AND THE SYMBOLS

A BOOK ON IMAGES OF GOD AND
THE PROBLEMS THEY RAISE

BY

GUSTAF AULÉN

TRANSLATED BY

SYDNEY LINTON

LONDON

S·P·C·K

1970

First published in 1970
By S.P.C.K.
Holy Trinity Church
Marylebone Road
London N.W.1.

Translated from
Dramat och Symbolerna
Published in Stockholm in 1965 by
Diakonistyrelsens Bokförlag

Translation © Sydney Linton, 1970

Printed in Great Britain by
The Camelot Press Ltd,
London and Southampton

231
Au51

SBN 281 02354 9

CONTENTS

Acknowledgements

Thanks are due to the following for permission to quote from copyright sources:

Chatto & Windus Ltd and Random House, Inc: *The Sibyl* and *The Death of Ahasuerus*, by Pär Lagerkvist, tr. Naomi Walford (1958 and 1962 respectively).

Hutchinson Publishing Group Ltd and Alfred A. Knopf, Inc: *Aniara*, by Harry Martinson, tr. H. Macdiarmid and E. Schubert.

James Nisbet & Co. Ltd and Yale University Press: *The Courage to Be*, by Paul Tillich.

Stockholms Stiftsrad: an article by Kerstin Anér in *Stockholms Stiftsbok*, 1963–1964.

Quotations from the *Revised Standard Version* of the Bible, copyrighted 1952 by the Division of Christian Education of the National Council of Churches of Christ in the United States of America, are used by permission.

Quotations from the *New English Bible*, *New Testament*, copyrighted 1961 by Oxford and Cambridge University Presses, are used by permission.

PREFACE

The main theme of this book is the Christian image of God. It begins with getting our bearings. This gives some indication of the range of varied problems that mark the present-day attitude to Christian faith in God. All kinds of questions are asked, and all kinds of answers are given. This book is not going to enter into apologetics. A god who needs defending is no God. What this book sets out to do is to attempt to make clear what is the image of God that characterizes and determines Christian faith.

To make an analysis of this kind against the background of present-day questions involves dialogue with it. But there is no need always and in detail to give an account of this dialogue. For it may be implicit in what is said.

What my book offers is basically only a perspective, or if you prefer, a vision. The Christian image of God is viewed throughout in dramatic perspective. There is no attempt at all to air all the issues of the Christian faith or to set forth a Christian creed. On the other hand, the perspective presented is so fundamental and the theme discussed is so central and so far-reaching that what emerges must to some extent be a picture of the whole. Drawing the contours must necessarily touch on a wide range of problems. Almost every one of them deserves far fuller treatment than can be given here. I am only too conscious how fragmentary and inadequate this presentation has to be.

While I should have liked to discuss many questions more thoroughly than I have, there are also others which I have intentionally avoided—because they cannot really be answered. Questions of this kind have not only often been asked. They have often been answered. This illustrates the very understandable curiosity of the questioners and the incredible presumption of the theological reply. Through the ages there has always been some theology which has forgotten the words of Jesus that "the Father is in secret" and Paul's word that "we know in part".

It is obvious that the main sources of the Christian faith, the writings of Scripture, must be fundamental and basic for any study of the Christian image of God. Many of the difficulties and misunderstandings of the testimony of Scripture originate because people have not understood the symbol language of the biblical writers. This symbol language can rightly be called the mother tongue of faith. There is much of it in the Bible. Indeed in *one* context it has to be used—whenever God is mentioned. Any statement about him, about what he does or says, makes use of symbol expressions, of images taken from the world of nature or the world of man. Symbols are the tools which the Bible uses to convey what is essential for the faith in God, the relationship to God, to which it bears witness. The biblical symbols for God and their significance are misunderstood both when they are regarded as adequate definitions and when an attempt is made to eliminate them by replacing them with other definitions that are supposed to be adequate. If symbols are regarded as adequate statements, insuperable difficulties ensue and statements of belief are confused with all kinds of quasi-scientific theories and ideas. If symbols are abandoned in favour of other supposedly adequate definitions, the world of faith is left behind. The living image of God of Christian faith is exchanged for an abstract conception of God, not only alien to Christian faith, but also, if it be linked with faith's image of God, likely to expose it to fatal and destructive influences.

The biblical symbols for God are many and varied. They glow in all the colours of the rainbow. Their many rays converge to a focus where their light shines steadily and clearly. This focus point is Christ of whom the Bible says that he "reflects the glory of God". This does not mean that the God who is here "seen" ceases to be the "Invisible" who "dwelleth in secret". But it does mean that the image of God has now been defined in such a way that it cannot later be surpassed or emended. Another way to put it is that the Christian image of God is reflected in the Christ drama where God goes to war with the destructive forces of the world.

The Bible symbols vary in the extent to which they can be used in modern conditions. Many, having a timeless character, are instantly usable. Some are expressions of another age, taken from the conditions and the ideas of their time, expressions which may have changed their meaning in the course of years and therefore need interpreting. There is the same need of interpretation in many of the New Testament images and expressions which are

heavy with Old Testament associations, immediately understandable in those days but not in ours. It is things like this that give
theology a far-reaching task of interpretation, with a high degree
of importance because the Bible documents set the compass for
so much. Inescapable as it is, the Christian vocabulary is not so
tied to biblical language that no expressions may be used except
those in the Bible. Just as the biblical writers took their illustrations
from the world of their own time, so this can be done—and to a
greater or less degree has been done—in every new age. Production
of this kind of language is primarily a task for Christian preaching
and writing, and theology is thereby given new material for its
studies.

In 1927 I published a book called *Den kristna gudsbilden genom
tiderna och i nutiden*.[1] The present book might be considered a
part II of that book, but it has a very different character from the
1927 book. That book was meant as a review of the history of the
concept. The present book is concerned wholly with the present-
day problem. But it relates to another of my books published in
1930 of which the English translation with the expressive title
Christus Victor reached a wide public, and still appears to do so,
though the first edition came out in 1931.

For two reasons it is worth commenting on the relation of
Christus Victor to the present book; first because the dominant
perspective in the two books is similar; and second because
Christus Victor has been much discussed, more widely than I have
been able to follow.

Christus Victor gives in pointed phrases a sketch of the history of
the doctrine of the atonement. Three main types are specified.
The ultimate difference between them lies in their images of God.
The main type, dignified in the book as the classic Christian view,
is marked by the dominant role played by the motif of battle and
victory. This motif, here called the dramatic perspective, is the
recurrent theme of this new book. Here it is presented with greater
consistency and wider scope. God's relation to the world is throughout viewed in this perspective. In other words it is made to illumin-
ate both "law" and "gospel".

With reference to the discussion of *Christus Victor*, I should
like to make a brief comment on two recurring objections. One

[1] *The Christian Image of God through the Ages and Today* (Translator's note).

claims that the human side of Christ does not receive due recognition in my book, which therefore has "docetist" tendencies. I can well understand that some of my statements could be regarded like that. My writing was directed against the tendency of scholastic theology to divide up the work of Christ into what he did "as God" and what he did "as man". In this present book I think the human side of his work will be found to emerge clearly. It was, after all, a single and unitary course of action, which may be viewed in two perspectives—as a purely human action and as a divine act of redemption.

The objections most frequently raised have been against my treatment of the doctrines of redemption of medieval and post-Reformation scholasticism. The objectors have risen in defence of these doctrines. I admit willingly that my criticism in what had to be a brief sketch was necessarily pointed and succinct, and that the intentions behind these doctrines were valuable and far better than their final result. But these considerations do not amount to a change of view from my side. The crux of the matter is that *in the very theological structure* there was a tendency to rational explanation, a rationalization, which had fatal results for the image of God, and which—countless examples could be given—was a direct invitation to a misinterpretation of the image of God, however unintended that might be. Neither the law, which they were concerned to support, nor the gospel could be asserted as radically as was needed. On both these points the dramatic perspective opens up wholly different possibilities.

Lund, Advent 1964   GUSTAF AULÉN

1 WHICH GOD?

To attempt to give anything like an exhaustive account of the present-day state of faith in God would be a hopeless task. The literature on the subject is enormous—almost boundless. It consists not only of theological and philosophical writings. The theme is widely dealt with in modern literary works, both in prose and in poetry. This is a very sensitive barometer and therefore often is at least as interesting as theoretical treatment of the subject. Almost all conceivable attitudes are represented: negative attitudes—sometimes aggressive, sometimes passive; groping and fumbling attitudes, marked by intensive wrestling with the problem; constructive attitudes and convinced Christian attitudes; and all of them in very varying degrees.

In this chapter we shall study and analyse some of the characteristic questions and arguments. In the first section, "Does God Exist?", we face the very common question which assumes that the central problem today is whether God exists or not. The next section deals with different kinds of "atheistic" arguments. We shall try to find out on what grounds they oppose faith in God, what it actually is that they oppose, and lastly what they set in place of faith in God—if anything. The next section will analyse some Swedish literary productions, Pär Lagerkvist's book, *The Death of Ahasuerus*, and Harry Martinson's *Aniara*. These books have been selected as having different backgrounds and orientations. Ahasuerus' opposition to "the cruel god" has a kind of theological background, while the image of God of which we catch a glimpse in *Aniara* is drawn against the conceptions of natural science. The books are complementary and together illustrate important sides in the religious problems of our time. In the last section we shall sum up the observations we have made. It turns out that the question of the existence of God cannot be treated as an isolated, theoretical question. In view of that, we shall finally consider the differences in "the religious question" at the present day as compared with earlier times.

Does God Exist?

The Fourth General Assembly of the Lutheran World Federation in Finland 1963 issued a message which included a passage on the present position of Christian belief in God. It said:

Man today no longer asks: How shall I find a gracious God? His question is much more radical and fundamental. He asks: God, where are you? He does not suffer from the wrath of God, but from a sense of his absence, not from his sin but from the meaninglessness of life. He does not ask for a gracious God, but he asks *whether God really exists* [my italics].

We may well admit that this brief description of the present state of belief in God matches opinions widely held. The question whether God exists is a characteristic question of our time. Its background may be, and often is, a strong sense of the emptiness and meaninglessness of life. It is also true that ideas of this kind are used to mark the difference between the present day and earlier times. People say: Once long ago belief in God had a firm and unshaken position, whereas today it has become a problem. Earlier it could be assumed that the existence of God was granted, undisputed. It was thought that we could prove his existence beyond dispute. It was no problem. The problems with which people wrestled were on a different level. They were concerned with the relationship between God and man, as we find in Luther's famous question: How can I find a gracious God? They were concerned with the salvation of the individual. Now, however, the situation is very different. The existence of God is by no means self-evident. The old proofs of the existence of God have long lost their power to convince. The belief that the created world was well suited for its purpose, and that life had meaning—all of it regarded as a firm basis for belief in God—has vanished from sight. The situation that has now arisen is marked not only by uncertainty and agnosticism, but also by negative attitudes of rejection of any kind of belief in God.

"Atheistic" currents are now widespread. Atheism may sometimes appear as passive, indifferent, uninterested in belief in God, sometimes as aggressive and hostile. Hostility is officially sanctioned among that huge section of mankind that lives under communist regimes. "Godlessness" is on the programme of the ruling party and has become a concern of the State. It is quite a different matter that in these countries the regime has to adopt a more or less compromising attitude to the Churches there. But aggressiveness and campaigns for godlessness are by no means limited to the Communist world. They are to be found widely in the western world where there is freedom of religion. First of all, there are the radicals in literature and the arts, who regard belief in God as something left over from the past, but doomed to fade away. They talk glibly of how "secularization"—by which they mean de-Christianization—is spreading through the traditionally Christian countries, and it is part of their propaganda to talk as if the process of secularization was inevitably advancing. Taking all this into consideration, one might say that the consequence is that the main question has become whether God exists or not.

There is some justification for reflections of this kind about present-day belief in God. Modern man finds it natural to question it, and to that extent the message of the Lutheran World Federation may be said to reflect modern tendencies. But I must confess that I was not a little surprised to read the sentences I have quoted in a message, behind the production of which there must have been a good deal of theological expertise. It can hardly be denied that the message is unduly formal and stereotyped. The questions are framed in an oversimplified way that does not correspond to the real problems of religion and of belief in God. This is true right from the first contrast drawn between the question of "a gracious God" and the question posed by the meaninglessness of existence. It may of course be true that the latter question has wider perspectives than the former, which is centred on the salvation of the individual. But there is still a close connection between the two questions. It would hardly be right to imagine that the problem of individual salvation as it faced Luther had no connection or association with a sense of the meaninglessness of life. Still less can we suppose that anyone who today seeks an answer to the emptiness and meaninglessness of life will find it without coming face to face with a power that bears the mark of goodness and mercy. Merely to imagine that there was in existence something that could be called "god" would be quite irrelevant. It would not affect or alter the meaninglessness. There would still be the same emptiness. The world would still be a world without mercy, a world "without grace".

This brings me to the most stereotyped and most debatable point in this differentiation of the problem of belief in God nowadays as compared with former times. Men write as if in former times people were seeking for a gracious God, but that nowadays they are driven to ask the "radical and fundamental" question whether God really exists at all. At first sight this may appear to be a clear and straightforward question: we must know first that God exists before we can start getting into touch with him and believing in him. The alternative we face would seem primarily to be to say either Yes or No to the existence of God. To use traditional terms we should have to decide between "theism" and "atheism". But in actual fact the issue is anything but clear and straightforward. It is of course possible to say that logically belief in God assumes the existence of God. But this does not mean that it is possible to treat the existence or non-existence of God as an isolated question to be decided before any sort of relationship with him is possible. To argue like that would be to assume that the term "god" was a single unambiguous "concept". But to assume that is to live in an imaginary world. There is no such unambiguous "concept of god". And therefore it is meaningless to isolate the question of the existence of God and to regard this as the fundamental question which has to be answered first. The most varied concepts may lurk behind the word "god". The immediate reaction to such an oversimplified question is: Which god do you mean? The question whether god exists cannot be meaningful if behind the word "god" there are, it may be, a number of diametrically opposed ideas.

When the message of the Lutheran World Federation contrasted the present-day questioning of the existence of God with the Reformation search for a gracious God, the motivation given was that "the religious question" had become different from what it once was, and that it was now asked under the pressure of the absence of God and the meaninglessness of life. That this is characteristic for man today is an undoubted fact. The problems of belief in God are closely connected with the theme of meaninglessness and emptiness. There is often talk of the silence of God, the absence of God. A classic formulation, one might say, is found in Pär Lagerkvist's *Aftonland*: "Who art thou, filling my heart with thine absence? filling the whole world with thine absence?" So in this book we shall consider the problem of belief in God at different periods, and see how far we can determine different attitudes.

But *one* thing has to be said right away. Whatever differences we may think we find, they never lie in belief in God having been at one time full of problems and at another self-evident and unquestioned. To draw such a contrast would be entirely unrealistic. There is no respite from problems. Belief in God never lives without conflict. It is not as if the talk about God's silence or his absence were something new in our time. We find it right back in Old Testament days. Even then God hides himself and is silent: "Why standest thou afar off, O Lord? why hidest thou thyself in times of trouble?" (Ps. 10.1). "How long wilt thou hide thy face from me?"(Ps. 13.1). "Keep not thou silence, O God: hold not thy peace, and be not still, O God" (Ps. 83.1). "Wilt thou hold thy peace, and afflict us very sore?" (Isa. 64.12). We might also remember the verse in the Psalter repeated as one of the words of Jesus from the cross: "My God, my God, why hast thou forsaken me?" (Ps. 22.1). Many such quotations could be given, from all ages. Take one from our own times, Bishop Einar Billing's hymn. It begins with ringing confidence:

> Rejoice in the Lord, O my Spirit. . . .
> for you who have God at your side,
> your lips should be filled with his praise.

But in the last verse but one, the hard struggle for faith finds pointed expression in the words:

> O Jesu, that peace which we all
> Desire is found only in Thee.
> In darkness we stumble and fall
> When thy light we no longer can see.
> My faith is a flickering candle;
> Thy faith won on Calvary's tree.
> Thy faith must suffice, Lord, for me.[1]

Men of faith through the ages have told of the battle and dire straits that always accompany the life of faith. If this fact is obscured or minimized, inevitably belief in God and the problems

[1] No. 380 in the *Swedish Hymnal*.

connected with it will be shown in a distorted way, without light
and shade. There is sometimes a tendency to make so much of the
peculiar and novel features of the problems of faith in God in our
times that the impression is given that all connection with the
questionings of past ages is now broken. This seems to be the case
when the relationship of belief in God to the modern view of the
world is mentioned. Anyone would think that this was a brand
new problem. Now of course the questions are asked in different
ways with the passage of years. But to screen off and isolate the
question in this way is unrealistic. Differences there may be, but
the continuity is stronger than the differences. If this is not
appreciated, it may be because the questions are not recognized, or
their relationship is not recognized, when they turn up in different
clothes with a different cut. Or it may be due just to not knowing
about the past.

In this I want to stress two things. First, faith in God is always
a fighting faith, never self-evident, never unproblematic. Secondly,
the problems connected with it admittedly differ from age to age,
but we should beware of regarding them in a standardized and
stereotyped way.

We now return to the statement of the Lutheran World Federation. They made a statement on the difference in the situation of
faith in God in times past as compared with today, and specified
that the special problem of today is "the radical and fundamental
question" whether God exists or not. We have indicated that there
is undeniably some difference, but that the problem is more
complicated than would appear from their statement. We have also
indicated that the question forced upon us—whether God exists—
is by no means so clear and straightforward as might be imagined.
It would be unambiguous only if we were dealing with an unambiguous "concept of god". Whereas now the question immediately arises: Which "god" is it to whom we are to say Yes
or No?

I should like to illustrate the issues that arise here with an
example that I take from Pär Lagerkvist's book, *The Death of
Ahasuerus*. The book leads up to a description of how at last
Ahasuerus reaches his "salvation". This has two sides, one positive
and one negative. On the negative side salvation consists in
Ahasuerus' having succeeded in seeing through god, and thus in
"overcoming" him. Which god? He has been fully described in the

earlier part of the book. The god who is overcome is "a cruel god". All the suffering and all the harshness of human existence testify to the cruelty of the god who "has power". All the evil in existence —suffering, sacrifice, cruelty—reflects, and is an expression of, god's craving for power. It is on this that all of it is based. The cruelty of god is also shown in his relationship to Christ. He too is a man sacrificed by god, cursed and forsaken. And this sacrifice, required by god, is nothing but one proof among countless others of his cruelty. When at long last Ahasuerus has seen through all this, god has lost his power over him. Ahasuerus has "overcome god".

But this salvation has also a positive side. It consists in Ahasuerus "bowing his knee" at the "spring". To drink at the spring gives peace, gives "salvation". The spring here appears as a symbol of "the holy and divine", "the holy self" that exists "behind all the sacred clutter". The deity—the god who has been overcome— stands in the way of and conceals the holy and divine: "god is what divides us from the divine".

Later we shall take up the question whether and to what extent this arguing the cruelty of god and the need to fight and overcome him depend on lines of thought in historical theology. All that we do here is to confront the argument propounded by Lagerkvist's Ahasuerus with the question: Does God exist? Ahasuerus answers No. God has been seen through and overcome. He can be written off, he "does not exist". And with this denial of the existence of the cruel god Christians could immediately concur. But at the same time it would be quite wrong to describe Ahasuerus' position as "atheist", as an expression of "godlessness". The "spring" at which Ahasuerus bows the knee represents the holy and divine. It quenches thirst, it gives peace. The holy and the divine are leads played out against god and all the "sacred clutter" connected with him. He says No to god, he says Yes to the divine. To ask "Does god exist?" does not cover the questions involved in belief in god in this book about the death of Ahasuerus. Formally it denies the existence of god. But what is actually denied is nothing but one idea of god, formed in one particular way. Nothing is definitely and unambiguously stated by the use of the word "god"—and nothing either by the use of the word "atheism".

No God?

The purpose of this section is to give an outline sketch of some
of the main types of "atheist" arguments. To begin with, what is
"atheism"? This might seem an easy question: being an atheist is
denying the existence of God. It might be claimed that there are
three possible standpoints: one may acknowledge the existence of
God or in other words believe in him; one may be "agnostic" and
take the "don't know" line; or one may be "atheist" and deny the
existence of God. But it is not really as simple as that. We noticed
at the end of the last section that Ahasuerus, declaring that he had
overcome god and written him off, with deep reverence "bowed the
knee at the spring", and we found it quite unreasonable to describe
his attitude as "godless". The "spring"—a not infrequent biblical
symbol for God—for Ahasuerus represented the holy and divine.
But just as it is possible to adopt a negative attitude to one concept
of God, or even for that matter to any concept of God without
entering the sphere of godlesness, so it is also possible to say Yes
to any number of propositions about God without necessarily
entering the sphere of belief in God. Something must be said at
this point about the meaning of belief in God, though this will be
more fully dealt with in Chapter 2.

It would be difficult to find anything which better combines
genius with simplicity than Luther's comment on this in his
Large Catechism: "That on which you set your heart and in
which you trust is in reality your God." Luther's point might
also be expressed: That in which man is most deeply involved,
is his god. What a person's god is like depends on what involves
him most deeply. When Paul Tillich finds the characteristic of
faith to be that in which man is "ultimately concerned" and says
that a person's god is what he is "ultimately concerned about",
he is on exactly the same line as Luther in the *Large Catechism*.
So it is not possible to reduce the issue of belief in God or atheism
to being nothing more than an acceptance or a rejection of some
theoretical statement about "god". Christian belief in God has a
very definite content. It is not belief in any sort of "god". However, this does not mean that it is merely a matter of opinion,
lying entirely on the intellectual level. It would be perfectly

possible for a person to claim to accept what he calls the Church's teaching while what really involves him most deeply is something very different from the God he claims to acknowledge—money or power-seeking or something else. Luther illustrates perfectly consistently his point that a person's god is the power in which he trusts and that has control over him by listing these "gods" as Mammon, Power, Honour, etc. His view—a very right view—is that it is part of the Christian faith to be at war with "false gods" like these.

It is this kind of perspective that we need to keep in view when we are talking about belief in God or atheism. It is not just a matter of opinions or dogmatic statements, but of our whole way of living. Behind the word "atheism" there may lurk "gods" of many kinds. Like Ahasuerus, people may oppose and reject the deity—the god whom they think of as the God of Christian faith—without ending up in godlessness in the real sense. People may also accept assertions about the God of Christian faith and at the same time dethrone him, replace him with very different gods. One has only to take a look at Nazism during Hitler's time. It had no official atheist programme, such as Russian communism has. Admittedly it was possible for prominent Nazi leaders to make violent anti-Christian speeches. But the typical attitude was not to attack Christian faith directly. That could be allowed to exist—provided that those who held it did not oppose National Socialism. In other words the God of Christian faith was dethroned by the god called *Blut und Boden* (Blood and Soil). And this god was a most bloodthirsty Moloch, whose gas ovens demanded millions of innocent sacrifices. It would hardly be possible to demonstrate more clearly the fundamental opposition to Christian faith, the anti-Christian attitude. Reichsleiter Bormann was undoubtedly right when he said in a letter of instruction that "National Socialism and Christianity are two incompatible concepts".

In what I have written I have been drawing attention to the complications in the issue between atheism and Christian belief. Without going into all these complications or writing a history of atheism or a document on the scope or activities of atheism, I have a more modest aim: to sketch some of the main types of atheism and their relationship to Christian faith. The greatest interest will lie in their varying criticisms of Christian faith—what they criticize and why. Another interesting question is what substitute they offer for the faith they reject, if indeed they have anything to offer.

Before we start on these atheist arguments, one small point deserves notice. Atheist criticism of Christian faith may be practical or theoretical. It may be directed against the way Christian faith is put into practice and turned into action or against the way it is expressed in theory and presented as doctrine. In both cases what is criticized is how faith has made its appearance in the course of history, how it has manifested itself in the Christian Church, in the various denominations. No one disputes—least of all the Christian Church itself—that there are many grounds for criticism. Indeed it should be emphasized that there is not only criticism from outside, but also from inside the Church, a never-ceasing criticism that cuts deeper than any criticism from outside can cut. So what we have to say about atheist criticism and argument is not written as apologetics. On the contrary, some of the central problems raised by atheist critics will be dealt with in the next chapter. But even there, the purpose is not to offer apologetics but to give a plain, matter-of-fact account of what is—and what is not—essential for Christian belief in God.

If we are dealing with present-day atheism, it is natural to start with the communist ideology. Of this, atheism is a regular ingredient. Atheism is official doctrine. Of course there are communists who are not atheists, and the Communist Party of Italy has recently surprised the world with a declaration that would appear to cut the party free from atheism. Is this a precursor of coming changes elsewhere? We cannot answer that question and we shall therefore have to stick to what has always characterized the communist party elsewhere up to now, where atheism has not only been an approved theory, but has also has initiated vigorous anti-religious aggression.

The question what is to replace the religion it has discarded has been clearly answered by communism. The communist ideology replaces religion and the communist ideal society becomes the goal—a counter-aim to the Kingdom of God of Christian faith, yet related to the dreams of earthly happiness of the messianic kingdom. Religion is regarded, in the well-known words of Marx, as opium for the people, or in Lenin's words, "bad vodka". It must be attacked because it is a hindrance to the realization of the ideal society. And it has been attacked wherever communist regimes have been in power, a very large part of the world. It is quite a different matter that this principle has had to be modified in practice by settlements of one kind or another with the Churches that exist in the communist States. Modifications and concessions of this kind do not mean that the principle, the attitude, or the aim have been given up. The Communist Party is the representative of the State and this means that hostility to religion is sanctioned by the State, and is given all the enormous resources of power and propaganda of a modern State. There have often been conflicts between Church and State through the ages. But there has not been a situation like that in the present communist world since the young missionary Church in the Roman Empire faced a State that was hostile.

The communist criticism of religion is partly practical, partly theoretical. In either case it is based on the views of Marx when he on the one hand criticized the behaviour of the Churches and on the other tried to prove that religion was opposed to science and must therefore be regarded as belonging to the world of illusion. As the emphasis in the social revolutionary ideology of communism lies on the promised ideal society, very naturally the stress lay on the practical criticism, and so it is worth while seeing how this criticism looked from the horizon of Marx. When he was out to fight for a radical change in the social order of his time, his opponent was first of all the ruling powers, particularly of the Prussia of his day. It was these that were preventing the social revolution at which Marx was aiming, oppressing the "proletariat" in a harsh and inhuman way. It is at this point that the Churches come into the picture. The criticism of them is that they were in alliance with the oppressive powers of the State, giving divine sanction to a class community and supporting the idea that there ought to be a social difference between the oppressors and the oppressed. The Church was attacked for preaching resignation, for preaching that injustices could be endured because they would disappear and be compensated for in a heavenly world of the future.

It is this line of thinking and the realities which undoubtedly lay behind it that is the explanation of communist criticism of religion. The criticism remains, whatever positive initiative can be—and indeed must be—entered up on the other side of the Church's account. It is not eliminated or weakened by referring to communism's hostile and resentful attitude to the Christian faith. We must remember that it is not only oppression but also passivity in the face of social injustice that is in direct opposition to fundamental Christian duties as expressed in the commandment to love one's neighbour, and the practical care of people that this requires. Secondly, it would be contrary to the universal perspective of the Christian faith (see Chapter 2, pp. 72–88) to judge the communism of social revolution only on its hostility to religion. From the point of view of Christian faith, anything that is done in the service of other people must be regarded as evidence that the law of God, the law of creation, is functioning, whether the people doing so acknowledge God or not. This is not white-washing the Communists or saying that everything that goes on in their world is in agreement with the law of creation—far from it. But it does mean that here, as elsewhere, there is a struggle between the things that accord with this law and the things that are opposed to it, between the constructive and the destructive forces.

Communism undergirds its criticism of religion on the practical side with a criticism of its theory. This too goes back to Marx who got his ideas principally from Ludwig Feuerbach, a philosopher of the Hegelian left. His main point, as in Feuerbach, is that religion is contrary to science and must therefore be rejected as nothing but illusion. The favourite communist slogan is that all study of history must be based on materialism and that the scientific view of the world is incompatible with religion. That the argument can be conducted on a very primitive level is illustrated by the applause which greeted the assurances given by the Russian cosmonaut that he did not see any god during his trip in space.

Apart from the cosmonaut's contribution, this theoretic refutation of religion contains virtually nothing that cannot also be found elsewhere. In this refutation, the difference between communism and what is found elsewhere lies principally in the dictatorial ways and the desire to decide dictatorially what opinions may be held or may not be held in general attitudes to life and the world. What is characteristic for the communist ideology is the social revolutionary programme, issuing in the idea—or rather in the dream—of an ideal social order, the goal of striving which gives meaning to life. At this point therefore a little idealistic metaphysics creeps in. It is in sharp contrast to the rational thinking to which on good grounds people refer in the building of the social order, and which on less good grounds they use as a weapon to crush religion.

The crown of the communist ideology is thus found to be a dogma entirely without cover.

In the communist world "atheism" is official doctrine. In the West the watchword is "freedom of religion". This takes different forms in different places. But the general rule is that democratic governments assert and apply the principle of religious freedom. We shall not here deal with these different forms of freedom nor with the extent of atheism in the Christian countries of the West and how it compares with the countries under communism. But what we shall try to do is to deal with some of the customary criticism of religion, which in traditionally Christian countries quite naturally takes the form of being a criticism of Christianity.

Returning for a moment to Feuerbach, tutor of Marx and so of all communist criticism of religion, there is one point in his criticism that we did not touch on. This criticism, Feuerbach says, is fundamentally a matter of human greatness. Man's ideas of god and statements about him are a transference to an imaginary divine being of all that man values most highly. This involves belittling man. Any statement about god is really nothing but a statement about man. Criticism of religion is therefore a work of liberation of man. When "god" goes, man comes into his own. He is set free from the feelings of inferiority caused by his idea of god. The criticism of religion is summed up in the phrase: Man is for man the highest being.

Marx follows up this side of Feuerbach's criticism. But for communist ideology with its markedly collectivist line, it plays a lesser part. Yet this theme has been one of the main criticisms of Christianity through the centuries since the Reformation, even though it has grown weaker and has more or less disappeared in the present century. This kind of criticism might be called *anthropocentric*. The distinctive thing is not so much that it talks about the greatness of man, but that this greatness is played off against Christian faith in God. It need not necessarily lead to outright atheism. It is perfectly possible to hold some sort of "concept of god". But this "god" is a dethroned god. Man has taken God's place. It is he who is "the measure of all things".

It begins with the Renaissance and this beginning is no weak and tentative one. Rather it is explosive. Starting from the phrase that man is the measure of all things, it bursts into a song of praise of the greatness of man and his divine nature. One of the leading men of the Renaissance, Ficino, begins his *Letter to Humanity* with the words: "Know thyself, O divine race in mortal dress!" Man is not only God's representative on earth, but is himself "God on earth", a rival of God, who cannot bear to see in God any perfection and power which he does not own himself. A deification of man of this Renaissance type is unparalleled. Its overtones were far too shrill for its music not to grate on the ear. But this did not mean that the theme which had been struck up was to fade into oblivion. It recurs in countless variations.

It would be the easiest thing in the world to pick out any number of instances from the philosophy of eighteenth-century Enlightenment, where polemics against what they regarded as Christianity's belittling of man was a favourite subject. It was all part of the confident optimism with which they viewed life and its meaningfulness. There is plenty of this kind of criticism of Christianity in the nineteenth century put forward against the background of the optimistic perspectives, developed or encouraged by the theory of evolution. Besides Feuerbach, there was the famous nineteenth-century figure, Friedrich Nietzsche, passionate preacher of "the death of God". The god whom Nietzsche attacks and pronounces dead is the God of Christian faith—as Nietzsche imagined him. This too is part of the battle against the belittling of man. But what this belittling is, Nietzsche interprets in his own way—along the lines of the title of his book, *The Will to Power*. Christian morality is regarded as "treachery against Life". Its values, as Nietzsche lists them, "virtues" such as humility, patience, sympathy, and so on, bear the stamp of inferiority. They lay hindrances in the way of the superman. The requirement of submission to God means a disarming and a repudiation of self. Christian faith debases man, especially through its teaching on grace: that all that is good is given man "by grace".

So far we have been considering two types of atheism, both of which offer substitutes for the faith that they reject. The communist ideology of the social revolution makes the coming ideal community the substitute for the belief in God which it combats. The anthropocentric type accuses religion of stifling human dignity, and regards the elimination of belief in God as a condition for human dignity's coming into its own, so that the meaningfulness of human life shall be clearly revealed.

But nowadays there is a good deal of criticism of religion and a good deal of atheism of quite a different kind. In this the greatness and dignity of man is in no way regarded as established and dependable. Talk of this kind is regarded as highly questionable. Actually man lives in a world of illusion, if we give way to the idea that our life has value and meaning. In other words this attitude is *nihilistic*. Ideas of god are just as meaningless as everything else in life. Here there is no room for the optimism of the atheism of the social revolution or for that of the ideology associated with the proud faith in Life of the Renaissance. To rid oneself of illusions means not to believe that life has a meaning. Undeniably, of course, an attitude of this type is deeply rooted in the past. Yet there are good reasons for describing it as a characteristic attitude of our time, palpably based on the tragic experiences of our century, and well documented in much of the literature of our day. Existential philosophy is the soil from which this attitude has sprung, and one of the authors specially noted for it is the French philosopher and dramatist, Jean-Paul Sartre.

The relationship of existential philosophy to Christian faith is of course not only negative. There are possibilities of positive association, which is not surprising when it is remembered that Søren Kierkegaard—with good reason—is counted as one of the spiritual fathers of this philosophy. Rudolf Bultmann, the noted German theologian, and many others have tried to build their theology with the help of existentialism. The foremost builder of this school, E. Husserl, could be interpreted both on the positive side and on the negative. For the negative view Sartre is a representative of literary eminence. He shares Feuerbach's attitude to religion in that he regards it as self-evident that religion is nothing but a projection of the human psyche. But he does not share the view that mankind's position would be strengthened if religion were abolished. From man's point of view it is a matter of complete indifference whether "god" exists or not. Either way it changes nothing in man's situation. The idea of god has usually been associated with the idea of a rational world order. But actually there is no rational world order. Life is meaningless. Nothing can fill or change its emptiness, not even the idea of god, which is just as meaningless as life itself. Sartre describes the meaninglessness of the idea of god in his book *Being and Nothingness* in these words: the deity "is an immanence which cannot be realized, an affirmation that cannot be affirmed, an activity that cannot act".

Since man is not placed under any superior, he is *free* to act.
Freedom makes demands, but it is not fundamentally an advantage.
Instead it is man's hard lot and meaningless fate. It is admittedly
very understandable that man has tried to avoid this predicament.
But all human striving of this kind is in vain, doomed to failure.
The supposedly super-empiric reality that he projects and calls
"god" is wholly imaginary. The only wisdom to be recommended
is that which lies in overcoming illusions, in the clear insight that
life is meaningless—and in *acting* accordingly.

Behind this very brief review of various kinds of atheist argument
there lie any number of further questions. Some of these will be
treated later. For the time being we limit ourselves to a brief
consideration of this criticism, in two points. First, there is much
of this criticism with which Christianity has every reason for
agreement. This is the case with all distorted images of God, which
have been thought to be Christian, but are not. They may be
abstract metaphysical ideas of God, springing from another root,
alien to the Christian faith. But they may also be genuine Christian
ideas of God which the critic has misinterpreted and misunderstood. This may be due to the critic's not having taken the trouble
to understand—not an unusual occurrence, particularly when there
is some resentment in the background, though I must at once
confess that theology is not without guilt in this connection.
Theology too has managed to create wrong images—with serious
after-effects. All this, however, gives all the more reason to stress
the title of this chapter: Which God? In meeting criticism, it is
essential to find out which idea of God it is attacking—whether it
is a Christian image or not.

My second point is the assertion that frequently recurs in
atheist argument that belief in God is imaginary, an illusion. The
critic may say: There are no reasoned grounds for believing in
God. By reasoned grounds he means scientific grounds, and he is
trying to establish that there is a conflict between science and
faith. He may then go on to say that statements of the Christian
faith involve logical contradictions, and all this only goes to prove
how unreasonable faith in God is. The prize example is the relation
between God's omnipotence and his love: if God is omnipotent
he cannot be Love; if he is Love, he cannot be omnipotent.

The history of the encounters of faith and science is loaded with difficulties. Severe conflicts have had lasting results. Belief in God has appeared as a competitor to science, for instance in contrasting the Old Testament accounts of creation with scientific research. On the other hand, science has put forward doctrinaire claims: nothing can be said about reality except what has been gained by pure empirical research. All belief in God is therefore immediately stamped as illusion. In a situation like this, boundary lines have to be drawn. Here faith ought not to draw attention to the gaps in knowledge left open by research. Instead of that, the boundary lines must make clear the nature of the difference between the religious and the scientific aspects. No belief in God can be derived from scientific research. Neither natural science nor historic study leads to any conclusions about God. It is the task of the philosophy of religion to determine the content of the religious aspect, and to investigate the possibilities of legitimating it and its context of meaning.

If, to begin with, a boundary has to be drawn between faith and science, this does not mean that faith is to be sealed into an ivory tower to live in an isolated world of its own. This is where the other objection comes into the picture, the objection aimed at what is logically contradictory in theological statements of Christian faith. It is one of the main tasks of theology to analyse the content and meaning of Christian belief in God. This must on principle be done with the aid of the same means as are used in any other kind of research. This means that the task of theology cannot be completed without close contact with other sciences, most of all with philosophy, and in particular with the kind that specializes in language analysis. The contradictions in logic which are incontestably to be found and pointed out in theological writings, have their root cause mainly in a lack of understanding of the symbol language which is the mother tongue of faith.

From the Horizon of Literature

For a study of the present-day problems in belief in god, one useful source is to turn to modern literature in prose and poetry. This provides a very sensitive seismograph, accurately registering what is happening in the depths of human living. It reveals samples of almost every conceivable attitude to religion. If we did not already know that posing the question as the simple question whether God exists or not is not the real issue, literature gives convincing evidence that it is a far more complicated issue than a simple Yes or No—if only that both Yes and No can cover very different motivations and very different attitudes.

It has sometimes been said that Swedish literature is less involved than that of other countries in religious problems and also less positive in its attitude. This may be true—I would not dare to hazard an opinion. Quick judgements of this kind are always more or less subjective. But two things are abundantly clear. First, that great numbers of people live without any close contact with the Christian Church or with Christian faith at all—this is often described by that word of many senses "secularization". Secondly, there are plenty of writers, not least in the world of journalism, who behave with marked arrogance as soon as Christianity is mentioned. On the other hand, there is undeniably a not insignificant body of literature involved in different ways in religious questions. In the Year Book published by the Christian Humanism Association an attempt is made to give a yearly review of this category of literature. Every year there is a considerable number of books to be reviewed.

Some present-day literary documents will be analysed in this book: Pär Lagerkvist's *The Death of Ahasuerus*, and Harry Martinson's *Aniara*. Poems by Hjalmar Gullberg, and many by others, could of course be considered. But these are no haphazard choice. They are complementary to one another in various ways. There is an affinity between them of a kind that may be considered characteristic of our times. At the same time there are wide differences in the problems they discuss and the positions they take up. Lagerkvist's book on Ahasuerus has to some extent a background of theological problems. The background of *Aniara* is scientific. In analysing these books, I am not attempting to determine the degree of religious feeling of the writers or their personal attitude to Christian faith. I am not trying to draw their portrait or make a psychological investigation. My interest is in how they frame the religious question, and how they argue it, with particular reference to the image of god which openly or below the surface is found in their questions and arguments. Their attitude to Christ will also be relevant, and so will the theological assumptions that lie behind their writings.

THE DEATH OF AHASUERUS

In the writings of Pär Lagerkvist, the religious problem has been
very much to the fore for decades. In novel after novel, poem after
poem, he is constantly wrestling with this kind of question. Three
of his many novels—*Barabbas*, *The Sibyl*, and *The Death of
Ahasuerus*—have a special position here. They form a group
because they are all connected with the drama of the Passion of
Christ. This is true even of *The Sibyl*, which deals not only with
the oracle-priestess in Delphi but also with Ahasuerus who visits
her in his journey round the world. The thing that happened at the
crucifixion on Calvary is the background to what these books tell
of Barabbas and Ahasuerus. They are both, though in different
ways, deeply affected by the drama of Calvary. Relationship to the
Crucified becomes the dominating factor in their life. It is for this
reason that, far more than in Lagerkvist's earlier production, these
books come to focus on, and to wrestle with, Christian problems.
At the same time the selection of the two figures, Barabbas and
Ahasuerus, gives a natural opportunity—not so unpremeditated
as it appears—to view the drama of the Passion as a distant stranger:
Ahasuerus is a figure of legend, and Barabbas' only relation to
Jesus in the Gospel story is that he was set free in place of Jesus.
In neither case does the author have to feel bound to accept the
person of Jesus as presented in the Gospels.

The final chapter in the Ahasuerus book gives us his message as
he enters a state of enlightenment. It is a chapter packed with
meaning and consummate beauty. Ahasuerus has at last reached
the point where he sees everything clearly. He has "understood",
he has seen through "god", and he has seen who Christ is. He
has come to the conviction that there is in creation something
holy before which he is prepared "to bow the knee". When he
says he has overcome god, this does not in any way mean that he
has come to any kind of "atheism" in the traditional sense. That he
breaks with god is due to the fact that "god is what divides us from
the divine". It is not saying No for the sake of saying No. The
intention is to make possible a positive religious attitude.

So our question becomes: Which god is it that has been overcome? The answer is unambiguous: it is a "wicked" god, a "cruel"
god and therefore a "detestable" god. The reason why the image
of god has become like this is that "suffering and sacrifice are

spread over the whole earth and throughout all time". The crucified
Christ is just one among the many in an endless procession. "All
mankind is crucified"—"man lies forsaken on his bed of torment
in a desolate world, sacrificed and forsaken".

Ahasuerus has the same view of god in the earlier book, *The
Sibyl*, when he and the oracle-priestess compare their experiences.
Admittedly there is a marked and significant difference between
The Sybil and this later book, a difference in Christ. In *The
Sybil* Christ represents god; he is, one might say, an incarnation
of the wicked god. In *The Death of Ahasuerus* it is very different,
as we shall see later. There is no difference in the actual image of
god. After talking with the Sibyl, Ahasuerus sums it up: "Yes,
god was incomprehensible, cruel and frightening." "God is evil.
The Sibyl was right in that. Heartless and malignant."[1] This was
what Ahasuerus had got out of what the oracle-priestess had said.
But actually the Sibyl had said not only this, but also something
very different. And when at the end Ahasuerus asks her if she
must not hate the god who has treated her so badly, the difference
between Ahasuerus and her is very clearly shown. The Sibyl begins
by saying that she does not know who god is, and therefore
she cannot either hate him or love him.

He is not as we are and we can never understand him. He is incomprehensible, inscrutable. He is god. And so far as I can comprehend
it, he is both good and evil, both light and darkness, both meaningless
and full of a meaning which we can never perceive, yet never cease to
puzzle over. A riddle that is not intended to be solved, but to exist. To
exist for us always. To trouble us always.[2]

After this very characteristic statement, the Sibyl goes on to
describe the ambivalence that her god possesses:

The most incomprehensible thing about him is that he can also be a
little turf altar where we may lay a few ears of corn and so be at ease and
at peace. He may be a spring where we can mirror our faces, and drink
sweet fresh water from our hands.[3]

For the Sibyl herself, god has meant both happiness and unhappi-
ness. She has felt the bliss that poured from him, the wonder of
"being annihilated in his blazing arms", of "sharing god's infinite
happiness in being alive". But god has also opened his abyss for

[1] *The Sibyl*, p. 146.   [2] Ibid., p. 148.   [3] Ibid., pp. 148–9.

her, "his evil depths". When the Sibyl looks back at her life, it is of the god that she thinks: "My life is what I have lived in you. The cruel, bitter, rich life you have given me. May you be cursed and blessed!"[1]

The Sibyl's image of god is different from that of Ahasuerus. For her the god is not only repulsive, detestable, and "accursed", but at the same time attractive and "blessed", a *mysterium fascinosum*. Ahasuerus' image of god on the other hand is predominantly cruel. This is shown by what Ahasuerus has to say about the relation between god and Christ. As we have already seen, his view of Christ changes gradually. In *The Sibyl*, Christ has a special position. There he is the Mighty One, who in his exercise of power represents the god. For Ahasuerus himself this means that he is struck by the curse that he has had to bear ever since. Ahasuerus tells the oracle-priestess that in his travels he has met people who believed in the Crucified, people who "seemed quite happy". They regarded Christ as good, and loving, indeed as Love itself. But, says Ahasuerus, "For me he is a malignant power which never releases me from its talons and gives me no peace." "Of his doctrine of love, I know little, only enough to be sure that it's not for me." Ahasuerus poses the question whether he really can be loving.

It is said that he gives peace to those who believe, but that he hurls into hell those who do not believe in him. He seems then to be exactly like ourselves, just as good and just as bad. Those we love, we too treat well, and we wish the rest all the evil there is. If we had the power that he has, we too perhaps would hurl them to damnation for all eternity, though we can't be sure. Only the malignity of a god surely could be great enough for that.[2]

In *The Death of Ahasuerus*, he continues to brood about Christ and his cross. The first stage in the change that comes over him we find in a meditation where his thoughts are circling round the remarkable fact that only Christ's cross has engraved itself on the consciousness of mankind, although his cross was only one among countless others. Indeed his suffering would not have been so difficult as that of many others who have been forgotten, because their suffering had no meaning. Whereas he knew that in his suffering there was

[1] *The Sibyl*, p. 150.   [2] Ibid., p. 25.

a meaning for all time, for all men; he must have been filled with it when he went up to his sacrificial death. It would be less difficult to endure what had to be endured. . . . It could not be the most difficult thing of all to walk up a hill and let oneself be crucified.[1]

In the final chapter of the book, Ahasuerus has seen through the significance of Christ and his cross: the curse that Ahasuerus has borne did not come from Christ but from god.

It was he who cursed me, not you. I know that: I've come to under-stand that at last. You just uttered what he prompted you to say. His was the *power* and the *vengeance*. What power had you! You yourself had been handed over, sacrificed, forsaken. Now I understand: you were *my brother*. He who pronounced the curse on me was my own brother, himself an unhappy, *accursed* man.[2]

The actual cursing has thus been transferred from Christ to god. Christ is a brother in the world of suffering, one among many in the world of crucified humanity. He has no special position. From this new starting-point Ahasuerus now speaks to Christ: "Who was it who made them crucify you, who consigned you to suffering and death? Who sacrificed you—you whom he called his own son, who made you believe you were so? Who demanded this sacrifice, which he demanded of so many others—the sacrifice that was never to be forgotten, the sacrifice of the chosen one himself? Who offered up the Son of Man?

You should know; you should know what he's like—you who persist in calling him your father, though he has never cared about you, never shown that he loves you; though he let you hang there when you cried out to him in your deepest despair: "Why have you forsaken me?" Have you forgotten this? Have you forgotten how he forsook you?[3]

Ahasuerus has at this point acquitted Christ; he has no longer any accusations to make against him. These accusations lapsed when Christ lost his special position. He was acquitted because he is on the same level as Ahasuerus. Like him, he is cursed and sacrificed, sacrificed by the god who "demands continual sacrifice —human sacrifice, crucifixion".

So Ahasuerus is finished with Christ. But he is also finished with god:

---

[1] *The Death of Ahasuerus*, pp. 55–6.   [2] Ibid., pp. 84–5 (my italics).
[3] Ibid., p. 84.

Now I understand it all. For now I have torn down the veil of the holy of holies and seen who he is. Now at last he has lost his power over me. At last I have overcome him—at last I have vanquished god! I have lifted the curse from my own shoulders. I have delivered myself from my destiny and mastered it. Not with your help or anyone else's, but my own strength. *I have saved myself*. I have conquered god.[1]

But this dethroning of god does not mean that Ahasuerus is finished with the religious problem, still less that he is taking up a position of irreligion or non-religion. This would of course have been the situation if he had stopped at "saving himself". If one saves oneself, it must mean one is self-sufficient, with no need to rely on anything but one's own capacity. Whereas religion, a religious relationship, always means that a person is somehow conscious of, and comes into contact with, something above himself, something superhuman, something to which humanity— to use Ahasuerus' own phrase—"bows the knee". When Ahasuerus begins to say what salvation means positively, it is all stamped with clear and deep religious feeling.

So Ahasuerus has *not* won salvation only through overcoming god. From his own point of view this victory should rather be regarded as a removing of certain intellectual barriers which for him had barred the way to salvation. That way he finds only when he has discovered and become convinced that "beyond all the sacred clutter the holy thing itself must exist".

Beyond the gods, beyond all that falsifies and coarsens the world of holiness, beyond all lies and distortion, all twisted divinities and all the abortions of human imagination, there must be something stupendous which is inaccessible to us. Which, by our very failure to capture it, demonstrates how inaccessible it is.[2]

But however much this inaccessibility is stressed, Ahasuerus still tries to visualize this holy and divine something through an image. The symbol he uses is "the spring". The god who divides us from the divine

hinders us from drinking at the spring itself. To god I do not kneel—no, and I never will. But I would gladly lie down at the spring to drink from it—to quench my thirst, my burning thirst for what I cannot conceive of, but which I know exists. At the spring I would gladly kneel. And perhaps that is what I'm doing now. Now that the battle is over at last and I may die. Now that at last I have won peace.[3]

[1] *The Death of Ahasuerus*, p. 85 (my italics).   [2] Ibid., p. 86.   [3] Ibid., p. 87.
CD

When Ahasuerus talks about how he has vanquished god, he points out in various terms that he had saved himself, that this had come about without the help of anyone else. But the whole of this aspect vanishes when he describes how he made this redemptive discovery. Here Ahasuerus declares in plain language that he was given help by someone else. This someone else is the peculiar pilgrim whose company he shared on his last journey.

There must be something [says Ahasuerus] which for man is of the utmost importance. *That he made me understand.* Something so important that it were better to lose one's life rather than one's faith in that thing.[1]

So the insight which saved him has been given to him through the help of a fellow man.

The importance for Ahasuerus of this man, Tobias, requires some consideration. Tobias is by no means presented as a strong helper, inspiring confidence. He is no pilgrim with confident faith. On the contrary, he is in perpetual doubt whether he really ought to be regarded as a pilgrim or not. Sometimes Tobias wants to give it all up: "It's not for me. For I don't believe in anything, and I hold nothing sacred, so far as I know. So how could I ever be a pilgrim?" His doubts go on like this all the time while Ahasuerus and Tobias are following slowly behind the other pilgrims towards the harbour from which they were to sail. Ahasuerus listens to Tobias' uncertainty and doubt and concludes: "Yes, he was indeed uncertain about everything." Tobias asks: "Tell me what it is I long for! I don't understand."

When the two travellers reach the harbour at long length, the pilgrim boat to the holy land has already gone. Tobias is overwhelmed. In this state of mind he suddenly leaves Ahasuerus. Now he wants to get away at any price. Ahasuerus looks for him at the harbour and sees at a distance how Tobias gets hold of a vessel with a crew of scoundrels who got all Tobias' money from him and said they would take him to the pilgrim country. Finally Ahasuerus sees the vessel disappear in the storm and darkness.

So it is this lost soul with all his doubts who convinces Ahasuerus that there is something so important that it is better to lose one's life than to lose faith in it. Ahasuerus indicates that it is the final scene—the eagerness of Tobias to get away whatever the cost—that decided him.

[1] *The Death of Ahasuerus*, p. 86 (my italics).

What he longed for, I don't know, but it must have been something of the utmost importance. Even if he perished in the storm, even if the rabble on that boat cheated him and perhaps carried him off to some quite other place, what he longed for must nevertheless have been of the utmost importance. That I have understood. There must be something that for mankind is of the utmost importance. *That he made me understand.*[1]

One wonders why it was a person of this type who convinced Ahasuerus. It seems quite unreasonable. It is hardly possible to give any definite answer. But there must be some significance in the fact that Tobias was so much a man of doubts, a man who had hardly got as far as: I believe—help thou my unbelief. It has been easier for Ahasuerus to feel akin to a man torn with doubts than to a man with firm and steady faith. So when at last an act of sacrifice breaks through out of all this doubt and uncertainty, and appears entirely unreasonable, the effect is overwhelming. Something else that this "pilgrim" has taught Ahasuerus also appears quite unreasonable: that there is something that is so valuable that it is worth sacrificing one's life for. It is perhaps worth remembering that it is not so uncommon in modern literature (Graham Greene, for instance) for faith to shine out of human lives that have been badly knocked about. The same idea also appears in the Gospels.

"At the spring I would gladly kneel." "The spring" is the word Ahasuerus turns to as a symbol for the holy, the divine. To drink from the spring gives peace, "salvation".

The idea of a spring occurs also, as we have seen, in *The Sibyl*. To begin with, it is interesting to compare what the Sibyl and what Ahasuerus say about the spring. The Sibyl tells Ahasuerus that in a valley near Delphi there was a spring that was holy. It gave peace just to stand there and look down into it, "it filled me with a sense of devotion and I came back at peace and strengthened and, in my own way, happy".[2]

Ahasuerus too wants to bow the knee at the spring. He wants to drink from it to quench his burning thirst. But his spring is not transparently clear like the Sibyl's. It has "dark depths".

I don't know what it hides in its dark depths. If I did I might well be terrified. But I desire to drink from it. It may be those very depths that can assuage my burning thirst.[3]

The hidden darkness, that might well terrify, is not terrifying.

[1] *The Death of Ahasuerus*, p. 86 (my italics).   [2] *The Sibyl*, p. 79.
[3] *The Death of Ahasuerus*, p. 87.

On the contrary, it is this that is full of promise, that gives hope, that "perhaps" can assuage his burning thirst. For the Sibyl god was—alternately—both frightening and attractive. When Ahasuerus makes the spring a symbol of the divine, it appears as a *mysterium* that is at the same time frightening and attractive, a *mysterium* where the *tremendum* and the *fascinosum* have been combined in unfathomable unity.

"The spring" is a symbol for "the holy", "the divine". When Ahasuerus identifies the holy with the divine he is using a word that many students of religion have regarded as specific for the religious sphere—for instance, Nathan Söderblom and Rudolf Otto. Without going into details, we can see that for Ahasuerus the word "holy" is clearly a religious word. The word "holy" here is not a word of moral significance, but simply religious. It is the divinely "numinous".

Now when "the spring" is made a symbol of what is holy and divinely numinous, we have first to note that the word is taken from the world of nature. It contrasts with the symbols for "the divine" that are taken from the world of man, the anthropomorphic symbols. When Ahasuerus conquers god, who is sketched with highly anthropomorphic features, he clears the decks of all anthropomorphic symbols. So the question is: What does the symbol of the spring tell us of the divine and holy? Does it tell us anything? Ahasuerus is concerned to emphasize how inaccessible for us the holy is.

Yes, unquestionably the spring as a symbol has something to tell us. It awakens certain associations. In view of what Ahasuerus says, there is no need to have resort to a word of many meanings like "mysticism", to which people usually turn when religious language ceases to run on anthropomorphic lines. In any case there is no question of that kind of mysticism which makes the soul pass into the "All-One" or whatever else it is called, the "mysticism of infinity" as Nathan Söderblom used to call it. Ahasuerus does not sink into the spring and disappear in it. To point the difference, we might quote some lines from one of C. J. L. Almquist's best-known romantic songs:

Run softly, O my soul, into the river, into the dark purple river of heaven! Sink softly, O blessed Spirit of mine, into the bosom of God, so fresh and good!

The symbol of the spring has very different associations. First of all it quenches thirst and so gives peace. The divine something that the spring represents is by nature *giving*. The spring gives the thirsty one what he is really seeking for and longing for. The symbol of the spring further stresses that there is no question of saving oneself. We have already seen that Ahasuerus has had to correct his statement that he had saved himself. Another human being has helped him. What is said about the spring puts this still more clearly. Ahasuerus has not himself produced the drink that quenches his thirst. But he has discovered that it is there. "The salvation" symbolized by the living water of the spring is a gift that Ahasuerus receives.

When we read the lovely words about the refreshing spring, we can hardly help remembering that the same symbolic language is found in the Bible. In Revelation 21.6 we read: "To the thirsty I will give water without price from the fountain of the water of life" (RSV). The same image recurs in John 4.10 and 7.37–8, Revelation 7.16 and 22.17. Without speculating to what extent the Bible symbols may have influenced Ahasuerus, we may rest content with noting that the Bible and Ahasuerus use the same symbol, and that in both of them it emphasizes that salvation is a gift, and that the most noticeable difference is that for the writers in the Bible it is a point of importance to say who it is that gives the drink of living water.

I have given a relatively exhaustive account of how Lagerkvist puts his argument in his Ahasuerus book. It is of great interest, not because it is particularly original, but, on the contrary, just because it is not original, for the two main points of the argument are among those that appear most frequently in discussion of Christian faith.

The problem that lies at the bottom of it is God's relation to evil. Ahasuerus knows well that the Christians speak of God as a "loving father". But he can find no meaning in such talk. All the nameless evil in creation is evidence against it. Since god "has power", is All-power, and since, therefore, everything that is evil comes from him and reflects his masterful power, god must be cruel, malicious, and detestable. The underlying theological basis of this argument is an abstract conception of all-mightiness, conceived of as all-causality. Now it cannot be denied that a concept of this kind is not unknown in the history of theology.

We find it particularly in theological writings with a scholastic background. It has always led to insuperable difficulties and has fatally obscured and destroyed the Christian image of God. We shall have ample opportunity to return to this point later. Here it will suffice merely to say that this kind of concept is not of Christian origin, and is wholly at variance with the Bible's dramatic perspective in which God is engaged in unceasing battle with evil, with the anti-God, destructive and demonic powers.

The second argument which Ahasuerus uses also has a theological background—God's relation to Christ. According to Ahasuerus, the sacrifice which god so callously demands of him is one piece of evidence among many of the cruelty of god. The theological background to this argument is the doctrine of the atonement which right from the time of medieval scholasticism has had such a strong position in Western theology, both Roman and post-Reformation. The emphasis in this doctrine is on the act of sacrifice by which Christ has given God "satisfaction" for the sin and guilt of mankind. Here too we are dealing with a theme which recurs in discussion of the Christian faith, and, as it is of great significance for the Christian image of God, will play a considerable part later in this book. Here in preparation, three things should be stressed: first, that Ahasuerus' presentation of the idea is not what was meant by this doctrine, but is a version of it that makes it crude; secondly, it is a version that we find it easy to turn to; thirdly, that this doctrine is a rationalizing of ideas that we find in the Bible, but a rationalizing that does not do justice to what Paul expresses as: "God was in Christ, reconciling the world unto himself."

Last of all, a few words about the religious problems raised in the Ahasuerus book. What are the religious problems that Ahasuerus is struggling with? He himself has hardly any problem of guilt. The defendant is not Ahasuerus himself but the god who is held responsible for all evil and all suffering in this hard and apparently meaningless world. When Ahasuerus finally finds something "holy and divine" behind all "the sacred clutter", this undoubtedly means that he has found something meaningful in all the meaninglessness. Yet this does not mean that the religious question is basically an intellectual one. It is obviously not. It is a deeply personal question. What Ahasuerus is seeking for is "salvation". That is what he finds when he bows the knee and drinks from the spring. The spring quenches his "burning thirst". It gives him peace. And so Lagerkvist describes Ahasuerus in his death as radiating tranquillity. It is clear that the spring as a symbol for the divine has a function close to that which the spring has in the Bible when it is used as a symbol for God. Ahasuerus describes the divine, of which the spring is the symbol, as an unfathomable mystery. But this does not mean that it has no quality. Let us put it this way: this that is holy and divine has the quality that makes it able to bestow salvation.

The arguments in the Ahasuerus book which we have now analysed undeniably help to illustrate the present-day problems of faith in God. The question to what extent Ahasuerus is a mouthpiece for Lagerkvist himself has not been taken up. But we might well listen—without comment—to one word of his, taken from the poem in *Aftonland* from which some words have been quoted earlier. In this fuller quotation, god is not described as "cruel", but as a "stranger" and a "friend". It is called "A stranger and a friend":

> A stranger is my friend, one whom I know not.
> A stranger from far away.
> Because of him my heart is full of trouble.
> Because he is not with me.
> Because perhaps he is not there at all?
> Who art thou, filling my heart with thine absence?
> Filling the whole world with thine absence?

ANIARA[1]

Aniara, published in 1956, is a great symbolic poem of our time, written by the Swedish poet Harry Martinson. The book has been translated into English. A shortened version in libretto form has also been adapted for the opera by a very modern Swedish composer, Karl Birger Blomdahl. This opera has been performed in different countries, both at the Edinburgh Festival in 1959 and later at Covent Garden.

The word Aniara, like many others in the book, is a newly coined word. Aniara is the name of a great space-ship, housing eight thousand people. It escapes from an earth polluted by atomic

---

[1] Translator's note: The Swedish original contained a fuller analysis of Harry Martinson's *Aniara*, and of the poems of Hjalmar Gullberg with some reference to the writings of Dag Hammarskjöld. For this edition Bishop Aulén has written a shorter analysis of Martinson's work.

explosions. But it is deflected from its course towards Mars and heads irretrievably into outer space. After a period of panic and desperation the passengers resign themselves to their fate. Life goes on as usual. Many seek consolation in escapist reveries. The ship's hallowed machine, the Mima, that superficially resembles a modern mathematical computer and whose activities lie beyond human analysis, is the main source of comfort to the pasengers of Aniara and their sole remaining contact with the Earth. The Mima is incorruptible and faithfully reproduces all that comes her way. When the atomic bomb smashes Dorisburg (the Earth), the Mima collapses under the strain of the terrible news she has to bring (from the preface to the English edition).

The voyage of Aniara is a voyage without goal. In Song 13 we read: "Through God and Death and Mystery she goes, our space-ship without trace or goal." At the end of the book it would seem that Death has the last word:

> By Mima's graveside, fallen in a circle,
> transformed once more to blameless dust we lay,
> impervious to the sting of bitter stars,
> lost and dispersed in oceans of Nirvana.

The poem could well be interpreted in this way, and the opera, I think, has emphasized this view. Whether this is a legitimate interpretation may well be doubted. The trinity, "God and Death and Mystery", is significant. A good deal is said about God, less perhaps directly about Mystery. Nevertheless, for Martinson himself it is Mystery that has the final word about man in time and space—the subtitle of Aniara is *A Review of Man in Time and Space*.

From our point of view we may observe first what Aniara has to say about God. Two perspectives are discernible, one cosmic and one ethical. In his article "Talking about God" in *Myth and Symbol*, Ian T. Ramsey says: "Perhaps scientific discourse may not be unhelpful. In particular, if activity is a central theological concept, it may be that we shall discover new models amongst whatever represents the scientific concept of energy."[1] In *Aniara* there are plenty of scientific symbols. A scientist, Tord Hall, has characterized *Aniara* as follows: "Poetry and science have become organically fused, and it is to the fact that the images

---

[1] S.P.C.K. Theological Collections 7 (1966), p. 93.

culled from science fit so neatly into its general pattern and purpose that the poem owes its overwhelming impact."[1]

According to "the second law of thermo-dynamics"—the law of entropy—the evolution of Cosmos moves from order to chaos. Song 77 describes a coal-black sun . . . which once glowed in a firestorm at the Cape of Time . . .

> until it was gradually, in accordance with
> the law of entropy, sucked up by the Photophag
> which left only cinders and shell behind,
> a gravestone on the empty plain of darkness,
> one of many thousand dark stones standing invisible
> in endless night in the cemeteries of space.[2]

These verses suggest a view of cosmic death. Space is often described as hard, as cruel. But at the same time Space can be described as Spirit, even as the Spirit of God. However, *this* Spirit is never described as cruel. It can be described as "elusive" and sometimes even as "the Spirit of Life". Of course, the view of God implicit in words like these is more or less pantheistic. The alternation of aspects found here is very interesting. We find the same alternation in the author's use of the symbol, *light*. When talking about the conflict between light and darkness, light— as usual in religious language—signifies the good and life-giving power, as opposed to the evil. On the other hand, light in *Aniara* is not only this divine element, it is also an invisible "dark illumination", the light of Röntgen and gamma rays. Thus light can be a healer, but at the same time it is a deadly threat to our existence.

This alternation demonstrates how the author is battling for Life against destruction. But it also shows the limitation of his endeavours. Having in mind the Christian faith in the resurrection of Christ, he finds it hard to understand the words of *mercy*: "where only *one* has burst the bonds of death to meet his God, while all the others . . . must lie in dust until the Judgement day." However, even the dead in some way sing the song of Life:

> Committed to the earth they lie in ranks
> in the blind ground beneath the winds of Spring,
> and there in unison they join the chorus
> of all blind chanting the songs of Rind [=the Earth].[3]

[1] Title page.   [2] *Aniara*, Song 77.   [3] *Aniara*, Song 49.

This certainly is not the song of the Book of Revelation, nevertheless it is a song.

We turn now to the ethical aspect of God. Aniara is a miniature
of the Earth. On the other hand, from a distance it is possible to
see with uncompromising truthfulness what is going on on the
Earth. From this point of view Aniara is a Judgement Day sermon.
Modern literature is often very good at describing the evil in
our world, its misery and its sufferings, its crimes and its mis-
deeds. In this respect *Aniara* excels. The songs describe these
things with a drastic power that could hardly be surpassed. Man's
guilt is as tremendous as his responsibility: "Prepare for doom.
The walls of wrath are closing around our fate—the fate we brought
upon ourselves." Man is presented as "the King of Ashes":

> There is protection against almost anything,
> against fire and damage caused by storm and cold.
> Yes, count up everything you can think of,
> but there is no protection against man.[1]

The life of man as seen from this point of view can be explained
as a conflict between light and darkness. But in fact there is not
much "light" to be discovered. The only beam of light is the work
of mercy and charity, symbolically represented by a girl called
Nobby, who in pure self-sacrifice is working for the prisoners.
This mercy is the only thing that gives value to life: "Without
the precious image of my Nobby, what would life have been worth
to me?" Such goodness is a rare exception: "When you have lived
long among fiends, such goodness is like an exotic garden."

We must now consider the relationship of God to this world
full of evil. There is only one thing that we "know": "We know
no more than that he [God] suffers deeply in every act that does
not wholly please him'" Otherwise there are plenty of unanswered
questions:

> How difficult in secret not to wonder—
> Has not the blood of sacrifice run dry,
> and why are executioners still with us?
> How difficult in secret not to wonder.[2]

The author's God is not a God without power. He speaks about
God's mighty power as contrasted with our helplessness. Nevertheless he does not accuse God. He issues no reproaches. He does not

[1] *Aniara*, Song 26.   [2] Ibid., Song 49.

derive the evil of the world from "the mighty power" of God. He "knows" that God suffers. Beyond that, his last words are: "in secret to wonder", "in silence to think"—without any answer. The space-ship Aniara goes through God and Death and Mystery. But the last word belongs to Mystery.

I conclude this short review of *Aniara* with a few observations.

1. In *Aniara*, we can find plenty of symbols chosen from the world of science. The poet has a deep respect for the work of science, for "the Friend of Thought". But he criticizes strongly another character, called the "Calculator":

> The Cynic, who is always close to hand
> to calculate our minimum of hope . . .
> A shrug, mimicking his victims in the past,
> is the Cynic's sole answer, or an icy grimace,
> reflex of his bitter loneliness.[1]

2. We do observe a certain tension between the two perspectives in *Aniara*, the cosmic and the ethical. We cannot find any rational theory of life here. Rather than giving definite answers, the poet prefers "in secret to wonder".

3. This attitude can be seen more clearly if we compare Martinson and Lagerkvist. We saw earlier how Lagerkvist's Ahasuerus defeated god because he was cruel. Why did he consider god cruel? Because he thinks of God's all-mightiness as being all-causality. Therefore all evil and all suffering in the world must originate in God. This means that the background of Lagerkvist's argument is scholastic theology—for scholastic theology always considers God's all-mightiness as all-causality. Martinson, on the other hand, never speaks of God as a cruel god. His attitude is "in secret to wonder". He is, as I should like to put it, "theologically innocent". But Lagerkvist, so far as he is dependent on scholastic theology, is not "theologically innocent".

Two Questions

What I have already written will have made it clear that the question "Does God exist?" is by no means as unambiguous as we might imagine when we think of it as the fundamental question

[1] *Aniara*, Song 45.

that has to be answered before dealing with the problems of faith. To attempt to answer the question—positively or negatively— would be meaningful only if it were possible to start from a reasonably well-defined concept of god. But as widely different ideas can lie behind the word "god", the task is impossible. In these circumstances to treat the question of God's existence as fundamental, requiring to be answered first, would be to try to answer a question without knowing what it means.

People have, however, regarded the question of God's existence as a primary question, possible to ask in isolation, and the reason for this is that they have posited a more or less defined concept of God. The background for this is the part played by the traditional proofs of God during the course of centuries. There has been a metaphysical idea of God, viewing him as a supernatural, super-human, extra-mundane being about whom certain statements could be made. In these circumstances the subject for discussion is whether these proofs are valid or not. If these proofs were shown to be untenable, it would lead to the conclusion that there were no reasons for saying that God exists. The whole problem as presented must be regarded as irrelevant for the Christian faith—first, because the God concerned is not this kind of extramundane metaphysical being, capable of being proved by reason; secondly, because the whole idea of rational proof of God's existence is incompatible with the relationship with God that is characteristic for Christian faith.[1]

So while we have to admit that to put the question "Does God exist?" is unproductive and as an isolated question impossible to answer, there are, nevertheless, other questions far more relevant and worthy of study. One of these is to ask the nature of the criticism that is directed against the Christian faith. Another might be put: What are people looking for when, openly or disguising their motives, they query the existence of God? We have been told that modern man has more or less stopped asking for a merciful God. Has the problem of faith in God become a different problem in the course of time?

Let us begin with the first question and see what we find. We might distinguish between, on the one hand, "criticism of Christianity", opposing Christian practice, and, on the other hand, theoretical criticism—though the boundary between them

[1] See also Chapter 2.

is not fixed. The former type includes the communist accusation that the Christian Church, allied with reactionary powers of State, has held back social reform. There is a similar charge in Bertrand Russell's book *Why I am not a Christian*, that the Churches have held back progress. Such accusations have often been made. All that needs to be said here is that undeniably it is not difficult to point to things in the history of Christianity which give justification for such charges. It is equally undeniable that there are many facts that point in the opposite direction. This makes it clear that this kind of criticism is argument from generalizations, where individual pieces of evidence are made to represent the whole. This gives the verdicts of these critics a highly subjective character, and that means that discussion on such a level cannot lead to reliable conclusions. It should further be emphasized that this criticism of Christian behaviour and conduct from outside is matched by equally pointed criticism from inside, by Christian self-examination, which realizes that to be associated with social oppression is so incompatible with a Christian attitude that it is really nothing less than patent betrayal of elementary Christian duty.

For us the theoretical criticism dealing with the principles involved is of much greater interest. We are dealing here with problems which we shall have plenty of opportunity to discuss in later chapters. All we do here is to register some of the critical arguments we have already met.

We begin with Feuerbach's thesis that all religion and all belief in God must be regarded as a projection of human wishes, and must therefore be dismissed as pure illusion. This thesis has since become part of the standard repertory of both official communist propaganda for godlessness and of many other critics. As we have seen, the group of existentialist philosophers who are critical of religion regard this interpretation as self-evident. No one is going to deny that both in the past and in the present there has been a good deal of religiosity springing from human wishes and dreams. Certainly it is not denied by Christian thinkers. The criticism of religiosity. that comes from this source—Luther, for instance—is far more searing than anything Feuerbach and his following have produced. But it is one thing to say that there is such a thing as wishful-thinking religiosity. It is quite a different thing to say that all belief in God must come into this category and to say that it is possible to verify this "scientifically". No such verification has ever been produced and it would be an extremely difficult thing to do. The assertion is an assertion and nothing more—just as it would be an unverifiable assertion if it were claimed that the existence of God could be scientifically proved.

A second category of criticism is represented by the argument that claims that Christian belief belittles humanity, and that this is a threat to man or robs man of values which are more important than those which faith in God believes it can guarantee. Inevitably a discussion involving values has to deal in subjective attitudes. This is shown by the fact that there is no agreement about which human values have to be protected against Christian belief. The values that Nietzsche with his superman ideal would want to protect are not necessarily identical with the ideal values of the philosophy of Enlightenment. The whole scale of values varies very considerably.

An offshoot of this discussion of values is also to be found in the nihilistic attitude that sweeps away any talk of values. So the argument based on values has here gone into reverse. Life has no meaning, there are no values to protect. The trouble with belief in God is that it is defending values that do not exist, and giving life a meaning that it does not have.

A third kind of argument has concentrated its criticism on ideas of the universe and stressed the problems based on the fact that Christian faith was from the first identified with an idea of the universe that has long since been outgrown. This brings us to one of the minor problems within the major problem of the relationship of faith to knowledge or rather to science. It is of course incontrovertible that the idea of the universe which we find in the biblical writings and in a good deal of later theology belongs irrevocably to the past. This has of course given rise to conflicts between faith or theology on the one side and scientific research on the other. This sort of conflict has been going on for centuries and in the nineteenth century was particularly severe. The conflict was insoluble so long as there was a theology which insisted on making the Bible an authority on scientific questions—and also so long as scientists, as often happened in that century, turned what they called the scientific view of the world into metaphysics with a negative key signature. But an attitude of that kind seems to be unknown in the science of the atomic age, as it expands with tremendous speed.

In dealing with problems of this kind, it is of fundamental importance that theology—if it is not to do harm to Christian faith —shall maintain the religious aspect unimpaired and distinguish clearly between the two perspectives of the religion of faith and the researches of science. While a distinction of this kind can in principle remove causes of conflict, it means at the same time that there must be no making use of modern scientific theories in the interests of faith, theories which might apparently seem to support some aspect of faith. It would be evidence of a failure to understand the content and conditions of faith if an attempt were made, for instance, to link belief in creation or divine intervention with modern scientific theories which presuppose some irregularity in the expected behaviour of the universe and allow an element of indeterminism to appear. To conduct apologetics of this kind would be to misunderstand both the intentions of science and the nature of faith. Belief in God does not try to find a niche in the "gaps" science may leave, nor is it limited to them.

We have pointed out that a clear distinction between the dimensions of religion and of science helps to clear away the conflicts that theology at times has battled with, sometimes to its own hurt. But a distinction of this kind does not mean that these dimensions have to be isolated from one another, as if they had nothing to do with one another. Nor does it mean that all the problems of belief in God and of views of the world are settled once and for all. One look at the facts shows that this is not so. Questions of this kind are being dealt with both in literature in general and in theological writings. The theme of our ideas of the universe has a way of cropping up wherever religion is discussed. We have seen something of this in Harry Martinson's *Aniara* with its scientific background. Here the problem was accentuated and made more pointed in the connection and the clash between the idea of space as empty and cruel and the idea of God as the "spirit of Life".

Modern theology too often confronts us with the theme of belief in God and views of the world. It is one thing to make a distinction in principle between scientific and religious perspectives. It is quite a different matter to decide how this principle is to be applied in different areas of the world of religious ideas. One instance of how theologically important the question of world views is, is the lively discussion in recent years of Rudolf Bultmann's programme of demythologizing biblical ideas. If we are to mention

in this connection Bishop Robinson's *Honest to God*, this is not
because the book has had any great theological significance—the
author himself would not claim that. But the wide circulation that
the book has had and the sensation it caused show unquestionably
the importance in wide circles of the issues of belief and world-
view. It also shows how little contact there has been between
theology and those of the public who are interested in religious
questions. As we shall be returning to this point, all that needs to
be said here is that rightly to understand the problem it is necessary to understand the language of symbols, the mother tongue of
faith.

But the question of "world-view" and its relationship to faith
has another side, an inner side. It is not a matter of the world-
view formed by scientific research. It is rather the actual character
of the world as seen from the perspective of human life on earth,
the problem of God and Evil in all its forms, of reconciling belief
in God with all the suffering and all the instances of human cruelty
and evil that abound in our time. It is an age-old problem, but a
torrent of present-day literature shows how the experiences of our
generation have brought it to the fore again. It is no mere chance
that this theme appears in the Swedish writers to whom we have
referred. In Lagerkvist's book on Ahasuerus it is the central theme.
The emphasis is that "suffering and sacrifice are found over all the
world and in all ages". A god who "has power" in these circumstances cannot be loving—he must be a cruel god. Elsewhere
Lagerkvist has put it differently: god is an "absentee" god, filling
the world with his absence. In *Aniara* the stress is on human evil,
hardness, and cruelty. God in this context becomes a suffering
god, and at the same time a god who flees "from man—the king
of ashes". A fleeing god becomes an absent god, who leaves emptiness behind him. But we must also remember the emptiness which
is part of the cosmic perspective in *Aniara*. The space-craft vanish-
ing into endless emptiness "without trace or goal" is an image of the
journey of mankind and perhaps also of the fate of the individual
human life.

It is time now to go on to the second question: What is it that is
being sought, what is it that people want to find when they bring
up the question of religion today? We remember what the Lutheran World Federation said in its message, that man of today asks,

"God, where are you? He does not suffer from the wrath of God, but from a sense of his absence, not from his sin, but from the meaninglessness of life." The positive side of this description is supported by evidence we have already considered. It could be duplicated any number of times. Thousands of voices today are asking about the "emptiness and meaninglessness" of life and about "the absence of God". The fact that there are plenty of voices telling us that even to ask the question is meaningless and in utter nihilism asserting that meaninglessness is the hard lot of mankind, only serves to emphasize the part this kind of thinking plays in modern times. Whether or not it is possible to maintain a nihilistic line of this kind, one thing is certain: even if individuals dismiss the question as meaningless, the idea that mankind should do so must be said to be unthinkable. The question remains.

If, then, it is possible for the positive side of the World Federation's statement to be verified, there is all the more reason to see whether this is also possible with the negative side, the thing that "man of today" is said no longer to suffer from or to feel to be a problem. We have earlier queried the historical theory that all too systematically makes different periods of time ask different religious questions. We should pursue this further.

Paul Tillich in *The Courage To Be* has made a most interesting attempt to describe how the problem of religion has appeared at different times. In Tillich's existential terminology, non-Being threatens man in three different ways, and this threefold threat produces three different types of anxiety. He emphasizes that this anxiety is existential, not neurotic. The main section about how non-Being threatens Being states:

Non-being threatens man's ontic self-affirmation, relatively in terms of fate, absolutely in terms of death. It threatens man's spiritual self-affirmation, relatively in terms of emptiness, absolutely in terms of meaninglessness. It threatens man's moral self-affirmation, relatively in terms of guilt, absolutely in terms of condemnation. The awareness of this threefold threat is anxiety appearing in three forms, that of fate and death (briefly, the anxiety of death), that of emptiness and loss of meaning (briefly, the anxiety of meaninglessness), that of guilt and condemnation (briefly, the anxiety of condemnation).[1]

Tillich tries to make out that each of these types of anxiety is particularly associated with a different period of history. In late

[1] Op. cit., p. 38.

Dᴅ

classical times, the period of the first Christian mission, "ontic anxiety" was dominant, anxiety for destiny and death. At the end of the medieval period, anxiety for guilt and damnation, moral anxiety, became prevalent. The question unceasingly asked was: How can I appease the wrath of God, get a share in his mercy, find forgiveness of sins? Now "as the modern age comes to an end", it is the spiritual anxiety that predominates, anxiety for emptiness and meaninglessness. "We are under the threat of spiritual non-being. The threats of moral and ontic non-being are, of course, present, but they are not independent and not controlling."[1] Tillich attempts to underpin his description of types by registering the sociological factors assumed to lie behind the characteristic questions of the different ages. It must be said that this is all on a hypothetical plane. But the typological ground plan is instructive and undoubtedly contributes to the characterization of the different stages. This is supported by the answers given at different periods to the questions of existential anxiety, by the emphasis of the primitive Church on salvation (*sōtēria*) as life and immortality won by Christ's victory, and by the Reformation stress on forgiveness of sins. What is to be regarded as the answer to the existential question of the present age is perhaps better left unsaid for the moment.

There is this to be said in Tillich's favour, that he is well aware of the danger of trying to force things into a hard-and-fast scheme. He says explicitly that, even if one type is dominant in each age, this does not preclude "both the others being present and in operation". He gives instances of this. I would stress this point even more strongly than Tillich does.

It may be right to present the three questions that Tillich mentions. But at the same time the connection between them also needs to be stressed. It is not only true, as Tillich says, that when one of them is dominant, the others are also there and make their presence felt. Rather it should be said that the "different" questions really involve one another, and that fundamentally there are not three different and separate questions, but they are different sides of one and the same basic question. To divide them up into compartments does not do justice to their deep connection with one another. This means that we can begin at either end, begin with one aspect or another, but we shall eventually have to deal not with one part, but with the whole issue.

[1] Paul Tillich, *The Courage To Be*, p. 58.

That the questions involve one another is clear both from the primitive Church and from the time of the Reformation. Let us think for a moment of Luther. Among the powers to whom man is in thrall he includes not only Sin but also Death and the wrath of God. To be under these powers of perdition means for Luther to be in utter despair at the meaninglessness of life. Release from this thraldom—salvation, *sōtēria*—he describes with the famous three phrases: forgiveness of sins, life, and eternal bliss—but these three are one undivided whole. *Sōtēria* here has the same wide scope as in the New Testament. It is one indivisible whole, because forgiveness of sins does not only mean remission of guilt, but from first to last a restored relationship with God—and with that "life and eternal blessedness". There are probably few questions that have been stereotyped more rigidly than the Reformation's radical view of forgiveness in the post-Reformation centuries. Two things are characteristic of the narrowing of the perspectives: on the one side, the idea that deep and complete consciousness of sin is a prerequisite on man's part for receiving God's forgiveness; on the other side, a moralistic aspect of sin, listing the forbidden acts that are to be considered as "sins". This makes Sin no longer a power that devastates and enslaves human life. It has ceased to be Sin with a capital S. The first aspect misjudges the real conditions of consciousness of sin—the fact that it is fellowship with God that more than anything else opens our eyes to the extent of Sin, its power and its depth. This kind of stereotyping has had powerful after-effects, and has contributed to the present-day questioning in religious matters taking a different form from the questioning at the time of the Reformation.

If in modern discussion it seems difficult to discover the inner connection between the three sets of questions, this may largely be due to the fact that nowadays we often use a different terminology and different symbols from those that were used earlier. But what are the wrestlings with the "cruel" god in Lagerkvist's *Ahasuerus* if they are not another form of wrestling with the "wrath" of God? The problem of evil in its various forms is a living problem indeed. What else could one expect? If there is today little talk of sin in this connection, the reason for this is largely a reaction against systematizing it, of which we spoke earlier. In any case: Sin in the sense of a demonic power of evil ought not to be beyond the grasp of modern minds or outside their experience. That the thought of meaninglessness and the thought of death are associated is clearly apparent. No doubt a description like that in *Aniara* of the last journey of the space-craft is a document characteristic of our day. What I want finally to say is that, whenever "god" is being looked for and asked for, against a background of emptiness and meaninglessness, it is always some kind of power and goodness and mercy that is really being sought. The world of emptiness and meaninglessness is "a world without mercy". Present-day religious questions are not really so very different from the old question about "a merciful God" as people sometimes imagine. Of course, "the religious problem" can appear in different forms, variations, and disguises, but fundamentally it is the same basic problem. The reason for this is that, in spite of all sorts of radical changes, the basic conditions of human life are and remain the same.

2 THE GOD OF FAITH

The faith mentioned in the title of this chapter is Christian faith in God. What we ask about God cannot be separated from faith. Just as it is impossible to speak of Christian faith without speaking of God, so it is impossible to speak of God without speaking of faith. Faith and God belong together. Our first task then is to define faith in the sense of faith in God, and we call the first part of our outline: Involvement. We then proceed to consider the tenses of faith. We stress that the primary tense of faith is the present tense. In all matters of faith, we live in the present tense. But when it is Christian faith, it is always inseparably related to something that has happened, to a perfect tense, and also to something that we look for, to a future tense. This will be only a sketch, because it will be further discussed in the final chapter of this book on "The Drama". When the first part of this chapter describes how God and faith belong together, it is easy to ask: Does not this linking of God and faith lead to an isolation of faith, and so prepare the way for the "secularization" that people talk of nowadays? After considering some of the demands made on theology in this connection, in the last section of the chapter we shall attempt to answer the question by considering the "universal perspective" of faith.

Involvement

Chapter 1 dealt with the question "Does God exist?". This question is often regarded as the characteristic, basic, radical question of our age, but we found that it was not nearly so unambiguous as we might have thought. The word "god" turns out to be a covering word for very different ideas. So there is little point in isolating the question of God's existence and, independently of what "god" means, trying to decide whether he exists or not. Further, behind the problem there lies the idea that it is a matter that can be decided on purely rational and "scientific" grounds. If god really "exists", people think that it ought to be possible to prove it in the same way as historical research can prove from documents whether an event in history took place, or as science can demonstrate facts in the world of nature. In other words, God ought to be an object among other demonstrable objects. Knowledge about God ought to be on the same level and of the same kind, they think, as the knowledge won by scientific research. It ought to be a purely objective and uninvolved knowledge, a knowledge that can be gained and can continue without any personal involvement on the part of the person who asks the question. If it were not possible to demonstrate any "divine being" on this basis, it would be tantamount to saying that the answer to the question "Does God exist?" was in the negative.

Putting the question in this way excludes it from the context where it is relevant and belongs—the context of faith. Here the words of Luther's *Large Catechism* are unquestionably true: "faith and God belong together". This phrase is no Lutheran monopoly. It is true wherever God is mentioned. There can be various kinds of faith, just as there are various images of God. But the question of God's existence is and remains a question of faith. God is not an object, to be objectively examined or the existence of which can be objectively proved or disproved. It just is not possible to place God in the category: "object". You can believe in God, or else not believe in God. *Belief* in God can be an object of investigation. You can find out what is characteristic of belief, what constitutes belief, and what belief has to tell us about its relationship to God—and incidentally about the God it professes.

But one thing must be said first, though we have already touched on it. We spoke then of the human problem of faith. Here we have to make a distinction between what constitutes faith and what are the conditions in which faith lives and makes itself known in the world of human life. If we turn to the New Testament descriptions, we find them speaking of human faith of different grades and types, strong faith, weak faith, doubting faith. Of the centurion of Capernaum, who sought help for his sick servant, Jesus says: "I have not found so great faith, no, not in Israel" (Luke 7.9). Faith can also be weak, but, even if it is as weak as "smoking flax", it will not be quenched (Matt. 12.20). Faith and doubt can exist side by side, and struggle together: "I believe; help thou mine unbelief" says the father who comes to Jesus with his sick son (Mark 9.24). Examples of different attitudes could be multiplied, even from the New Testament, still more if we listen to the witness of humanity through the ages down to our own time. In the evidence of psychology there is ample verification of the Bible text about "fighting the good fight of faith". The rich and varied problems of faith are fully illustrated. Faith in the conditions of earthly life is always a battling faith, a faith in conflict with opposition. It is always in an area of risk. It may grow or diminish. To "increase in faith" (see 2 Cor. 10.15; 2 Thess 1.3) always involves overcoming opposition.

But we are not going to describe the battle of faith and the difficulties it has to face, nor discuss the "measures of faith" that —in the Bible phrase—have been "dealt" (Rom. 12.3) to every man. What we are concerned to do is to try to indicate what constitutes the faith that is given in varying measures.

First, then, faith in the Christian sense is *to be involved*. No involvement, no faith. Naked assent to the existence of God is not faith, it has nothing to do with faith. However many statements or doctrines about God people assent to, about his "being" or his actions, this does not entitle them to be regarded as within the sphere of faith. It is of course undeniable that faith has something definite to say about God and how he acts. But this is no theoretical insight that people can assent to as they assent to the things that research discovers about historical events or scientific findings. In the world of faith there is no "objective" neutral ascertainment of facts. To believe, to have faith, means taking up a personal position. To believe is to stand in personal relationship with the "God" of whom faith speaks, and this relationship has the character of involvement. God and faith "belong together" in such a way that the man who believes knows he is involved with the power whom he calls God. In this relationship, God is felt to be the one who involves, and man the one who is involved: God is the active one, man is the object of his action; God is the one who overcomes resistance from the side of man, man allows himself to be overcome, surrenders himself, devotes himself to God.

When we try to define this more closely, two points emerge: the involvement of faith is marked by *confidence* and by *obedience*. We mentioned a little while ago Jesus' generous recognition of the centurion's great faith. He had complete confidence, and this could be paralleled many times in the Scriptures. It is enough to quote the Old Testament passage referred to in the first three Gospels: "Thou shalt love the Lord thy God with all thy heart and with all thy soul and with all thy strength" (Deut. 6.5; Matt. 22.37; Mark 12.30; Luke 10.27). The *Shorter Catechism* of Luther agrees with this—to "love God above all things and to set all faith and trust in Him". When faith has also the character of obedience—"the obedience of faith" (Rom. 1.5, RSV)—this obedience is of a twofold nature. The word "obedience" states something about the relationship to God, that God here is Lord and Master. But, as obedience, faith is directed outwards and functions through the second commandment, to "love thy neighbour as thyself".

Trust implies obedience and obedience implies trust. Trust and obedience together illustrate the total dependence of faith on that "power" to which faith gives the name of "God". This means that for faith relationship to God is not just something of relative importance, more or less, but instead is something of decisive, final importance. In English writers this is often expressed as of "ultimate concern", an expressive phrase difficult to translate into other languages. To speak of God and of relationship to him is to speak of something that is of ultimate concern. Relationship to God is something of utmost importance, encompassing and determining human life in all its situations and functions. Involvement applies not only to the religious side of human life, but to human life as a whole, indeed to world life as a whole.

Relationship to God, faith in God is therefore different from any other form of belief. There have always been, and still are, plenty of other forms of belief which attach decisive importance and dignity, "ultimate concern", to various phenomena in the spiritual world. One of these, in Bible terms, is "to worship and serve the creature more than the Creator" (Rom. 1.25). Paul is here thinking of various kinds of idols. But the line he takes is on principle of much wider application. There are any number of examples—honour, power, the worship of race or class or State— all well known in our time. We have experienced the devastating results when something that belongs in this world, race for example, is made the decisive factor for humanity.

As soon as anything is vested with all-important dignity, we are dealing with "faith" of one kind or another. Faith of this kind may be said formally to be on a par with faith in God. Both are matters of decisive importance. The similarity is actually only formal. What is really important is *what* is given this great importance. From this point of view there is a radical difference between faith in God and the forms of faith that are directed to phenomena in the finite world. Phenomena are not capable of sustaining the importance and dignity that is assigned to them. They become a substitute for religion. But the God confessed by faith is not an object among other objects. He is not an object at all. To say so is inappropriate and misleading. It is just as inappropriate to speak of God as a "being" among other beings—nor does it improve matters to use the phrase "the Highest Being". All such definitions are relativizing and therefore irrelevant. They are therefore out of place in Christian faith. To speak of God as a "being", even if the highest, is from the point of view of faith a down-grading of God. This, however, does not mean that faith stops short at negative definitions and is only prepared to say what God is *not*. Faith has much to say of the God in whom it puts its trust, to whom it offers its obedience, on whom it is entirely dependent. But even then faith is not talking about what God is "in himself", but what God is for faith.

If the question of God is inextricably bound up with the relationship of faith, this does not mean that an analysis of faith would deal only in anthropocentric perspectives, and so become part of the psychology of religion. It is of course possible and perfectly permissible to carry out a psychological study of the phenomena of religion, to analyse human religiosity. But, however significant such investigations are, they cannot succeed in discovering the nature of faith. Faith depends on relationship with God. Any analysis that leaves this out may explain many things, but will not explain what is characteristic for faith. It is not functioning on the level where faith is. "God" cannot be eliminated from the picture without faith ceasing to be faith. If faith in trust and obedience is wholly dependent on "God", this means that everything in the world of faith revolves round God and him alone. Everything we have said so far about the character of faith can be summed up in the single word: theocentricity. No anthropocentric description here is adequate. It would be in conflict with what is most essential for faith, that life in the world of faith has a centre outside the Self. Luther expressed this drastically, expressively, and concisely when he said: *fides rapit nos a nobis et ponit nos extra nos*—faith takes us out of ourselves and sets us outside ourselves. This means of course that God is at work. It is he who by involving us, by faith, takes us out of being shut in on ourselves, and who makes himself our centre in place of the Self.

The theocentricity of faith means that faith is focused on God and him alone. Its trust and obedience is all for God. Admittedly there is Christian language which speaks of faith in other connections, particularly of faith in Christ. This we shall come back to, later. All that needs to be said here is that this language never means that faith is to be divided, split, and focused on two rival objects. It is undeniably characteristic and essential for Christian faith that it is focused on Christ. But this never means that Christ is a rival of God. Faith in Christ is faith in the God who acts and makes himself felt through Christ. We find the classic expression of this in the statement in St John's Gospel: "He that believeth on me, believeth not on me, but on him that sent me" (John 12.44).

If faith is defined primarily as involvement, in which God is the one who involves, and if this involvement is marked by trust and obedience, this implies that faith has the character of fellowship with God. There is no reason for using the word "mysticism" here. Fellowship with God, as we saw in the last chapter, is no monopoly of mysticism. A faith in God without fellowship with God would be nothing but a travesty. If we listen to what the Bible says about faith, we find any amount of evidence that faith is regarded as fellowship with God, for example, "our fellowship is with the Father, and with his Son Jesus Christ" (1 John 1.3). The expressions used to describe this fellowship may vary greatly. But the thing itself is always there in some form.

Tense

It is possible to talk of religiosity without talking about God. Religiosity can have Self as the centre. But it is not possible to talk about faith in the Christian sense without God coming into the picture and becoming the centre. It is because of this that we have been emphasizing the theocentric character of faith, faith as a relationship of trust and obedience towards God, faith as fellowship with God. The involvement concerned takes place in time and space, now and here, in this world where man lives, in this time which is now. But at the same time the God who involves is raised above the world of finitude and over the limits of time. Therefore faith as fellowship with God, as sharing in what belongs to God, is to be anchored in the world of eternity. Eternity is a characteristic category of faith. Everything in the world of faith is stamped with the mark of eternity and is seen in the perspective of eternity, *sub specie aeternitatis*. To use a theological term, we might say that everything has an *eschatological* character. "Eschatology" here does not only mean something in the future. The aspect of the future, the looking out towards what is to come, is undeniably an indispensable and constant ingredient, something that will always be part of faith as fellowship with God. But this eschatological aspect, this aspect of eternity, is not only something in the future. It is here as soon as God comes into the picture, as soon as God is in action, as soon as faith speaks of God's "kingdom", his "dominion", his "sovereignty", or of his "activity" here and now in the midst of this fleeting world, in the passing of time.

If we listen to the witness of the Bible, we find how this aspect of eternity is the constantly recurring refrain in all its songs of praise, its doxologies. There are such phrases as: to God "be honour both now and for ever" and to God "belong honour and might for ever and ever". But this dominant category of eternity can also be linked with time as in the trinitarian song of praise which has become by far the most commonly used doxology of Christendom: "Glory be to the Father and to the Son and to the Holy Ghost, as it was in the beginning, is now, and ever shall be, world without end." We find here three forms of time—he who was, is, and shall be—all put into the perspective of eternity. But, as relationship to God is for faith primarily a relationship to the God who "acts", the time system of faith comes to be that which happened, that which is happening, and that which shall happen; or, if you prefer, that which has been done, that which is being done, and that which is going to be done. The question now is how these three forms of time relate to one another.

THE NOW OF FAITH

There is a way of looking at things, more or less traditionally established, which reasons as follows: there are two actions of God which belong to the things that have happened once and for all.

The first is the act of creation which, according to Genesis, took place "in the beginning". That is now concluded and belongs to the past. But among things which have happened there is also God's act of redemption, which was fulfilled and concluded through Christ. In this act of redemption God has revealed himself, and this revelation is fulfilled in Christ. What now remains and is still awaited is the "final judgement" which will come some day, and will lead on into the final consummation the other side of the limits of time.

In this scheme it is remarkable that there is no real place for Now, for what is happening at this present time. It almost suggests the idea that, after the act of redemption was completed and his "revelation" was concluded, God would, as it were, have gone into retirement, and would now be marking time until the moment for his final intervention in the last judgement and the full realization of the kingdom of God. One thing is obvious: in so far as this scheme is applied consistently, faith ceases to have a direct, immediate relationship to a God who involves us. Faith is no longer related to a God who acts in the present, but to actions of God in the past—creation in the beginning and redemption through history culminating in the death of Christ on the cross. Actually, however, it would be a relation not to these actions, but to the accounts of them in the Bible. Faith would then be primarily giving credence and assent to these accounts, and the decisive question for faith would be the authority of the Bible accounts, and whether this can be demonstrated reassuringly enough to be an objective guarantee for faith.

Now it is of course undeniable that Christian faith is inseparably bound up with Christ and dependent on God's act of redemption that was completed in him. We shall return to this. But this does not mean that faith is reduced to a theoretical insight, an acceptance of a doctrine, a "tenet" about what God did once in the past. Any view of that kind is entirely foreign to the Bible account of what faith is. For nothing can be more obvious than that faith is personal involvement—to use the term we have already used. The view that reduces the idea of faith and makes it only a matter of past history is utterly foreign to the Bible, which knows nothing of the idea that God's activity would be limited to a certain period of time and that after that he would cease to reveal himself. The same is true of Christ. When St John's Gospel tells us of Christ saying:

"My Father is working still, and I am working" (John 5.17, RSV), the word "still" does not mean "only up to a certain time" or "for a little longer"—it is a permanent "still".

The God of the Bible is the living God, a God ever active. The work of Christ, the work of redemption that God accomplished through him, is in the Bible view completed, but at the same time it is a work that is always going on, because Christ is the living Lord. Here we must also remember the place of the Spirit in the biblical writings—sadly neglected by theology. The Bible has much to say about the Spirit, and it is always speaking of God's activity in the present, the work that is ever new. The Spirit "gives life", the Spirit "gives rebirth", the Spirit "guides into all the truth", the Spirit "bears witness with our spirit". When the Spirit is in action, what has been said or done in the past is no longer only in the past; it is brought to life, brought into the present. The Spirit makes "the word" alive. It is no longer an extraneous, doctrinaire authority that man does his best to force himself to acknowledge, but it is an inward conviction. We might also put it thus: what happens is that the Spirit reveals the eternal content in what has happened, has been done, has been said—and this makes it a living reality in the present.

All this goes to show how strong is the emphasis on Now in the world of faith, and how basic this aspect is. The vital condition of faith is that God "is working still". If faith were not a relationship with God in the world of Now, it would have no possibility of existing. It would also be meaningless to speak of God's actions in the past or in the future. Without the present tense of faith, there is no perfect and no future tense. If we are to speak at all of God's acting or of his revealing himself, it is inseparably bound up with this action and this revelation being perceived in the present. The acts by which God makes himself felt are classified in Christian language under three heads: creation, judgement, redemption. All three refer to the present. In 2 Corinthians 6.2 we read: "now is the accepted time; behold, now is the day of salvation". The same might be said of creation and judgement: now is the day of creation, now is the day of judgement. Unless they were concerned with something that happens in the present, all these three aspects of God's action would lose their meaning and be abstract metaphysical ideas or nothing but mythology—which is basically the same thing. The act of creation loses its meaning and is changed into a metaphysical and mythological theory about "the origin of the world", if it is reduced to being only an initial action performed once in the past, if creation were something that has stopped, if it were not an action of God, constantly going on anew.

It is the same with judgement: it would lose its meaning if all we can look to is a final judgement. All prophesying about a coming judgement would lose its basis in reality and appear as mythology without any content if faith did not sense the God who judges in the present, and sense something of what God's judgement means. The same is also true of salvation: to talk about an act of redemption that God performed far back in history, completed when God "in Christ reconciled the world to himself" would appear wholly unrealistic, as nothing more than empty mythology, if God's redemptive act had no relation with the present, if it were not carried into effect in the here and now.

We have dealt here with God's acts of creation, judgement, and redemption, as ever continuing, and of the relation of this his threefold activity to the here and now. This means that the God who involves man in faith, thereby carries out a creative, judging, and redeeming work. The involvement of faith is marked by this threefold activity. When we remember that faith has been described as confidence, obedience, dependence, and fellowship with God, it is tempting to associate confidence and fellowship with the idea of redemption, entire dependence with creation, and finally obedience—as opposed to disobedience—with judgement. There might be something to be said for this kind of link. But this kind of division into a system of categories has its risks, and easily leads to separating things that belong together. In any case it is far more important that analysis is concerned to map the connections, the affinities, between the actions of God that current Christian usage calls creation, judgement, and redemption.

If, then, we think first of the relationship between creation and redemption, it is so intimate that redemption would lose its meaning if it were not at the same time regarded as an act of creation. However salvation, *sōtēria*, is interpreted, it is in any case clear that it is not, and cannot be, self-salvation, and that it has its basis in God's dealings with man. Resistance is overcome, a new relationship with God is established, is created. Something

entirely new has come into being, something that did not exist
before. There has been a new creation. We read in 2 Corinthians
5.17 (RSV): "if any one is in Christ, he is a new creation". This is
one piece of evidence among others that God's creative activity
has not ceased, but is still going on now.

If we then turn to the relationship between salvation and judgement, it may at first appear that they are two contrary ideas, in as
much as judgement is something that divides, while salvation is
something that unites God and man. Nevertheless, there is an
indivisible and clear link between the two. Judgement presupposes
law: no law, no judgement. If there is judgement, the law is being
applied. We have just seen that salvation involves overcoming
opposition, the opposition that prevents salvation coming into
effect. It is here that law comes into the picture. It would be quite
misleading to speak of the law as a series of directions and commands, given at a certain moment in history. It is rather a divine
function in continuous action, disclosing what it is that prevents
fellowship with God, disclosing what is antagonistic to God and
antagonistic to humanity. This disclosure is felt by man as accusation and judgement. This function of God in the law is not in
itself an act of salvation. It does not create any fellowship with
God. But it is inseparably linked with his continuing work of
salvation, carried out in and through the gospel, breaking through
judgement so that God accepts the person who is under judgement
and receives this unacceptable, unworthy person into fellowship
with himself. This work of salvation is inscrutable. It is a mystery.
No motives or reasons can be given for it without making it cease to
be what it is. The God who saves does not eliminate or weaken
his utter opposition to all that is antagonistic to God, all that is
destructive. He does not stop unmasking it. On the contrary, in
the work of salvation, this unmasking is most strongly expressed.
Judgement and salvation come into dialectic relationship with one
another. There is at the same time both opposition and an unbreak-
able link. This dialectic relationship cannot be changed into a
temporal, psychological relationship, in such a way that the act of
judgement would always represent a preliminary stage in the economy of grace. To interpret it so would be to provide motives and
reasons for the act of salvation and that would deradicalize the
radical gospel.

It now remains to have a look at the relationship between

creation and judgement. This will be dealt with more fully in the last section of this chapter. We have already spoken of salvation as an instance of a continuing work of creation. In this combination of creation and judgement there is the same kind of continuing work of creation. It is marked by battle against the destructive forces at work in the world. But we are now dealing with a creation that lies on the level of law and of works. When "the law" comes in and the judgement that follows from it, it is not only as a defence and barrier against all that is destructive, but also as forcing and driving on works in the service of life and constructiveness, actions that are creative and that for faith bear witness that God's work of creation is still in progress. This leads to wide perspectives: in all this work—whether negatively opposing or positively constructing—faith discovers how God creates in and with his universal law, and all this whether men who are his agents are conscious of it or not. God's relation to creation is not partial but total. His activity is not limited to those people who—in faith—are conscious of it. In these circumstances it is no more possible here than in connection with salvation to regard the law as merely certain fixed commands or directions. The phrase that God works through the law—or if you prefer—as the law, expresses God's active reaction against anything that destroys his creation. And this is shown both by the fact that God in judgement puts a stop to the advance of destructive powers and by the fact that he compels actions by which creation is fulfilled.

This section has attempted to show the connection between the actions of God that in Christian language are called creation, judgement, and salvation. This connection is so intimate that we might well speak of one homogeneous activity of God seen in three aspects. The singleness of his activity is more clearly seen when we realize that there is one common denominator for his different ways of acting. His action always appears, so far as faith can perceive it, as being directed against something. There is always something that is to be overcome. This is true not only in the case of acts of judgement and salvation, where the conflict with the powers of destruction is clearly visible, but also in acts of creation, when this is seen as part of a continuing creation. Creation appears here as creation versus destruction, versus chaos. This conflict is the background against which God's actions are seen by faith, the context of meaning in which they are set.

THE PERFECT AND FUTURE TENSES

We have stressed the part played by the present tense in the world of faith. We are now to consider the relationship of faith to the past and to the future, to what has already happened, and to what has yet to come to pass. If Now has been the starting-point for our analysis of the tenses of faith, this is because faith exists as a relation to God at the present moment. If we were to leave Now out of our perspective and think of faith only as a relationship to something that has happened in the past, and possibly also to something that will happen in the future, faith would cease to be an "involved", personal, existential relationship to God. It would cease to be what it really is. It would be changed into an assent to things that had happened in the past, to the interpretation of these events by men, and of occurrences expected in the future. Faith in God would be changed into faith in a given teaching about God. All talk about God's actions, whether in the past or in the future, would appear as unfamiliar and unrecognized talk. Disconnected from a present-moment relationship to God they would all become irrelevant.

But once this point has been made, it must at once be added that what happens in the present is inseparably linked with what has happened in the past. Relationship with God at the present moment cannot be isolated. The God who involves people in the present moment, who "is working still", is the same God who was working in the past. What happens now is a direct continuation of what was happening in the past. Faith does not isolate man. Rather it places man in a wide context. What God is doing at the moment is one link in a chain of action, and this continuity gives faith both its foothold and its meaning.

In what has happened in the past there is one point in the past with the magnetism to draw our glances. For Christian faith Christ is the centre in the continuity of God's activity. If we listen to the original Bible evidence, we find this reflected in many formulas, in various ways attesting that what Christ did was of decisive and final significance for our relationship to God, and that this has given him a unique position. There is in Philippians 2 that eulogy of Christ which says that God has "exalted" Christ and "given him a name which is above every name" so that "every tongue should confess that Jesus Christ is Lord, to the glory of God the Father". This exaltation has come about because Christ "made himself of no reputation" and "became obedient unto death, even the death of the cross". The "exaltation" then was due to Christ in his human activity having fulfilled in obedience the task God gave him to do. The meaning of this action is shown in the Bible in different images—as an act of reconciliation, which is an act both of Christ and of God at the same time: "God was in Christ, reconciling the world unto himself" (2 Cor. 5.19); as a sacrifice that puts away sin (Heb. 9.26); as a destroying of the works of the devil (1 John 3.8); as an overcoming of death, "he hath abolished death, and hath brought life and immortality to light" (2 Tim. 1.10). All these statements have this in common that they stress the revolutionary, the unique, and the decisive factor in what Christ did. At the same time they bring to the fore the whole series of questions which through the ages has been asked about the person and the work of Christ. But it cannot be denied that these questions which have basically always been concerned with the meaning and validity of the Bible evidence have for various reasons become more pointed in our day. Part of the reason for this is the historical Bible criticism, working both on the historical problem of what really happened and on analysis of the Bible's own interpretation of what happened. But there are also other problems that come into the picture: the distance that separates the language of the Bible from that of our time, as well as the wider question of the character of religious language and its ability to find expressions for what it has to say. This is the sort of question with which we shall deal.

The question we now come to is the place of Christ in the continuity of divine activity, or to use traditional terminology, the relationship between "revelation" in Christ and the general, universal revelation of God. To begin with, it is clear that Christ is set in a context reaching backwards and forwards. Backwards lies all that the Old Testament recounts, forwards lies the life of the Church that bears the name of Christ. Backwards, as described in the Old Testament, is a chequered stretch of religious history, forwards is an equally chequered stretch of church history. But in both cases this is not all. The continuity backwards is also a witness to divine activity in the realm of preparation and promise, leading to the fulfilment which came when "the fulness of time was come". And the continuity forwards is not only a piece of very confusing human history, it is full of witness to how Christ continues and brings into effect the work that he completed during his earthly life, to how his Spirit has never ceased to carry out his work of making the message of Christ living and effective, thereby adding continually to the areas of life under his control.

Christian faith in God is christocentric. What God did through Christ is of decisive importance for our relationship to God. As a result, this action of God determines our image of God. No image of God can claim Christian dignity unless it conforms with the way God acted in Christ. The Bible says: the only begotten Son "has made him known" (John 1.18, RSV); "he that seeth me, seeth him that sent me" (John 12.45); "he that hath seen me hath seen the Father" (John 14.9).

But christocentricity is not in any opposition to universality. Universality is a pre-condition for christocentricity, which rightly understood opens people's eyes to the universality in God's work. Christocentricity would be misinterpreted if it were used to draw up limits for God's work, or if it were imagined that God's actions before the appearance of Jesus were on different lines or had different aims from those revealed later in his work in Christ. This needs now some comment.

First, the Bible always preserves inviolate the universal aspect of God's action. The New Testament sees the history which the Old Testament relates as a preparation for, and a promise of, what was to come "in the fulness of time". But let us first have a look at the Old Testament's own attitude. It never ceases to tell how the people of Israel were the object of God's "special" action, how God has "chosen" them, made a "covenant" with them, made them the object of his care. But this does not imply any limiting of the universality in God's work. The Bible does not limit God's activity to Israel. This is shown not only by the fact that the first three chapters of the Old Testament make the universal perspective of God's relation to the world and humanity form the background of all that is said in the rest of the Bible. It is also shown by the fact that the Bible never allows the idea that God's activity comes to an end at the frontiers of Israel: God uses other peoples as his instruments, Assyrians, Babylonians, etc.; he can take a Pharaoh or a Cyrus into his service. Finally, it is undeniable that over and over again in the Old Testament we find the idea that what God does with Israel is of significance for other people, that it has universal address; what happens in Israel is preparing for the realization of God's worldwide sovereignty over all nations.

The universal perspective is found even more clearly in the New Testament, where it is inseparably linked with Christology. What Christ does is done for all nations: "make disciples of all nations". In an analysis of how the christological perspective is linked with God's universal activity, there are two points of view, both of "cosmic" character. In one our attention is drawn to what happens through the "exaltation" of Christ—in the symbol language of the Bible: God "set him at his own right hand in the heavenly places, far above all principality, and power, and might, and dominion, and every name that is named, not only in this world but also in that which is to come" (Eph. 1.20–21). In the other our attention is drawn to God's act of creation in the beginning. This comes about through the "the Word" who was in the beginning: "All things were made by him; and without him was not anything made that was made" (John 1.3). It would be difficult to state the universality of the christological perspective more emphatically than is done here.

The phrase about God's creating through "the Word" throws light on the second of the two points to be commented on: the suggested contradiction between God's work through Christ and his "earlier" activity. The primitive Christian Church energetically opposed the gnostic theories of Marcion and others that the "creator god" was a different and lower god than the "God of salvation" revealed in Christ. When the early Fathers did battle with ideas like these, they were in full agreement with the Bible view. The very phrase that everything was created by "the Word" makes this clear. The real content of that phrase is that the God of creation and the God of salvation are one and the same. The ideas about God that men hold may vary—they do widely in the Old Testament. But in spite of this, God remains the same. This not only means (as it says in Ps. 102.27, quoted in Heb. 1.12) that his "years shall have no end". It also means that God always acts on the same lines and with the same goal. The God of Christian faith does not act sometimes in one way and sometimes in exactly the opposite way, capriciously and inconsistently. He always acts in accordance with "the law" that judges and spurs on, he always acts also as the God of "salvation", and in both cases as the God who is always creating afresh. His work through the law and his work of salvation do not serve different purposes. They both aim their attack at the destructive forces and both serve the on-going work of creation. The theory that distinguishes the Old Testament from the New by saying that in the Old Testament God acts only through the law and in the New Testament only through the gospel, meaning only as a God of salvation, does not tally with the evidence. God's work of salvation did not begin with the work Christ did during his days on earth. The Old Testament also has many clear instances of God as a God "of whom cometh salvation". And the salvation that God brings through Christ does not mean that he ceases to work through the law.

For Christian faith the Bible is the basic evidence for the character of God's on-going work, and for the direction that this takes. But this does not mean that faith would wish to draw up boundary lines within which it would wish to confine God's activity, or would wish to regard the Bible as doing so. Anything of that kind is unknown to Christian faith. It would seem presumptuous and irreverent. It is quite a different matter that the Bible is an authoritative witness to a series of actions of God, a continuity of them, leading on to, and finding fulfilment in, the work to which the apostles' preaching in the New Testament bears witness.

So what we find there is a continuation of something that has already happened, already been done or spoken, of demands that have been made and of saving actions. But this continuation is at the same time completion and fulfilment. The work of Christ is seen from a double aspect. The work he does at the same time is completion, fulfilment of law and of gospel. In the Sermon on the Mount we find a perfect expression of fulfilment: "Think not that I am come to destroy the law, or the prophets: I am not come to destroy, but to fulfil" (Matt. 5.17). This verse would be misinterpreted if the fulfilment of which it speaks were to be applied to "the law" alone. The expression "the law and the prophets" is a summary of all that God has done with Israel during the time of the old covenant—it applies equally to the work of salvation and to the work of the law. In John 1.17 we read: "the law was given by Moses, but grace and truth came by Jesus Christ." That verse would also be misinterpreted if we were to draw the consequence that the law of God had now ceased to apply—even the Johannine writings speak of the continuing validity of the law, of "a new commandment" which at the same time is "an old commandment which ye had from the beginning" (1 John 2.7–8). The thing that disappears through the grace that comes with Christ is not the law, but "the curse of the law" (Gal. 3.13), the condemnation the law brings: "There is therefore now no condemnation to them which are in Christ Jesus" (Rom. 8.1). The law is fulfilled in the work of Jesus—that is to say the law of creation, the law of the Creator is revealed in the fulness of its radical quality, and, what is more, it is fulfilled by him who was obedient unto death. Further, the gospel of God's salvation is revealed in the fulness of its radical quality. This comes about not only through its being presented as a message, but also in action: the forgiveness of sins is announced, new life is created, "as many as received him, to them gave he power to become the sons of God" (John 1.12).

When the work of Christ is seen under the double perspective of the law and salvation, there is another double perspective in the Bible that corresponds to it: it is seen as both a work of Jesus the man and a work of God himself. As "made of a woman, made under the law" (Gal. 4.4), he is in battle with temptation and in solidarity with all mankind obedient to the task given him, and he completes this act of obedience right through to the final sacrifice of his life on the cross. His life is a life in obedience to God, and his death the sacrifice that completes this obedience. But at the same time his life and suffering in battle with hard opposition is bringing God's saving power into the world. And when this happens in point of fact it is God who through this human action brings about his "counsel" of salvation: "God was in Christ, reconciling the world unto himself" (2 Cor. 5.19). His sacrificial death was not the end of the story, the cross was not just a martyr's cross. The Bible constantly links sacrifice and victory, death and life, passion and exaltation. The sacrifice was in itself a victory, death a way through to life, the passion a premiss of exaltation that gave Jesus the "name above every name", Kyrios, the Lord (see Chapter 4).

We shall return to the varied images with which the Bible interprets the work of Christ. As for the meaning of that victory, the Bible regards it as a victory over the powers of destruction, or, as the Bible puts it, over the devil, sin, and death. We read in 1 John 3.8: "For this purpose the Son of God was manifested, that he might destroy the works of the devil"; he has "appeared to put away sin by the sacrifice of himself" (Heb. 9.26); "who hath abolished death, and hath brought life and immortality to light" (2 Tim. 1.10). The meaning of statements like these is not to make the unrealistic suggestion that the victory of Christ has disposed of these powers of destruction, so that they cease to exist or to function. Ideas like this may appear in Christian theology or poetry. But they do not appear in the Bible. The victory that Christ has won over the hostile powers is his *own* victory. It is *he* who has overcome the devil and sin, and death has lost its power so far as he is concerned. It is before him that the hostile powers have been forced to retire. He stands there as victor. So far as he is concerned, the victory is complete.

The victory that was won—the victory of sacrifice—was an individual victory. But according to the Bible it was not just an episode which now belongs to the past. It was a break-through in the battle against the powers of destruction that is constantly going on in the world of human life, or, looked at from the other side, a break-through in God's relationship to men. It creates a new situation with new possibilities. It is not an end, it is a beginning. The work of Christ has not come to an end with what has happened in the past. The victory that was once won is the introduction to a continuing action, to an activity that is now no longer limited to, or hindered by, time and space. This is the meaning of all that the Bible with its symbol language has to say about the "exaltation" of Christ, about God's giving him the name above every name, about his setting him "at his right hand" in the heavenly world above all powers and lords, about God's giving him to the Church—*ecclesia*—to be head of all things. Bible statements like these draw our attention to Christ's on-going exercise of power, by which the victory he once won is now steadily carried into effect in the world where hostile powers are still at work, the world that still lives in a state of sin and death.

His victory once won did not mean—as we remember from the texts we have quoted—that the demonic powers are finally destroyed, that the reign of sin has come to an end, that death has been eliminated. But because *he* has broken the tyranny of these powers, because they no longer have any power in relation to him, he can continue and complete his victorious work, his work of salvation. Where he is in action, where men are involved and controlled by him and his Spirit, there the work of liberation is being carried out in present tense form: there "the works of the devil are being brought to nought", there "sin is being put away"; there he is "the Lamb of God that taketh away the sins of the world". There "the power of death", death as the forces of decay, "is destroyed", for there man is given a share in the life of incorruption. What happens there can be summed up in the words of St John, put into the present tense: as many as receive him, to them gives he power to become the sons of God. So new links are continually being added to the continuity, the spiritual union, the "Church", whose head is Christ. But what is done is at the same time God's own work: it is he, the Spirit of God, who involves, controls, overcomes opposition and creates the faith that consists in confidence and obedience.

It now becomes clear how the various tenses of faith relate to one another. What is happening has its basis, its sustenance, its life out of what has happened. What has happened is made real and reveals itself as a power—"the power of God unto salvation" (Rom. 1.16)—in what is happening. So there is not only a connection, a continuity between what has happened and what is happening, but there is also a reciprocity. What is happening at present is given substance by what has happened, at the same time as the meaning of what did happen is shown by what is happening. There would be no point in talking about God's actions in the past unless God were also one who "still works".

As faith also speaks in the future tense about what is going to happen, this eschatological future is anchored in the reciprocal action between what has happened and what is happening. Without this anchorage all talk about what is going to happen the other side of the limits of time would be reduced to unfounded fortunetelling. But this anchorage has a firm hold because actually every statement about what God does, whether in the past or in the future, is a statement with an aspect of eternity and is eschatological in character. As soon as God comes into the picture, there is always something eschatological about it, something connected with "the last things", something that in this sense too is of "*ultimate* concern". "Eternal life" is therefore not only something in the future, it is also at the same time something in the present: "this is life eternal, that they know thee the only true God, and Jesus Christ whom thou hast sent" (John 17.3). The eschatology of the future is not just loosely attached, it is part and parcel of faith as fellowship with God. But, on the other hand, this "time to come"—about which at present we hope—is not identical with, nor merely a straight-line continuation of, what now is. What is to come differs from what now is, in the same way as the perfect differs from the fragmentary: "when that which is perfect is come, then that which is in part shall be done away" (1 Cor. 13.10). The life of faith in the present is lived out in conflict and imperfection. And God's power is here a power that comes into effect through conflict with violent opposition. "Perfection" is what distinguishes the life of the world to come from the world of the present. There will then be something which "eye hath not seen and ear hath not heard", something that *cannot be seen* in present conditions. It will be a life where all opposition is definitely overcome and God's power is revealed as the sovereign power: "*Now* is come salvation, and strength, and the kingdom of our God, and the power of his Christ" (Rev. 12.10). It is analogous to Paul's description of the final act of the drama of history: everything will be subordinated to God "that God may be all in all" (1 Cor. 15.28).

We used the expression "the final act of the drama" just now. It was not a casual choice. There has been a dramatic perspective running through all that has been said about the tenses of faith. It all reflects history filled to the brim with dramatic tension and battle. But it is a drama where the principal character never appears on the stage. He is expected to reveal himself in the final act of the drama. But until then he remains the Unseen. His remaining concealed in this way does not mean that he does not make his presence felt, that he is not in action. We might illustrate how it appears from the point of view of Christian faith by remembering Strindberg's play, *Gustav Vasa*, where the principal character does not appear on the scene in the first acts, yet holds the threads in his hands all the time and makes himself emphatically felt. In God's drama with mankind, the principal character through the acts that are played during the passage of time remains the Unseen. But he makes himself felt through the human agents who appear on the stage—first and foremost through him who in the Bible account of the drama is called the Only Son.

A drama can be written and produced in such a way that the decisive action for the drama as a whole is concentrated on one particular scene. What happens there throws light over what has

gone before and determines what is to come afterwards. It is just
like that in the drama of life, God's drama in which faith is not
only a spectator but also an actor. Christ has the key part. His
action throws light on what has gone before and determines what
is to follow afterwards. Here, through him, it is revealed *how*
God acts and what is the goal of his action. This means also that
the features of the image of God are determined by what happens
here. In Bible language this is expressed as: "the glory of God in
the face of Jesus Christ" (2 Cor. 4.6); Christ "reflects the glory of
God" (Heb. 1.3, RSV); "he that hath seen me, hath seen the
Father" (John 14.9). The meaning of this is not that God has
appeared in visible form, that Christ was God walking about on
earth, or that God had thereby ceased to be the Invisible. He is
still—to use the words of Jesus—the Father in secret.

But this Invisible is none the less the "principal character" in
the drama, around whom everything circles. God as the invisible
principal actor—this means that he can only be sensed through what
happens and that his "image" can only be "drawn" by means of
symbols. God cannot be determined and defined with "adequate"
terms and expressions. He is not an object for "viewing". "We
walk by faith, not by sight", says Paul (2 Cor. 5.7), and of this
faith, the Epistle to the Hebrews says that it is "the conviction of
things not seen" (Heb. 11.1, RSV). What is seen, what can be
viewed, can be described and defined in more or less adequate
terms. But this is not possible with what is invisible, the Invisible
One. Here we have to turn to symbol language. That language is
the mother tongue of faith.

Two later chapters in this book will deal with these questions—
one with the symbols and one with the drama. Before that, in this
chapter, we must take up one important and many-sided problem.
We have already attempted to establish that the question of God is
a question of faith, a question to which only faith can give a positive answer, and also that our image of God is determined by our
relation to Christ. Does this imply a limitation and isolation of
faith and the world of faith? Does relationship to Christ mean
a limitation of God's activity? Does the fact that "faith and
God belong together" involve an isolation of the religious element,
delimiting it to an area closed in on itself, shut off from the rest of
the world? It is with these questions that we shall now deal.

Isolation?

So far this book has been setting out the theme: God and faith belong together. The question of God, however you may answer it, is a question of faith. It loses its meaning if you treat it as a theoretical problem to be solved with rational reasons, for and against. Faith in God exists, and can only exist, in the form of personal involvement. But if this is so, it raises at once a whole series of new questions: Does not this linking of God and faith lead to an isolation of the world of faith? Does not this world of faith become a closed area of life, shut in, screened off, exclusive, and out of contact with the rest of life? Is not this exactly what has been happening, progressively becoming more so, today?

It is not at all surprising if "the isolation of religion" has become a burning question. What else is possible? The reason is on everyone's lips, the word secularization. That is not to say that this word is unambiguous. It is not so. Still less is the reaction to it uniform. By secularization people mean in the main the process by which areas of thought, philosophical and scientific, and areas of life, especially the areas of morals, have been set free from any relationship to, and any dependence on, religious issues. We are not here concerned to investigate either the extent or the causes of this secularization. The only issue we shall deal with is the relation of theology to this process of secularization.

There are plenty of people who say that theology has to bear its share of the blame for what has happened and still is happening. The accusations are couched in a variety of terms; so are the recommendations given to theology on how to break out of this isolation. One main theme is the contrast between the theological climate in earlier times and now. In earlier times people had a much broader foundation on which to build. People reckoned with reliable proofs of God's existence, a rational knowledge of God, with natural religion, the rights of natural law—and consequently some natural theology. "Religion" then was not a closed and isolated area of life. It had as a matter of course contacts in every direction, and so therefore had theology too. Nobody thinks now that it would be possible just to go back to that situation. It is fully realized that critical philosophy discredited the old proofs of God's existence and so destroyed the basis for a supposedly rational knowledge of God. But people are still looking for a substitute for what has been lost. They are still looking for a new form of natural theology. We find an argument typical of the modern age in *Soundings: Essays concerning Christian Understanding*, published in 1963. The first article is entitled "Beginning all over again". The main thesis of the author, H. E. Root, is that the health of theology and of *faith* depends on the health of natural theology. The issue of natural theology is given very great importance; if it were unable to survive, it would mean admitting "the triumph of the secularized, post-religious attitude". According to the author, the "post-religious" attitude is the outlook for which "the question of God, of the meaning of life, the nature of reality and the destiny of man no longer have power to involve". For the moment we can leave the question how to provide this substitute, and merely take note that the demand for a new form of natural theology obviously charges theology with having neglected important tasks. It is a charge with wide perspectives. It is aimed not only at Karl Barth, who used to oppose any idea of a natural theology, but is also aimed at theological ideas with roots considerably further back in the history of theology.

Let us now listen to another charge, this time from Bonhoeffer's famous and much-discussed *Letters and Papers from Prison*. The term "secularization" does not appear, so far as I can find, in Bonhoeffer's letters. But the thing itself is very much there. Bonhoeffer describes it in the words: the world has come of age. "Coming of age" means that man "has learned to cope with all questions of importance without recourse to God as a working hypothesis"—in the field of science, art, and even morals this is taken for granted. When Bonhoeffer here speaks of a world coming of age, this does not mean that he regards this as negative, but rather that it has also a positive side. "Coming of age" is not therefore to be made a target for theological polemics or apologetics. The demands which it makes on theology are of a different nature. The world's coming of age "is to be understood better than it understands itself". The coming of age which is to be preserved is not that which makes man the measure of all things, but instead that which is "rightly understood" when it is seen in the light of relationship to God. It must be confronted with God "at its strongest point". This demands a wider theological perspective.

Relationship with God must not be restricted to "the peripheral questions" of life, or only the question of salvation. "I should like to speak of God," it says, "not on the borders of life but at its centre, not in weakness but in strength, not, therefore, in man's suffering and death but in his life and prosperity." Strong emphasis is placed on this worldliness: "We shall find God in what we comprehend, not in the incomprehensible; it is not in the unanswered questions, but in the answered ones that God will allow himself to be grasped by us."

In very pointed and intentionally shocking language Bonhoeffer announces his theological programme: to reach a non-religious, a worldly interpretation of theological ideas. Terms like this are easy to misunderstand, and have often been badly misunderstood. "Religionless" must lead to misapprehensions unless we are quite clear that "religion" in Bonhoeffer is a word that strikes a poor note, almost meaning egocentric, exclusively individualistic religiosity, whereas "faith", as contrasted with this religiosity, is a word of honour. To interpret "worldly" means to accentuate "the deep this-worldliness of Christianity", but it must not be taken to mean that faith is shut in in "this world". The this-worldliness for which Bonhoeffer pleads is "the deep earthiness which is full of discipline and which is lived face to face with death and resurrection".

It can be discussed whether Bonhoeffer, or the English volume of which I spoke, is pleading for a "natural theology". Some things point in that direction. But his strong christocentric orientation holds him back. He declares that a general belief in God is no genuine experience of God. On the other hand, what happens when one meets Christ is a genuine experience of God. Our relationship to God is not a "religious" relationship to what we imagine to be "the highest being"—"our relationship to God is a new life in existing for others, in sharing the life of Jesus". In accord with this he declares: "My theme is the claims of Jesus Christ upon a world come of age." The programme Bonhoeffer develops, or rather outlines, is concerned with a widening of the theological perspective, with fierce criticism of all theology that limits itself to the question of salvation, viewing it from a one-sidedly individualist and exclusive point of view.

Criticism of theological isolationism can also take the form of demanding an acceptance of that view of the world which, it is claimed, is now taking shape through modern scientific research. The background to these demands for a new orientation is provided by the lively debates in earlier times about the relationship between faith, theology, and world-view. There had long been, particularly in the nineteenth century, a battle between, on the one hand, a faith in God that was more or less closely bound to "the ancient view of the world", treating the Bible story as teaching about the origin of the world, and, on the other hand, natural science starting out from Newton's mechanics and regarding the universe as celestial machinery, functioning with mathematical precision. The conflict was insoluble, and destined to end in favour of science, so long as the Bible was regarded as an authority on scientific questions. For theology the first task was to show how belief in creation really meant something different, and was on a different level from scientific theories on the origin of the world and its development. As soon as the religious perspective is allowed to tell its own story, belief in creation becomes independent of science with its world-views that change with the times.

But if faith in God is one thing and "scientific world-view" another, this does not prevent there being a relation between them. This is what is really being sought when people critize theology for isolationism. This criticism considers that modern revolutionary science gives new openings for fruitful contact. Much has been written on this, and much more will be written, in varying degrees of expectancy. One of the boldest voices is that of Kerstin Anér, in a witty article written with journalistic sparkle, entitled "Crown of Creation". Theology gets a touch of the lash for so seldom attempting to express the gospel in the world-view of the 1960s: "So it is the laymen who will have to do it, and to begin at the other end: begin with the world-view of our own times, where boundaries for imagination and thought are being burst through all the time."[1] It sounds very like the English document, "Beginning all over again". The article goes on to paint the fantastic development of research. In the words of an expert, modern nuclear physics are to be understood in much the same way as the symbolism of lyrical verse.

The world to which we have to adjust ourselves today has grown in all directions unbearably. Upwards into space until not even light travels fast enough to reflect back to us. Downwards to anti-protons and

[1] *Stockholms Stiftsbok* (1963), pp. 18–25.

"strange particles", and nobody knows what they may be. Inwards to the depths of unconsciousness far below the bottom of our personality. Out beyond the beginning of time with cities planned ten thousand years ago and human bones half a million years old. Forward to changes we can surmise but know that we cannot even imagine. As against this, most of us have a sort of home-spun religion from the days when the farmstead ran a couple of acres in any direction.

The writer points out that the new world-view basically goes well with Christian perspectives.

The difficulty is not to fit Christianity in to the universe of our times; for a century or two the difficulty has been to fit it to as narrow a world-view as that of Newton and Darwin. Now we are beginning to come out of it, and Christ can once again recover his cosmic dimensions.

She then quotes from the Bible: "for in Christ all things were created, in heaven and on earth, visible and invisible, whether thrones or dominions or principalities or authorities—all things were created through him and for him" (Col. 1-16, RSV). The world-view best able to "spread its wings" in the space age is the one that two thousand years ago said: "What we shall be, we know not yet."

In her article Kerstin Anér seems to make two points. First, the perspective of the Bible is really by no means so narrow and shut in as people often think when they talk about the Bible being bound to the world-view of antiquity. Secondly, contact with modern scientific research helps us to become aware of the cosmic perspective of the Bible. To this I should like to add some words from Martin Lönnebo's interesting *Kyrklig kraftsamling, en debattbok* (1963). Of contact with scientific thinking he says: "traditional thinking" is often "dangerously near a doctrine of the double truth". He goes on:

Natural history research ought of course to be classified within theology as the authority on existence. It studies "God's book", it explores God's magnum opus, and is producing the finest "*natural theology*" of our day.[1]

Note that the writer puts "natural theology" in quotation marks, to indicate that it is not natural theology in the traditional sense of the words.

Many more instances could be quoted, but this is enough to

[1] Op. cit., p. 52 (my italics).

start us considering the problems and the way the questions are framed. There is a general pattern of criticizing theology and at the same time making demands on it. Is it justifiable to criticize theology for neglect and for islolation—and, if so, what has gone wrong? Can theology meet all the demands made on it? Many deep issues have been raised. People ask for a "natural theology". But natural theology has not always had a good reputation—one would hesitate to follow some of the tracks it opens up. Are there justifiable motives behind the demands? What are people aiming at? What can be attained? The question of faith and world-view is no new question. Theology has struggled with it through the centuries. But it keeps on being asked, and asked in new forms. And finally, behind it all there is the old and ever-new question on the relationship between faith—faith in God—and the knowledge that is won through scientific research, both of natural science and of history. Faith is not founded on, and does not arise through, scientific research. It always involves "personal commitment". Does this mean that faith has to live in isolation, or even to be banished to the world of illusions? Or has faith something of importance to say to the world in which we live?

Before dealing with the more important of these questions, let me lay down some general lines. It might first be asked whether the proposition that "God and faith belong together" does not predispose people to isolate theology. Does not this view of things, the idea that God can be "grasped" only in and through faith, mean that the world of faith is fenced off as an area of life on its own, and therefore isolated? Now, as we have already seen, one of the main tasks of theology is to analyse Christian faith. Theology cannot make God a direct object of study. What it can study is faith, faith in God. What it has to do is to understand faith, understand its content and meaning. Here, as in all research, there must be analysis by every possible means. It is not possible to conduct a theological work of this kind in isolation. It must be related not only to other branches of theological research but also to virtually all the research that is going on to map and understand the world in which we live.

But it is one thing that theology cannot be isolated from other kinds of study—it is an entirely different matter how faith is isolated and whether theology contributes to this isolation. Two things need to be said. First, *if* theological analysis of the content of faith leads to an isolation of the world of faith, the basis of this is that the perspective of faith has somehow been too narrowly constricted, which is to say that the analysis has not been conducted in a way that does justice to the object of study. Secondly, the task of analysing the content of faith—the task of "systematic" theology—is and will always remain one of the principal tasks of theology. But the wide field of theological study has other tasks too. And one of them, important in this context, is the task of the philosophy of religion, which in one form or another has to deal with the legitimacy of the perspective of faith.

Now for the general lines I promised. Behind the "natural theology" of earlier times there are two main motives: people wanted through rational proof to lay a firm foundation on which faith—or, as it was usually termed, "revelation"—could continue to build; and at the same time people wanted to assert and express the universality of relationship to God. There is no possibility of natural theology coming back in that form. Rational proof has been disposed of by philosophical criticism. Besides, it would undoubtedly involve a considerable risk of a reinterpretation of Christian faith. On the other hand, it is also apparent that the elimination of natural theology has its obvious risks, particularly the narrowing of the universal perspective of faith. This double-sided relationship between natural theology and Christian faith can be explained only by saying that natural theology in its unserviceable and misleading form contained something that was necessary for faith—the present-day call for "natural theology" in a new form is explained by this. So what is needed is to separate the essential content from the unserviceable and unsafe frame of ideas in which it was cased. This can be done only by making clear what is involved in the universality of relationship with God. To do this would not be natural theology in the traditional sense of the term, but would be a substitute for the old natural theology—though only so in part. The theme behind the first main motive of natural theology—the firm foundation—has not yet been touched upon. To provide a sure basis, such as rational proof was meant to provide, is not possible. But the theme will recur. It is inevitable. It leads us to the issue of the philosophy of religion: Is it possible to legitimate the perspective of faith, and if so, how?

Universal Perspective

When in earlier centuries people talked about natural theology, there were two complexes of ideas in their minds. One was the proofs of God's existence thought necessary to lay the foundation for a purely rational knowledge of God. The other was natural law, thought of as justice resting on human reason or on its own inherent nature, containing absolute demands valid for all time and goals appropriate to them.

People wanted to prove the existence of God. But of which God? We have already stressed that the word "god" can be a word to cover the most varying concepts. It then becomes meaningless to isolate the question of God's existence and—independently of what is meant by the word "god"—try to answer the question whether he exists or not. To give a positive answer to a question put in this way would mean that one said Yes to the existence of a "being" about whom nothing was stated and who could therefore only be said to be an x. When human thinking has for centuries been busy trying to put forward rational, sound proofs of the existence of God, the arguments have of course not been concerned with anything so meaningless as an x of this kind. What they have been trying to demonstrate has really been a rationally constructed concept of God, a "highest being" conceived in a certain way. The statements made about this highest being were made in contrast to human imperfection and limitations. God was thought of as all-powerful, in contrast to the limited power of man; as omniscient and all-wise in contrast to the limited knowledge and wisdom of man; as moral perfection in contrast to the moral imperfection of man. It was this kind of concept of God that people wanted to secure by proofs of the existence of God.

There is no need to describe how the concepts of God and of natural law have been shot to pieces by the drum fire of philosophical criticism. It has often been said of the ruins that they stand as a beautiful witness to man's search for God. It might almost be more correct to say that they not only bear witness to that search but also to an actual faith, and a faith that was not content to remain faith. But, if our age has brought up again the question of natural theology—or at least a substitute for it—it would be well

to bear in mind the risks linked with the natural theology of old.
It was not a case of Christian faith, as had for so long been imagined, being simply able without complications to build on the
foundation of natural theology. There were considerable risks, as
was natural when it was really a matter of combining entirely
different things, an abstract concept of God and the living God-
in-action of Christian faith. The nature of these risks can be
illustrated by observing how proofs like the cosmological and
moral proofs were able to affect the image of God of Christian
faith.

The cosmological proof argued that existence as a whole must
be derived from God as the first cause, conditioning all. God's
all-mightiness is therefore regarded as being all-causality. God then
is the cause of all that happens. But this supposes something that
the Christian faith clearly denies. For to Christian faith it is
certain that God is *not* the cause of all that happens, and that on
the contrary there is much in existence which is in radical opposition to God, and with which he is in conflict. However, when people
had nevertheless allowed themselves to be led into accepting the
theory that God was the cause of all, it could only lead to insuperable complications. In the lumber room of theology there are
quantities of compensating, compromising "solutions" that
have attempted to reconcile the unreconcilable, or so far as possible
conceal how unreconcilable it was. People tried their best to
neutralize the damage that poured out like a torrent from the
theory of God's being the cause of everything, and that would
otherwise have turned the God of faith into "a cruel god"—to
use the words of Lagerkvist's Ahasuerus.

The moral proof of God's existence, however it is formulated,
comes into conflict with the image of God of Christian faith. The
difficulty of presenting a proof in the strict sense is of course
insuperable. If we turn to Kant's proof, it is not a proof in the
strict sense, only something called "a practical assumption".
What is assumed is the moral order which has its origin in God
and which is also watched over by him. God displays his righteousness by punishing the evil and rewarding the good. God becomes
the God of avenging righteousness. Retribution is given the final
word. Now of course the idea that God judges evil is firmly
anchored in Christian faith. But when this idea is made the
starting-point for our image of God, and also is given the last word

on it, there is no longer any room for the radical gospel. There is no room for the unfathomable love of God which breaks through the system of justice. This radical gospel does not mean that God now ceases to act as judge. But it does mean an overcoming of the moralism which is inseparably linked with all forms of moral proof of God, including Kant's practical assumption.

But the linking of Christian faith with a supposedly rational knowledge of God involves not only a risk of the fatal effects on the image of God which we have pointed out. There are two further things to be noted. First, this linking conceals the fact that the God of faith, as we have already seen, is entirely different from the abstract concept of a God of rational proofs or the "highest being". An abstract concept of God—an ultimate cause or anything else—is entirely different from the living God in action of whom faith speaks. Nor can the God of faith be reduced to some "highest being", which must always involve some relativization: God would be a being beside other beings in our world of existence, even if he were the highest. The very attempt to provide a proof for the existence of God must appear strange to faith, in conflict with the very nature of faith, and resulting in an entirely different relationship to God than that which faith knows. Secondly, the attempts to prove the existence of God were intended to lay a firm and secure foundation for knowledge of God and for faith in God, but the result was, as history shows, the exact opposite. If it were possible to state reasons for the existence of a divine highest being of this kind, it must also be possible to state reasons for his not existing. When the God of faith was linked with the God of rational proof, or even identified with him, criticism of the process of rational proof could also be regarded as a criticism of faith and of its God. This link meant that faith was in risky and hazardous company, and had no occasion to remain in company with it.

Linking Christian faith with a rational knowledge of God, and making it in fact dependent on it, had proved fatal. It was therefore in principle in the interests of faith that the link should be broken. And broken it was. This was mainly due to philosophical criticism. But, if anyone expected that this would have led to a clearer and more adequate theological view of faith and its perspectives, this was by no means the result. Actually, when the history of the process and consequences of breaking the link is reviewed, it turns out that not only the link had its risks, but also the elimination of a rational knowledge of God had its risks. When the link was broken, what came into the danger zone was the universal perspective of faith. While they were linked, this universal perspective had been represented more or less by the "natural theology" of the rational knowledge of God, which of course had universal application. Relationship with God applied to the world in its totality—it did not permit any limits to be drawn up to screen off and fence in this universal application. Now it was this universal perspective that came into danger when rational knowledge of God was eliminated. If there was no rational knowledge of God, if instead it was just a matter of faith "taking up a position" on the basis that faith and God belong together, if therefore all statements about God were merely statements of faith, then it would be easy to consider that faith, as it were, had a monopoly of God and that God basically could not have any relations with "the world" except those that come through faith. The risk in other words was that we might end up in what could be called an exclusiveness of faith, an isolation of the world of faith. In fact, it was not only a risk. It is undeniable that we can find obvious symptoms of this kind of exclusiveness. But it is equally undeniable that exclusiveness of this kind means a narrowing of Christian faith. Let us look at these two undeniabilities.

There is a chapter in the history of theology that shows strikingly how the tendencies to exclusiveness work and how the universal perspective is narrowed. It is the chapter of the law of God. When people used to try to work out how it functioned, they distinguished between the "first" and "second" use of the law, as they called it. The "second" use of the law was that God used the law to show up and condemn human sin so that he could afterwards meet man with the gospel of salvation. This "use" of the law was always thought of as directly linked with "salvation", and working in its service. But here it is particularly the first use of the law that we should note. Behind this term lies the idea that by his "law" the God of creation was still actively at war with the destructive forces of the world. The function of the law was to counter and block anything that would damage creation, to create order instead of chaos, fellowship instead of division, building up mutual service instead of injury. From this aspect "creation" appeared not only as a work completed some time in the past but as something continually going on, as a work in which God could use people as his instruments whether they were conscious of it or not, whether they confessed his name or not. In other words God's relation to the world was not limited to a relation only to the people who had been involved in faith by him. Faith is entirely dependent on God. But God's relation to the world is not dependent on faith. It exists before faith and independently of it. It is not only something that can come into being in the course of living, but it is given in and with life itself, whether man is conscious of it or not. God's relation to the world is not particular but universal.

This universality of relationship to God is inseparably linked with the perspective of creation, but not with any doctrine of creation at all: not with that view of creation that limits it to being a work carried to its conclusion once in the past "in the beginning", and that by doing so changes belief in creation into a theory about the origin of the world alongside other theories. If God's relation to the world is given with life itself, this means that creation is— and can only be regarded as—a work of God in continuous progress: life is being constantly created anew. As given, "created" by God, it is also in a permanent relation to him. This view has received its classical expression in Luther's explanation of the First Article of the Creed, where it says that "God has created me and all beings" and where it goes on to say how God protects "from harm, danger and all evil".

When it says here that God "maintains" creation and protects from harm, it is not just a matter of preserving creation, but the work of creation is continuing in battle against the destructive forces. It is here that "the law" comes into the picture. But this law is not just a series of fixed commandments but a demand which the varying situations in life make upon a person in his contacts with others, a demand to resist and do battle against everything that threatens these contacts with chaos, calamity, and ruin. The demand—the law—works as a barrier, an impeding, protecting factor—that is one side of the matter. But it also functions as a driving force in the service of construction. Any work, of whatever kind, that in one way or another promotes living together, is by that very fact serving creation and continuing the work of creation.

In and through this demand, meeting men in their various situations in life, the God of creation is still at work. The picture of what is happening would be distorted if "the law" were separated from the ongoing activity of God, and described as an ordinance once given by this God who then, as it were, withdrew from his creation. When the law functions, God functions. When the law functions as an impeding factor, it reveals God's radical opposition to all that is destructive and evil—his condemnation of all that leads creation to ruin is revealed in the consequences that follow when the destructive forces are allowed to run riot unhindered. When the law acts as a promoter of actions in the service of the common life, this reveals how the work of new creation is still in progress.

In this ongoing double work of God through the law he uses men as his instruments. His ability to use them is not conditioned by whether they acknowledge him or not, nor does it depend on their degree of goodness, so that God would be able to work only through "good" people. Here again it is true that "none is good but God alone". The perspective of how God can work through human instruments in the service of creation and for the advancement of the common life of mankind does not involve any idealization of man. If God could work only through good people freed from selfishness, no such work in the service of creation would be possible at all. When, however, work of this kind is nevertheless going on, it is a work that is driven forward in spite of all human selfishness and indeed in opposition to it. But it should be added that this perspective stands guard against any depreciation of mankind that might occur in theological presentations of human sin.

To summarize: our theme was the universality of relationship with God. Two things have been emphasized: that this universality was due to the fact that relationship with God was given in and with life itself; that this relationship, implicit in creation, finds expression in God's ceaseless action through the law, the demand, which has a double function—to protect and to fulfil the work of creation. This view has been linked with what theology through the centuries has had to say about "the first use of the law". However, this view of the universality of relationship to God is no new thing, nor a speciality for the doctrine of the first use of the law. Rather these are ideas that are anchored in the world of the Bible and are there developed far more vividly and picturesquely than in theological writings on the first use of the law. The central theme of the Bible is the description of the election of Israel, finding its fulfilment in the work of Christ, when the "old covenant" was replaced by a "new covenant". But this election is not opposed to, and is no limitation of, the universality of relationship with God. On the contrary, it is set within the frame of the universal perspective and cannot be rightly understood without it.

In other words, the election does not imply any narrowing of God's activity, nor any disengaging of his relation to creation as a whole. Both Old and New Testaments bear witness to this.[1] The election, both that of Israel and that which finds fulfilment in Christ, does not mean that it is only here that God works. It does not imply any exclusiveness, still less any guaranteed privilege that might be claimed. Time and again in the New Testament ideas of this kind are controverted. It does not help to say "Abraham is our father". It is no guarantee. These words of Jesus can contradict it: "Many shall come from the east and west, and shall sit down with Abraham, and Isaac, and Jacob, in the kingdom of heaven" (Matt. 8.11). What Jesus says in the Gospels is actually continual pointed criticism of drawing an exclusive line. Chorazin, Bethsaida, and Capernaum are warned that on the day of judgement it will be more tolerable for Tyre and Sidon and Sodom than for them (Matt. 11.21–3). It is the Samaritan, in contrast to the priest and the Levite, who by showing mercy has acted in accordance with the law of God. These passages all go to show that God's activity is not regarded as being limited to the Chosen People. Similarly Paul in the first two chapters of the Epistle to the Romans writes of how God is in action outside the area of the elect. In either case, it is viewed from the aspect of the law, once as judging, and the other time as positively spurring on, compelling, and activating. In the first chapter it deals with how God "in wrath" judges unrighteousness. In the second chapter we find the well-known words about the Gentiles "which have not the law"—the law of Moses—but who still "do by nature the things contained in the law" and thereby "shew the work of the law written in their hearts".

It is to be noted that what Jesus says is placed in exactly the same context as what he had just been saying about Capernaum and Sodom. It is a question of what will be revealed in the judgement

---

[1] See pp. 57–8 above.

when—as St Paul says—not the hearers of the law but "the doers of the law shall be justified". This passage about the Gentiles and the law has been interpreted in many ways. But, however it may be interpreted in details, it is certain that it cannot be a declaration that the "Gentiles" are independent of God, without any relationship with him. What Paul means is exactly the opposite, that the law of God, the law of creation, is at work in those who know nothing of the commandments of the decalogue; in fact that it was God who "wrote", who drove forward the *work* of the law in their hearts. It is clear that "the law" is not regarded here as definite, set commands and instructions, but instead as an active power, a divine *dunamis*. Paul speaks of the gospel as a *dunamis* of God unto salvation. He might also have called the law a compelling and creative *dunamis* of God.

This Bible view of how God works through the law and of the universality of relationship to God is preserved in the doctrine of "the first use of the law" even though in somewhat stereotyped form in that the law is thought of less as *dunamis* of God than as commandments and ordinances promoting a *iustitia civilis*. In addition to "the first use of the law" people were glad to speak of "the natural law". Both these terms could be used in the same sense —the natural law being then regarded as identical with the law of creation, or rather of the Creator. But it was also possible to disengage the natural law from this connection. This was what happened in the seventeenth and eighteenth centuries when it was "secularized". It was then thought to be set up on a purely rational basis, to consist of definite, unalterable ethical standards involving human rights valid for all. As being a law wholly based on reason, it was thought to be the self-evident basis for the ordinances of the common life of mankind. It took over the functions earlier ascribed to "the first use of the law", and served as a substitute for the law of God—until its position was undermined by the crushing effect of philosophical criticism, denying the possibility of building a system of rights on a rational basis. As they then said, there could be no place for any law or system of rights, generally valid—only for views of what is right, in competition with one another.

It will be remembered that we said that not only by maintaining but also by eliminating "rational knowledge of God", natural theology, and natural law, Christian faith in God would be subjected to risks, and that in the latter case the risk was that the perspective of faith would be narrowed and faith itself would become isolated. This was really much more than a risk. It is a fact that Christian faith today lives in a highly "secularized" world, that earlier contacts between what is humanist and what is Christian have been weakened or broken, and that all this leads to isolation. It is this which lies behind the demand for a new natural theology. People may not be very clear what they are wanting. There can be no return to the old natural theology. But they want something in place of it. We are reminded of Bonhoeffer's not particularly clear words about a "non-religious" theology and about a "wordly interpretation of theological concepts"—even if he himself would never have spoken of natural theology and still less of natural law. He had made much too close acquaintance with the Nazi form of "the natural law", determined by Blut und Boden. He preferred to speak of the divine "mandates", the divine commissions, and wanted in this way to illustrate how God met man not only "on the frontiers" but also "in the midst of life".

We are not going to attempt to give a general analysis of all that has contributed to "secularization" and "isolation", expressed in the cleavage between what is humanist and what is Christian. We are only concerned with the question whether, and to what extent, the Christian attitude can have contributed to this. Intentionally I write "the Christian attitude". This is not only a matter of theology. The problem is wider than so. Yet we do first have to pay attention to what has happened in the world of theology.

The first thing we notice is that when rational knowledge of God—and with it all natural theology and natural law—went by the board, the whole theological concept based on "the first use of the law" went too. It had fallen under suspicion because of its connection with the natural law. The consequences were widespread. It was this that had borne up the idea of the universality of relationship with God, there was a relationship even where there was no conscious, professing faith. As this aspect was eliminated, the tendency grew to limit the activity of God to the area of faith and to set "the world" outside it. The universality of relationship with God had come into the danger zone and disappeared more and more from sight. This meant at the same time that the perspective of creation more or less ceased to function. The universal activity of God had been linked with, and realized in, the thought of how God was still at work in and through the law of creation. In other words, the universality of relationship with God had been included in belief in creation, though, be it noted, in a view of creation as an ongoing work of God.

There was, of course, no rejection of the idea of creation as such. People went on speaking of creation, but only as an act carried out in the past, "in the beginning". The thing that has been suppressed is the relationship of creation to the present time. And with that, belief in creation has in reality ceased to function. A concept of creation that reduces it to an act in the past, thus transforming it into a metaphysical concept related to the "ultimate cause" of rational knowledge of God, no longer functions in our day. It needs to be a belief in creation with direct relation to, and relevance for, the present time; a belief in creation according to which relationship to God is given in and with life as such, and according to which God is one who, in battle with the destructive forces of the world, is still continuing his work of creation.

In so far as belief in creation has in this way ceased to function, God's activity becomes *de facto* limited to his work of salvation, the work by which he involves people in faith. A shift of this kind is to be noted in pietist currents, and an attitude of this kind has often made itself felt in theological works right down to the present time, even in some that are anything but pietist.

These lines of thought led to a considerable narrowing of the universal perspective of Christian faith. There was, for instance, a changed view of the law and its function. With the elimination of what was called the first use of the law, the action of the law was limited to what was called its "second use": to show up and to judge human sin. Basically the law was in the service of salvation; it prepared for, and made possible, that act of salvation by which God took into fellowship sinful man when conscious of his sin and penitent. This gave man power to fulfil the demands of the law, which he had not been able to do, because "the natural man" cannot. It is easy to see that a conception of this kind must lead to drawing a border line between what is Christian and the world outside the Christian sphere, between Christian and profane, both through what is assumed and what is denied. It is also easy to see that there was a great danger of Christian *hubris* creeping in.

The logical consequence of this line of thought would be that the natural man could not do anything "good", anything in conformity with God's demands; and secondly that these demands could be fulfilled by the man who was "born again" through salvation. Neither statement was capable of verification. The former, the negative statement, is false even from faith's own point of view. It draws up limits to God's activity which cannot be drawn. The man of faith has to admit that he does not have any monopoly of doing good works in the service of his neighbour or of creation. He has to admit too that people who do not acknowledge God can do things that put him to shame. The latter statement, the positive one, is only half the truth. It is true in so far as there is plenty of evidence that faith or fellowship with God can drive men to willing and sacrificial service. But it would be false idealism to attempt to conceal one thing that is shown up more than anything else by meeting the *agapē* of God—that all human activity falls short and is tainted by sin. There is no place here for conceit, only for humility; none for *hubris*, only for *humilitas*.

Christian faith in salvation is therefore not of a kind to call out any self-centred exclusiveness. Nor can ideas of this kind appeal for support to Christ. The warnings to Capernaum and Bethsaida are still valid today. Their target is not only the Pharisaism of their times, but all forms of Christian exclusiveness. If faith in salvation is used in this way, it is a sure sign that it has lost contact with faith in creation, which in turn is losing its meaning so that man is dethroning God as creator.

In actual fact any limitation of the universality of relationship with God must be branded as alien to Christian faith. To say that this is the consequence of God and faith belonging together is to confuse things that should be kept separate. The statement that God and faith belong together means that faith is dependent on God. It also means that any assertions about God and his actions are assertions of faith. But it does not mean at all that God and his activity are dependent on faith, that God can act only by using as his instruments people who believe in him, as if faith had a monopoly of God's activity. Christian faith draws no such boundaries, no boundaries at all to God's activity. It is not necessary to try to derive the universal perspective from any supposed rational knowledge of God. It is an essential element in Christian faith.

Summarizing this, we find neither natural law nor natural theology in the traditional sense. To begin with, it is not natural law in the sense of general or universal moral principles derived from reason. But we find that what is preserved is the universal perspective that natural law supported. The law is what the demand is anchored in, given with life as it is formed and created, as it is still in process of being created. It functions in and with relations to other men and to things, to nature as a whole, as they are given in creation. The demand is for what builds up as against what breaks down, what serves creation and helps towards its fulfilment as against what harms it, and is destructive. This demand is given in the very structure of creation and is therefore primary in relation to all human attempts to fix general or universal moral principles. If principles of this kind are ranked above it, the result is not morals but moralism. K. E. Lögstrup says: "Our existence is essentially moral and immoral in its own potentialities, and does not become so as a result of principles."

For Christian faith this demand, given with life and its relationships, is not only a demand of creation but also necessarily of the Creator. The demand is a demand that the Creator constantly renews in the shifting situations. And what is more, every realization of the demand means that the Creator is in action, maintaining creation and fulfilling it in the face of all that is destructive and undermining, that for this his ongoing work he takes people into his service whether they confess his name or not.

In this law of creation, all other "law" is included. The law is one and indivisible just as the demand of God is one and indivisible. What the Bible has to say about the law and "commands" of God does not mean that here is another "higher" law than that of the Creator, but is instead a giving of a concrete form to, a making explicit of, the one indivisible law. When in his Epistle to the Romans Paul mentions some of the ten commandments and continues thus: "and if there be any other commandment, it is briefly comprehended in this saying, namely, Thou shalt love thy neighbour as thyself", what he is trying to say is that the requirement of loving care of one's neighbour is a fundamental human requirement, implicit in human relations as given in creation, real and inevitable. This perspective of our common humanity keeps guard against, and demolishes, all tendencies to Christian isolation. The faith in whose view God's creative work is ever going on in everything that is constructive and that counters the advance of destructive powers has no interest in any suggestion of a Christian monopoly, nor for the prestige claims that go with it. The universal perspective is a platform which makes contact between Christian and non-Christian not merely possible but inevitable.

As this requirement is implicit in life itself, and its immediate relations with human beings and with nature, it is a constant requirement, ever inevitable, ever renewed under changing conditions. But these changes do not bring any change in the nature of the requirement. The alternative remains, constructiveness or destructiveness. Our generation has experienced more rapid and more radical change of conditions than any previous age. The fantastic discoveries of science and the breath-taking advances of technology have changed the world. Powers previously unimagined have been put into the hands of man. This has meant equally unimagined possibilities of a constructive nature. But at the same time we are well aware that these powers can equally well be used for destruction. Atomic power for present-day man is both a factor of hope and a factor of fear, with boundless risks for man and nature. To take one instance where the fear factor seems to predominate, we may think of modern biochemistry's possibilities of profoundly changing human nature. Brain-washing gives us some idea of the possible risks. Facts like these make us realize the requirements that are implicit in life itself and its immediate relations to human beings and to nature—make us realize the requirement and heighten our sense of responsibility. Another example of revolutionary change in relations between the peoples of the world is what we call help to developing countries. The measures that force themselves upon us, whether we want them or not, illustrate the compelling power of the requirements inherent in the common life of man as such.

This seems to answer the question of natural law and to be a substitute for it, even if only in outline. By far the most important thing, as we have stressed, is that the universal perspective of Christian faith is not infringed or narrowed. But we have still not finished with the questions connected with the demands for a new natural theology. What is it that people want or ask for from theology? It seems in the main to be to get either their scientific or their philosophical bearings.

We go back to Lönnebo's remark that a study of nature is producing the best "natural theology" of our time. We go back to Kerstin Anér's talk of the theologians neglecting to "express the gospel in terms of the world-view of the 1960s", "bursting all the bounds of imagination and thought". Her view is that modern science gives a very different scope from that of the narrow view of the world of Newton and Darwin, with which theology wrestled so long in the past. Now she may say this, but, if so, it is not because present-day science has formulated a fixed new view of the world, but rather because it is most hesitant to do so, because—in contrast to the studies of an earlier age—it refuses to sketch a world picture of metaphysical structure. Does it want to put forward any view of the world at all? There are good reasons for leaving that question unanswered. Certainly the scientists are not concerned to produce theology of any kind. Now it must be conceded that when Lönnebo spoke of it, he put quotation marks round the words "natural theology" by way of indicating that they were not to be taken too literally. What he means is not that we should get our theology direct from science, but rather that the increasing knowledge given to us by science about the universe we live in concerns all of us and therefore greatly concerns theology. If it is doubtful whether present-day science wants to put forward any view of the world, this alone challenges the statement that the task of theology is to express the gospel in terms of the view of the universe of the 1960s. One of our Swedish theologians who has shown great interest in contact between theology and science, Gösta Lindeskog, has good reasons for his statement in a document on "Science and the Bible" that "the gospel is in no way dependent on views of the world, whether the Bible view of the world or any other views".

In principle, it is not only the gospel but the whole of Christian faith that is not dependent on changing views of the world. Faith is no more restricted to the idea of a three-decker universe— heaven, earth, and underworld—than it is to the idea of time limited to a few thousand years. It is independent of whether people think in terms of very limited space and very limited time or in terms of the unimaginable extent of millions of light years in time and space, as we shall see in the next chapter about the symbol language of faith. The Bible often says that God "dwells" in heaven and has his "throne" there. But even the Old Testament shows that people realized the inadequacy of ideas of locality and their symbolic nature. So too with God and time. He for whom "a thousand years are as a watch in the night" and who is "from everlasting to everlasting" (Ps. 90) cannot be fitted into any time scheme, calculable or incalculable.

When it is realized that the language of faith is symbol language, faith ceases to be restricted to changing ideas about the universe, whether of Bible times or later. Faith can move freely and unembarrassed in a universe where, to quote Kerstin Anér "all limits for imagination and thought are constantly being broken through". It does not feel strange when faced with the breathtaking perspectives that modern science sketches, often in symbol formulas. But this freedom does not mean that theology regards what happens in the world of science as no business of hers. Theology cannot help confronting her analysis of the meaning of faith with contemporary thinking where science is so dominant. And if we include its consequences in the area of technology, the scope for dialogue is still further extended.

When we face the problems connected with natural science and the way we think about the world, we have to remember that our view of the world can mean different things. The observations and discoveries of astronomy and nuclear physics are one thing, the philosophical consequences of these scientific results drawn by scientists or philosophers in constructing a total view, a worldview in the true sense of the word, are quite a different matter. Science as such produces no world-view, and therefore to speak of "the scientific view of the world" is inappropriate. Science can, if you like, produce the material to construct a world-view. But to produce a world-view in the real sense of the word, a total view, requires the use of other factors. We have to move over into the world of philosophy. Present-day science has been much more modest than a century ago when mechanistic materialism was confidently proclaimed as *the* scientific world-view. Nowadays we should probably say that that world-view has been largely discredited, but that current philosophical theories are too widely divergent to make possible any coherent world-view to replace the one that is discredited. These shifts in thought are of course of great interest from a theological point of view.

Sometimes, however, some theological writers have been much too quick in using these shifts for the sake of apologetics. The same is true of statements with a religious flavour made by prominent scientists such as Einstein. The risk lies in reading into these statements far more than they have a right to, which only means that they are misinterpreting the position taken by scientists and bringing theology into disrepute. John MacQuarrie in *Twentieth-Century Religious Thought* discusses these problems; he says of the perspectives that discredit "the old naturalism": "Perhaps they call only for a more refined naturalism."[1] This warning against misuse is justified. It is perfectly clear that science does not offer any natural theology on the basis of which theology could build a superstructure.

The perspective of faith is different from that of science. This perspective of faith—this content of faith—can be made an object of independent research. It is the main task of systematic theology to do this. It can be done whether or not the perspective of faith can be legitimated. But theology cannot leave this question disregarded and unanswered. It is here that the philosophy of religion comes into the picture. Legitimation of faith is a question of the relation between faith and knowledge. The problem of faith and the knowledge which research gives us is part of the wide problem of the relation between faith and knowledge in general.

It was this range of problems that lay behind Lönnebo's fear that we might finish up in "the doctrine of the double truth". It lay too behind Root's intensive demand for a new natural theology in *Soundings*. When earlier I mentioned his article, I gave no account of what sort of substitute for natural theology he was looking for when he rejected its rational proofs. He approaches the problems rather tentatively, and does not attempt to conceal it. There is some uncertainty about it, due partly to the fact that the term natural theology is hardly suitable in the context. Nevertheless, there is an argument here worth noticing. Root thinks that a precondition for the natural theology he seeks must be that we gain insight into the inwardness of the lives we lead. He asks where best we can seek this insight and answers: in poets, novelists, playwrights, and film producers. In creative art we see ourselves afresh, we come to understand ourselves better, and we come into contact with the sources of the imagination that can give nourishment to a natural theology. The best handbook for present-day natural theology is not second-hand theological

[1] Op. cit., p. 251.

treatises, but living work by artists who are "in touch with the springs of creative imagination".[1] We can disregard the term "natural theology" which here is almost confusing. The point of the argument is that purely theoretical scientific research is not the only way in which we can gain insight into the conditions of our existence, and that there is an affinity between artistic language and religious language, the language of faith.

This gives us a starting-point for philosophical studies of the possibility and meaningfulness of religious language, the language of faith. Studies of this kind have been made relevant through modern analytic philosophy. This makes possible some useful work on the philosophy of religion, which I shall deal with later. In this book I am not aiming at writing a philosophy of religion. But, as the next chapter is to deal with some of the questions connected with religious language, the symbol language of faith, some philosophical perspectives will come into our field of view.

This section has been dealing with the universal perspective of faith. I have not been aiming at getting back to earlier ideas about natural law, nor to present any new natural theology. But the relationship to them has not been merely negative. The justified tendencies in what is said about natural law and natural theology have come to expression in the form of the universal perspective of Christian faith. What I have been aiming at could be described in a formulation by Ragnar Bring: "to allow free scope to whatever it is that natural theology is the wrong expression for".

[1] *Soundings*, p. 18.

3 THE SYMBOLS

Symbol language is the mother tongue of faith. In this chapter we are going to deal in outline with some of the problems in this connection. But far from all. In a review like this, it is not possible to discuss, for instance, all the problems connected with modern language philosophy. The questions we shall deal with are these. First, we shall establish why symbol language is the mother tongue of faith, why when we talk about God and everything that belongs to him, we are obliged to use symbols. This will be illustrated by contrasting the terms "concept of God" and "image of God" taking our material from two present-day theologians, Tillich and Brunner. In the next section we shall illustrate the imagery used by the Bible in speaking about God, the symbols for God which the Bible takes from the world of man and from the world of nature. Finally, we shall look at the imagery used by Jesus and the image of God which he sketches in contrast with some Jewish ideas of his time.

When we have looked at these Bible symbols, we shall return to the question of the function of symbols and show both their power to express ideas and their limitations—quoting Brunner in this context. The broad lines drawn up here will be detailed in the next two sections. One will deal with present-day discussion of "demythologizing". In this section, with Bultmann as the prime representative of demythologization, the term demythologizing will be contrasted with the term derationalizing. We shall show that the insight which lies in the use of symbol language leads to a derationalizing, which is opposed not only to what is called rationalism but equally to scholastic theology. This derationalizing, however, does not mean that reason is excluded from our analysis of the potentialities of symbol language, and that we end up in irrationalism, full of logical contradiction. The concluding section will therefore deal with the meaning of symbols.

Concept of God and Image of God

Symbol language is the mother tongue of faith. When faith makes a statement about God, it has to use symbols, images, metaphors. There is no "adequate" language for us to use, for the simple reason that the God of whom faith speaks is not one object among others in the finite world, which can be analysed and described exactly like other objects. He is not part of the finite world. All the expressions we can use, however, are taken from this world. They cannot therefore adequately define anything except what belongs to this world. This is not to say that everything that belongs to this world can be made an object of adequate definition and exact description. Even the sciences which are regarded as the most exact, mathematics and natural science, find that they have to make use of symbol language. The same is true of poetry, drama, and all literary writing in its attempts to reveal and interpret the hidden depths of human life. So symbol language is not peculiar to faith in God. But in this case it is the only language available. If we were to try to replace symbol language with supposedly adequate definitions, thus making God an object of our analysis, this would mean that man had made "god" an object among, or perhaps "above", other objects.

Something must here be said about the relation of faith and theology. It is faith in God that is the object of theology. The task of theology is to chart and clarify the meaning and content of Christian faith. This task has many sides. Having said that symbol language is the mother tongue of faith, we find that it is an important task for theology to study symbol language, its potentialities, and its functions. This task would be twisted and distorted if theology laid claim to be able to say more than faith can say with its symbol language, that is to say, if theology laid claim to give an exact definition of the being of God. In doing so, theology would abandon its central task of making clear the content of faith. It would be operating on its own, without regard to the proper object of its study.

The difference between the theology that has faith as the object of its research and the theology that operates on its own with the aim of giving an adequate definition of God and his being may be illustrated by contrasting the terms "image of God" and "concept of God"—the image of God that develops in and through the various symbols used by Christian faith on the one hand, and on the other a supposedly rational concept of God.

We shall take up later the nature and function of symbols. We start with some preliminary definitions. The symbols for God used in the Bible are taken from the world of nature and the world of man. To take an instance, we find in several places that God is "a rock". The word is used in a figurative sense. God is not identified with a rock, neither Mount Zion nor any other rocky mountain. Yet the word "rock" in its proper sense contains something that makes it usable as an image of God. The word points out beyond itself in a definite direction—it intimates something important about God. In all this, when used about God, the word preserves its character as a symbol. It is not regarded as an adequate definition, for it would then be possible to use it in any context. The serviceability and the meaning of the word depend on the context in which it is used. The word "rock" is meaningful as a symbol of God in Psalm 18.2 (RSV): "my God, my rock, in whom I take refuge". In other words, the meaning and the serviceability of the symbol are dependent on the context in which they appear.

Now there is no great risk that a symbol taken from nature might be regarded as an adequate definition of God. The risk may be very much greater when the symbol is taken from the world of man. Take a word most widely used as a symbol of God, the word "love". It might well be asked: Is not this an adequate definition? Does not the Bible itself say, straight out: "God is love"? Yes, undoubtedly this is a most usable and meaningful word. But at the same time we have to remember that the word is taken from the world of human relationships and has many and varied meanings. There are many different kinds of "love" and not all are suitable as symbols of God's relationship to man and to the world. Still less can God be identified with human love, as such. It is perfectly clear that here too we are dealing with a symbol, and that the content and meaning of that symbol depend on the context in which it is set. *One* such context—and there are many—is: "By this we know love, that he [Christ] laid down his life for us" (1 John 3.16, RSV).

Before leaving this theme, we must ask: "If it is possible to speak about God only in the form of symbols, does this not have fateful consequences for our knowledge of God?" It can be objected that it is all "only symbols". To this the answer is that symbols are by no means "only symbols". To contrast symbols with reality is quite unrealistic. It is a way of viewing them that is entirely foreign to the eyes of faith. When faith speaks of God as a rock or of God as love, the very last thing this is is meaningless symbols or words with no cover. It is something that for faith is the supreme reality. Further, that we can speak of God only with the aid of symbols is not just a recent invention based on modern theories of knowledge—it is firmly anchored deep in the New Testament. There we find no direct philosophical theories of knowledge. But undoubtedly we do find this. For Jesus himself God is the Father who is in secret. He offers no theoretic teaching, no doctrine about him. But when—in the words of St John's Gospel—he declares God, this is done in images and parables, where it is not done in direct action. Paul is absolutely convinced that knowledge of God has been given to us. But in the conditions of our life on earth this knowledge is "in part" in comparison with what it will be when we "understand fully" and see "face to face".

We return to the "concept of God" and the "image of God". The concept of God, built up on a philosophic basis, rational and regarded as adequate, has had a great part to play in the history of theology. We might describe this history as a struggle between a concept determined by reason and an image drawn from the Bible. The great feat of theology was to combine and amalgamate these two separate factors, though the process led to difficult and indeed insuperable complications. Without further ado, we pass on to the present position when clashes of this kind are reflected in modern theological thought, and when the idea of an adequate concept of God still has its after-effects even in circles which are critical of an earlier generation's rational concept of God. Let us look at two outstanding modern theologians, Paul Tillich and Emil Brunner.

Paul Tillich's philosophical and theological thinking has a background of existential philosophy. He does not want to be a spokesman for any rational or natural theology in the traditional sense. But still he wants, speculatively one might say, to reach a concept of God, supposedly rational and ontologically expressed. What makes him of interest to us is that he is well aware of the meaning of symbols and even myth as the forms of expression of religion. He is all against devaluing the function and power of symbols, shown by scornful talk of their being "only" symbols. With good reason he points out that symbols are able to open the way to levels of reality that are otherwise inaccessible for us, and to open the way to the corresponding dimensions "in our soul".

From his starting-point in philosophy, Tillich gives an analysis of man's "existential situation". We have already dealt with his interesting sketch of this.[1] He wishes then to confront man's existential situation with the Christian message. This means confronting the questions implied in the existential situation with the answers implied in the message. The answers are not to be derived from the questions—the answers presuppose a "revelation" from the side of God—nor are the questions to be derived from the answers. But, if the answers are to have any meaning, Tillich says, it must be assumed that the questioner has some idea of the God he is seeking. The question of God has its basis in man's consciousness of his finiteness, and this implies then that he also has some idea of something non-finite, something absolute. Man cannot help posing the question of the ultimate ground of being, and this becomes a question of what has ultimate, absolute importance for man, what is "man's ultimate concern". The thing that is being sought for here cannot be regarded as an object we can reach. It must be something raised above the subject–object relationship, something above all objects, yet at the same time something in which we can share. And this absolute—the thing we call "God"—is then *Being itself*. Tillich is in this rejecting the idea that God is a being, one being among others; God is not the highest of beings, he is Being itself. Tillich is also able to use other definitions, regarded as parallel definitions: God is the ground of being, the power of being. According to Tillich a definition of God of this kind is the only univocal statement that can be made about God. Apart from that, it is only possible to speak of him in the form of symbols.

This line of argument, briefly outlined, gives rise to a number of questions, in particular three: Is this definition of God, this concept of God really univocal? Has this answer really been taken from the sources from which, according to Tillich, it ought to be taken? How is this concept of God related to the Bible image of God?

[1] See p. 39 above.

The first question has to be answered in the negative. There is no univocal meaning here according to a philosopher as well-disposed towards existentialism as Macquarrie. To say at the same time that God is "being itself" and "the ground of being" is to take the word "being" in two different senses. Being itself, as ultimate, can have no ground. The "ground of being" must be taken as the ground for particular beings. Still more obscure and ambiguous is the expression "power of being", which may mean either the power that is exerted in being or the power to be. What Tillich really meant with his parallel formulas, Macquarrie[1] does not venture to decide.

In the second question, according to Tillich the answer to the questions which are asked in man's existential situation are not to be derived from the questions, but from the Christian message. But it can hardly be claimed that the concept of God as "Being itself"—whatever the meaning of the formula—is derived from that source.

So we come to the third question: whether the definition of the concept, "Being itself" can be harmonized with the image of God that meets us in the Christian message. Here we are confronted by the same difficulties that have always been associated with concepts of a similar nature. To speak of God as "Being itself"—however that is to be interpreted—opens up entirely different perspectives from those of the Christian message when it speaks of a living and active God, a God who is in action against everything that opposes him. If God is Being, as such, this undoubtedly invites us to obscure, reduce, or eliminate the category of opposition and conflict that is such a notable feature of the image of God in the Christian message.

If we pass on from Tillich to Emil Brunner, we find in him too an attempt to determine what we might call a primary concept of God. He stresses the activity of God, God in action, in a very different way from Tillich. God is not Being as such, but the absolute Subject, Subject *per se*. This definition is based on philosophical premisses of which Brunner gives an account. The philosophy he refers to is neither existentialism nor the speculations along Platonic, neo-Platonic, or Aristotelian lines that were common in theology earlier, but rather an "I-and-Thou" philosophy akin to the thought of the present-day Jewish philosopher,

[1] *Twentieth Century Religious Thought*, p. 367.

Martin Buber. This absolute Subject is a subject "for some end", a subject that communicates itself. Just as you cannot describe the nature of radium without speaking of radio-activity, so communicating-activity is God's nature. So you cannot first determine the nature of God and then begin to talk about the love of God as "ethical quality", an "attribute". God's nature is the radiating out of spiritual energy.

In an article on Emil Brunner's Doctrine of God,[1] Anders Nygren has analysed this thinking. He says that Brunner is right in his view that we cannot think of God's love as an ethical attribute, and has a good word for Brunner's intention to avoid regarding God as an object. Nevertheless, by his philosophical definition of God as absolute Subject—in spite of his not intending to—Brunner has come to make God a "something", an "it", an object. The ontology Brunner is intending to build up may be an improvement on the Greek metaphysics of old. But this does not prevent speculation based on the "I-and-Thou" relationship making God an object when it uses philosophical ideas to define God's existence. God as "Subject *per se*" and "Subject for some end" is clearly something other than the God of whom the Bible speaks. Brunner himself is also clearly aware that there is a tension between philosophical reflection and the Bible message, the "revelation" on which elsewhere he means to build. But he regards that tension as inevitable. What we find in the Bible message "in a poetic form, childish or without reflection", he says, theology is to present in a rational, studied, and scientific form. The risk in doing this Brunner describes like this:

The more reflection, exact definition, stringent logical argument, rational classification, method and systematization, dominate in Christian doctrine, the more scientific it becomes, and the more removed it becomes from the original truth from which it started and on which its claims are based.[1]

Brunner regards theological work as a kind of tug-of-war between speculation and faith, where they have somehow to balance one another. Of this Nygren rightly says:

It is an anxious situation for theology if the more consistently it proceeds, the more it distorts its object, Christian faith; if logic and faith in

[1] Anders Nygren, "Emil Brunner's Doctrine of God", in *The Theology of Emil Brunner* (1962), p. 177 ff.

theological work are played against one another so that "at every point" [Brunner's words] they hamper and interfere with one another.[1]

This raises a number of questions. It is all very well to say that one has no intention of regarding God as an object to be used for rational definition. But this is what actually happens when God, as distinct from man who is subject in a relative sense, is defined as the absolute Subject. The importance that Brunner attached to this definition is shown by the fact that he not only regards the definition as a basis for theological work, but also declares that the task of the whole of theology consists of nothing else except expressing the meaning of the statement that God is the absolute Subject. Later, when Brunner is to solve this theological problem with the help of "revelation" and in doing so defines the nature of God as Love, one is surprised at the imagery he uses. Can such an image as radio-activity, which incidentally can hardly be applicable to an absolute Subject, really guide and direct our thoughts, or does it not really lead them in a very different direction than that of what "the revelation" has to say about divine Love? This brings us to the main question, whether it is justifiable to define by setting the absolute subject over against the relative. Does not a definition of this kind involve the same dangerous tendency as we found in Tillich's "absolute being"— and as is associated with all rational definitions of God's being? If God is absolute subject, he must really be regarded as subject in all that happens. God as absolute subject seems to imply a consistent monism. But, if so, there is a great gulf fixed between this concept of God and the image of God where the divine love is opposed to, and at war with, whatever is not derived from God. Brunner, of course, does not want to draw conclusions like these. But that is one thing. It is quite a different matter what his definition really leads on to.

Brunner's and Tillich's concepts of God are built up in entirely different ways. Both are in their own way akin to earlier concepts. To hear Tillich talk of God as the absolute being brings to mind Spinoza's *Deus sive natura*. Brunner's absolute subject is activist. It brings to mind God as the highest of humans. Of course he does not mean to think of God like that. But that is where it leads when that which in man is relative—being a subject—is

[1] Anders Nygren, "Emil Brunner's Doctrine of God", in *The Theology of Emil Brunner* (1962), pp. 177 ff.

raised to the absolute in God, who then becomes, as it were, the superhuman subject.

Whatever differences there may be between these modern attempts to determine a rational concept of God, they, like all earlier attempts, are alike in that God, whether they intend it or not, comes to be regarded as an object accessible to our thinking, an object which we can define adequately. This leads, as we have seen, to tensions with the image of God we get from the symbols of the Bible. It means too that we place on theology a task which it has not the power to perform. Theology cannot undertake to make statements about "God in himself". And it can therefore not fancy itself capable of producing adequate definitions of God's being, as such. Its task is limited to faith's relation to God as it makes itself known in the witness faith bears to the living, active God. It is this witness to God that theology makes the object of its analysis. It is of course particularly inconceivable for theology to make God a direct object of study when faith itself finds it impossible in time and space for God to be seen "face to face".

Christian faith has unquestionably definite statements to make about God. But these statements are made in the language of symbols. The symbols, the images, it takes from the world of nature and the world of man. It is conscious at the same time that in relation both to nature and to man God is "different". It is not possible to identify God with nature on a *deus sive natura* basis, nor with the highest in humanity. Adequate definitions here are out of the question. The language of faith is and will continue to be symbol language. For a theology whose task is to analyse faith's relation to God, the primary activity will be to study this language which is characteristic for faith, its scope, its potentialities, and its limitations. But before we start on this, we shall make a rapid inventory of the symbols used in the Bible.

Biblical Symbols of God

The thesis that symbol language is the mother tongue of faith is fully established by the way the Bible speaks about God and all that belongs to God: "the Lord's throne is in heaven" (Ps. 11.4), or "Heaven . . . is God's throne" (Matt. 5.34). Christ is "the bread which came down from heaven" (John 6.41). Christ "is taken up from you into heaven" (Acts 1.11).

Statements of this kind in the Bible are clearly linked with a view of the world that is different from ours, indeed one that has long since vanished. Does this mean that they are meaningless and are to be discarded? This seems to be the view of Bishop Robinson in *Honest to God*. He is tireless in controverting the idea of a God "up there". As against such an antiquated idea, he wants to talk of God "in depth", and with Tillich to "define" God as the ground of being and as ultimate reality, clearly intending to provide an "adequate" idea of God. The enormous sales of *Honest to God*, both in Britain and in Germany, make it appear that many people regard Robinson's dismissal of a God "up there" as a remarkable work of theological liberation. If this is so, it is a frightening illustration not only of how slender is the contact between, on the one hand, people who are interested in religion and are looking for something and, on the other hand, the work of serious theologians, but also how widespread unfamiliarity with the Bible has become. But it also illustrates—if proof is needed—how powerfully the problem of faith involves people. This makes unavoidable certain questions and demands both upon theology and, still more so, on Christian preaching and teaching. The importance that Robinson's book may have will lie principally here.

Apart from this it has to be said that in his book Robinson has simplified his problems almost to a primitive level. In contrast to his precursor, Tillich, he makes no serious attempt to understand the symbol language of faith. With combative eagerness he attacks the Bible symbols that are connected with heaven, while at the same time he himself uses other symbol expressions, "ground", "depth", as if they were adequate definitions of God. The result is that his propositions suffer from a lack of clarity and that his attacks strike on open doors. One is reminded of the Russian cosmonaut who did not see God as he flew round the world in his sputnik. Of the way Robinson deals with Bible expressions such as "came down from heaven", "ascended into heaven", "sitteth on the right hand of God", one of Robinson's critics in *The Honest to God Debate* writes with good reason: "To reject such forms of speech surely shows as much theological naivety as to take them literally."[1] Both these forms of naivety are calculated to make the

---

[1] H. McCabe, *The Honest to God Debate*, p. 175.

message of the Bible seem strange, inaccessible, and irrelevant. To choose to understand everything in an absolutely literal sense is not to understand. One cannot understand what the Bible is talking about without understanding the language it uses, symbol language, the mother tongue of faith.

With this in mind, let us now have a look at some of the Bible symbols. They are varied over a wide range, so that this will not be an exhaustive study, not even a full list of them, but just a summary as a necessary background for our work.

To begin with, though the Bible uses a wide imagery in its language, it refuses to allow any representation of God, as we see from the strict condemnation of image-making in the Ten Commandments. The point of this condemnation is clear. It is to protect the "highness" of God, that he is above all that he has created. It is to prevent God's being dragged down into the world of created beings, and there made an object among other objects. The prohibition of images is an expression of, and a protection for, the unlimited reverence that is the fundamental attitude towards God. The Bible—both in the Old Testament and to some extent in the New Testament—can tell of visions of God, though with marked limitations. There are no representations of God. In the story of Moses, the vision is linked with the fire in the burning bush, and with the fire and storm on Sinai. For Elijah, the voice of God comes neither in fire or storm but in a still, small voice. Isaiah, in the vision when he was called, saw the Lord sitting upon a throne, high and lifted up. In the New Testament the Spirit is seen in the form of a dove and of tongues of fire. The Book of Revelation, like Isaiah, has visions of the throne of God.

But though the prohibition of images has been strictly observed in the Bible, this is not true of the Christian Church. An image of the Trinity that was not infrequently used in the Middle Ages, the Throne of Grace, represents God as elderly, with the Son on his knee, and the Spirit above in the form of a dove. It goes without saying that this highly anthropomorphic representation is likely to give a number of false impressions: God as a man, and an old man at that! This is almost the opposite of what the Bible says about God, the Eternal, for whom "a thousand years are as a day". With such imagery, there is good reason to regret that the Old Testament prohibition of images has not been respected by the Christian Church. In comparison with this, the frequent representation of God as "the all-seeing eye", enclosed in a triangle, is comparatively harmless.

Pictures have otherwise been used in the Christian Church mostly to represent Christ. We shall not attempt here to analyse the wide range of them in painting, in sculpture, and in other forms of art. There is of course no reason to object to this kind of representation. It has great importance. It reflects too, most sensitively, the reaction of different generations to the figure of Christ. But it is clear that not all pictures of Christ serve their intended purpose, and that the pictures can give a very different impression from that given by the Bible. The figure of Christ has sometimes been sentimentalized or reinterpreted in other ways. But we shall not go further into this—or we should have to present the whole history of Christian thinking from the viewpoint of art.

SYMBOLS FROM THE WORLD OF NATURE

Symbols of God in the Bible are taken from the world of nature and the world of human life. Both types occur in the Old and the New Testament, even if those from the world of nature are relatively infrequent in the New Testament.

Some of the most frequent symbols in the Old Testament are Rock (Ps. 18.2; 62.2; 89.26; 2 Sam. 22.2), Fortress (2 Sam. 22.2; Ps. 18.2; 31.3; 71.3), and the related word Refuge (Ps. 9.9; 46.7; 91.2). A good example is Psalm 18.1–2: "I will love thee, O Lord, my strength. The Lord is my rock, and my fortress, and my deliverer; my God, my strength, in whom I will trust; my buckler, and the horn of my salvation, and my high tower" (horn is a symbol of power and strength). The word "my" illustrates the meaning of the symbol and its context. God is the firm or strong rock where I have my refuge (Ps. 62.7), he is "the strength of my heart" (Ps. 73.26), "the rock of my salvation" (Ps. 89.26).

Linked in content with these images there is another frequent symbol, taken from the world of birds. It speaks of taking refuge under "God's wings" (Ruth 2.12; Ps. 91.4) or under "the shadow of God's wings" (Ps. 17.8; 36.7; 57.1; 61.4). We find also "in the shadow of thy wings will I rejoice" (Ps. 63.7). This is re-echoed in the New Testament in Luke 13.34 when Jesus tells of how he would have gathered the children of Jerusalem "as a hen doth gather her brood under her wings".

Another kind of symbol taken from the world of nature is the word "fountain", "well", or "spring". It may be used directly of God: "they have forsaken me the fountain of living waters" (Jer. 2.13), but also in phrases such as : "with thee is the fountain of life" (Ps. 36.9), "the river of God which is full of water" (Ps. 65.9). Isaiah 12.3 speaks of "the wells of salvation". The theme of all these phrases is that God appears as the Giver: "thou givest them drink from the river of thy delights" (Ps. 36.8, RSV). That God's fountain is at the same time the fountain of life and the fountain of salvation illustrates the unity of the God who is Creator and the God who is Saviour. The same symbol recurs in the New Testament. In the Book of Revelation, "he that sat upon the throne" said: "I will give unto him that is athirst of the fountain of the water of life freely" (Rev. 21.6). And we should also remember in this connection the water that Jesus gives which shall be "a well of water springing up into everlasting life" (John 4.14).

So far all these symbols are from the earth. A symbol which is connected with the heaven is the symbol of "light". God covers himself "with light as with a garment" (Ps. 104.2). In Isaiah 60.19 we read: "the Lord shall be unto thee an everlasting light, and thy God thy glory". This combination of light and glory often recurs: "Thou art more glorious and excellent" (Ps. 76.4). When light is used as a symbol for God, it is used as a contrast symbol. God's light contrasts with darkness and night, which are forced to withdraw when God's light shines. God's light can shine through the darkness and turn it into light: "If I say, Surely the darkness shall cover me: even the night shall be light about me. Yea, the darkness hideth not from thee: but the night shineth as the day: the darkness and the light are both alike to thee" (Ps. 139. 11–12). The New Testament also makes frequent use of the symbols of light. In 1 John 1.5 we read: "This then is the message which we have heard of him [Christ], and declare unto you, that God is light, and in him is no darkness at all". God is "the Father of lights, with whom there is no variation or shadow due to change" (James. 1.17, RSV). To be "God's children" is to be "the children of light". As in many other instances, the symbol for God can be applied to Christ. He is "the true light", "the light of the world". The contrast with darkness is strongly marked. When people "love darkness rather than light", the reason for this is that their "deeds are evil"—but to "come to the light" means salvation (John 3.19–21).

We saw that God is described as "the Father of lights", implying a link between the symbols of light and heaven. When God and heaven are linked, it is often said that God "is" in heaven, "dwells" in heaven, that his throne is in heaven or that heaven is his throne. In the later writings in the Old Testament and in the New, "heaven" may be used as a synonym for God. "The heavens do rule" (Dan. 4.26). When Jesus asks: "The baptism of John, whence was it? from heaven or of men?" (Matt. 21.25), "heaven" is synonymous with God. The same is true when John the Baptist says: "A man can receive nothing, except it be given him from heaven" (John 3.27). In the same way St Matthew's Gospel keeps on referring to "the kingdom of heaven" where the other Gospels speak of the kingdom of God.

In relating God and heaven in this way, the intention is not to localize God to heaven and, as it were, shut him in there. "If I ascend up into heaven, thou art there: if I make my bed in hell, behold, thou art there" (Ps. 139.8). God "is" in hell just as much as he is in heaven. We see clearly how impossible it is to "localize" God in the words of Solomon at the dedication of the temple: "the heaven and heaven of heavens cannot contain thee; how much less this house that I have builded?" (1 Kings 8.27). Yet in St Matthew's Gospel we can read that God "is in secret" just as much as that he "is in heaven". There is also a quite different New Testament way of saying where God dwells: Paul writes to the Romans about the Spirit of God "that dwelleth in you". If we consider the symbol of heaven, the main intention of the symbols is quite clearly not localizing God in terms of space. The context in which the symbol is used shows that it is meant to express God's greatness, majesty, power, dominion, inscrutability, and the limitless scope of his activity. When God "looks down from heaven upon the children of men" (Ps. 53.2), he "sees" everything. "His glory covered the heavens" (Hab. 3.3). "As the heaven is high above the earth, so great is his mercy toward them that fear him" (Ps. 103.11). "As the heavens are higher than the earth, so are my ways higher than your ways, and my thoughts than your thoughts" (Isa. 55.9).

This shows that the symbol of heaven can refer to God's activity and that, from one point of view, it is a function symbol. So are all the other symbols taken from the world of nature, like all the Bible's symbols of God. Words such as rock, fortress, etc., say something very definite about how God functions. It is not without significance that the Bible takes its symbols for God not only from human life but also from the world of nature. Nature symbols may be less able to express meaning, but, on the other hand, there is less danger about them than with anthropomorphic symbols. To speak about God as a rock or a fountain makes it quite clear that it is a symbol. There is no risk of God's being identified with a rock or a fountain. At the same time both these images have something timeless and unchanging about them. A rock does not change. It remains what it is. On both these points anthropomorphic symbols have obvious risks. One risk is that its character as a symbol is obscured and that, for instance, God's "love" or "wrath" may be gauged with human measurements. Another risk is that a word which the Bible uses about God may in the course of time alter its meaning.

SYMBOLS FROM THE WORLD OF HUMAN LIFE

First of all, there are a number of symbols linked with the human body: the face, arms, hands, eye, ear, and mouth. The face is often associated with the symbol of light, as in "the Lord make his face shine upon thee", "the light of thy countenance". "The light" reflects God's "glory": "Honour and majesty are before him; . . . ascribe to the Lord glory" (Ps. 96.6–7, RSV). The Lord makes his face shine. But he can also turn his face away, hide it, cast men from his face. The face of God can either unveil and condemn or it can save. "Thou hast set . . . our secret sins in the light of thy countenance" (Ps. 90.8); "The face of the Lord is against them that do evil" (Ps. 34.16). But, on the other hand, the formula "The Lord make his face shine upon thee" is a frequent expression of God's saving action: "cause thy face to shine; and we shall be saved" (Ps. 80.3, 7, 19).

The symbols, arms and hands, express the power of God. "The eternal God is thy refuge, and underneath are the everlasting arms" (Deut. 33.27). God's arm is mentioned in connection with battle and victory. "Thou hast with thine arm redeemed thy people" (Ps. 77.15); "thou hast a mighty arm" (Ps. 89.13); "his right hand and his holy arm hath gotten him the victory" (Ps. 98.1). God's hand, or his right hand, is spoken of in the same way.

HD

"Thy right hand, O Lord, hath dashed in pieces the enemy" (Exod. 15.6); "in thine hand is power and might" (1 Chron. 29.12); "thy right hand upholdeth me" (Ps. 63.8); "the right hand of the Lord doeth valiantly" (Ps. 118.15).

The symbols *eye*, *ear*, occur frequently with their corresponding verbs, to see, to behold, to hear. The symbol *mouth* is seldom used but the corresponding noun and verb, *word* and *speak*, are common, both in the Old and the New Testament.

Sometimes the opposite is true—God is silent, he says nothing. God is asked not to do this—"Keep not thou silence, O God: hold not thy peace" (Ps. 83.1)—just as he is asked to hear, to listen, to bow his ear to the voice of prayer.

There is a widespread and important category of symbols taken from human relations—Lord, King, Shepherd, Father.

The word "Lord", which is frequent in the Old Testament, represents several Hebrew expressions. It is also frequently used in the New Testament. But, as the Church grew, this name was used as a name of honour for Christ, Kyrios, a name which differed from Messiah in that it was understood in the non-Jewish world.

The name *King* is also used of God throughout the Bible. In the Old Testament this symbol was largely based on the "sacral kingship" in Israel, and the "king ideology" which permits the king, who can be described as "God's Son", to function in worship as "high priest after the order of Melchizedek". It was against this background that there arose later the hope of a coming Messianic Redeemer-King. That is why in the New Testament Christ is referred to as king: "Blessed be the King that cometh in the name of the Lord" (Luke 19.38). The Book of Revelation calls him "King of Kings" (19.16). But the name King is still also used of God: he is "the King eternal" (1 Tim. 1.17).

The symbol *shepherd* is used in the Old Testament about God and in the New Testament about Christ. The best-known passages are Psalm 23 and John 10. The symbol brings out the shepherd's function of caring and the entire dependence of the "sheep" on the shepherd. But in neither passage is there the atmosphere of idyll that we find later in Christian writing. The word shepherd is a name of high honour akin to Lord and King—as we see when St Matthew's Gospel refers to the prophecy: "for out of you [Bethlehem] shall come a leader to be the shepherd of my people Israel" (Matt. 2.6, NEB). The work of a shepherd includes battle against the powers that threaten to damage, destroy, or scatter "the flock", which brings us to the words of Jesus about giving his life for the sheep.

With the symbol of *Father* there are some differences between the Old and New Testament. In the Old Testament this name has a limited use, but in the New Testament it is the central name for God. There is the same difference in relationship to God. In the Old Testament God is first and foremost the father of the people, of Israel. Isaiah writes: "O Lord, thou art our father" (64.8). It is the sacral king who is first thought of as having an individual relationship to God as father, for the king is an intermediary between God and the people. When some of the psalms speak of God as father, with a strong personal emphasis, it may be because these psalms were originally royal psalms.

In the New Testament "father" becomes the name of God above all others, the symbol that reflects all that has been given by the gospel in fulfilment of the promises during the time of the old covenant. God as Father is the God who saves, the God of love and grace, "the Father of mercies and the God of all comfort" (2 Cor. 1.3). God is the universal Father: "the Father, of whom are all things, and we in him" (1 Cor. 8.6); "One God and Father of all" (Eph. 4.6). But he is in a special way the Father of the new people of God. As earlier, the collective aspect is strongly present: God is *our* Father. But this collective aspect is in no way in contrast to the individual personal aspect: God is at the same time the Father of the individual, "thy Father" (Matt. 6.4). The special sonship which, according to the New Testament, is the property of the new people of God, is linked with, and mediated by, the still more special sonship which is here ascribed to Christ—a theme treated elsewhere in this book.

In Chapter 2 we mentioned important functions—Creator, Redeemer, Deliverer, Saviour, Judge—and all these are linked with activities in the world of human life. Inventors and artists create, law courts judge, and people are delivered, helped, and "saved" or freed from all kinds of dangers, distress, and need. When words of this kind, familiar from their use in work and social life, are applied to what God does, this too is an instance of symbols being used. It is not intended that these human activities should give an adequate definition of what God does. The same analogy applies to many of the expressions that were earlier used in theology to describe "properties" of God: love, goodness, grace, mercy, faithfulness, righteousness, wrath, power, etc. It is most important that their character as symbols should be left intact. Otherwise anthropomorphic expressions of this kind will lead to an anthropomorphism that will ruin the image of God they are meant to convey. God's love and righteousness and wrath are not meant to be copies of human love and righteousness and wrath. God's love is not just something in line with human love, which in itself is far from unambiguous, but it is also something that contrasts with human love. We find illustrations of this in the imagery that Jesus himself used. When it is said of God's love as revealed in and through Christ, that it "passeth knowledge" (Eph. 3.19), this means that it cannot be modelled on human love as a gauge any more than human fatherhood is the standard when God is said to be the Father "from whom all fatherhood, earthly or heavenly, derives its name" (Eph. 3.15, J. B. Phillips).

Two points are to be noted here: first, that all these symbol expressions about God and the way he works get their meaning from the context in which they appear, and secondly, that they cannot be isolated and separated from one another as if they were entirely different things. Admittedly there can be a tension in the Bible between, for instance, love and wrath. But this does not mean that there is a radical contradiction between them, and that basically they cancel one another out. The anger that shows how fundamentally opposed to evil God is is by no means incompatible with his love.

While on the subject of these symbols, something must be said about the Bible use of the words *might* or *power*. We have already dealt with a number of power symbols: Lord, King, Majesty. All function symbols are in one way or other really attempting to show God's "might". In the New Testament we find many references to God's might or power. Once or twice the word "Might" is a synonym for God. But the Greek word *Pantokrator*, meaning Ruler of all, occurs only once in the New Testament, in 2 Corinthians 6.18 (where it is translated "the Lord Almighty"), apart from the Book of Revelation where it appears nine times. So the term "almighty" and cognate words appear in the New Testament virtually only in an eschatological context. The word "Almighty" in the Creed represents the Latin translation, *omnipotens*, of the Greek *pantokrator*.

But if the word "almighty" is conspicuously absent from the New Testament, which, with the exception of the Book of Revelation, only once speaks of God as the "Almighty", this does not mean that God's "eternal power" and "mighty power" is regarded as on a par with other "powers". God *is* the ruler of all, sovereign in power. If one wished to use the word omnipotence, it would not contradict what we have been saying, provided that omnipotence is not regarded as an abstract, rational concept of omnipotence of the kind that later appeared in theology. Omnipotence must not be regarded as all-causality. God exercises his power in conflict with the anti-God elements, those who resist him. This perspective of antagonism and drama appears more and more strongly in the Old Testament, and becomes a dominant element in the New. God's relationship to the anti-God forces is not seen as causality—God is not the cause of what is opposed to him—it is seen as action. God's power shows itself in definite actions in the service of the process of creation and redemption. God *is* sovereign throughout, but his sovereignty is not fully revealed on earth. According to the New Testament this will not be fully revealed until the present age is replaced by the coming age. This is why the word "Almighty" recurs in the Book of Revelation. "There were great voices in heaven, saying, The kingdoms of this world are become the kingdoms of our Lord and of his Christ; and he shall reign for ever and ever" (Rev. 11.15). "And I heard a loud voice saying in heaven, Now is come salvation and strength, and the kingdom of our God, and the power of his Christ" (Rev. 12.10).

These few symbols of power will suffice for the purposes of this book, which deals throughout with this problem.

Among the Bible symbols of God, there are two that are in a class by themselves: *eternity* and *holiness*. The thing that distinguishes them from others is that they are both direct contrasts to everything else in human life. Whereas the symbols that we have already mentioned—love, anger, might, and all the others—are all words that are also used of human beings, the terms eternal and holy are words that the Bible uses only about God and things in relation to God. Both words express the divine in contrast to the human. Eternity and holiness are used about people only in those cases where God has taken people into fellowship with himself and given them a share in what belongs to him, his eternity and his holiness. This does not mean that these are adequate definitions of God, still less that we are here dealing with abstract concepts gained through the exercise of reason. It would be more true to say that the contrast these expressions throw into relief is specially able to mark the limitations of the use of symbols. The fact that these two symbols are so special makes it clear that both "holiness" and "eternity" have been regarded as the characteristic categories of religion. Nathan Söderblom and Rudolf Otto regarded "the holy" and Anders Nygren "the eternal" as the specific category of religion.

On the subject of God's eternity, there is a difference between the Old and the New Testament. In the Old Testament eternity is almost regarded as time extended without end. It is these ideas of long duration and long continuation that lie behind the expressions that God is an "eternal king", that his kingdom is an "eternal kingdom", and that his mercy endures "from everlasting to everlasting". In the New Testament God's eternity means that God cannot be fitted into categories of time, he is ranged above this world and its fluctuations—in him there is "no variableness of light and darkness". On the other hand, man is part of the world of time, of finiteness, or transience. If man is to have a share in the world of eternity, of eternal life, he must have a share in God, fellowship with him, or, as it can be described in New Testament language, he must "come to know" God. Jesus says in John 17.3: "This is life eternal, that they might know thee, the only true God, and Jesus Christ, whom thou hast sent."

God's *holiness* has often in the history of theology been regarded as a "moral quality", an expression of God's radical opposition to every kind of sin. It is indisputable that God's holiness is contrasted with human sinfulness. But it is equally indisputable that this is by no means the primary aspect of God's holiness. If we ask what that is, we can hardly find a better presentation than that in the vision of the prophet Isaiah in chapter 6: the Lord is sitting upon a throne, high and lifted up, and his train fills the temple. Round him stand the seraphim, crying to one another: "Holy, holy, holy is the Lord of hosts: the whole earth is full of his glory." All this is highly significant: holiness as God's being high and lifted up, his sovereignty and "glory" (*kabhodh* in Hebrew, *doxa* in Greek), the context of worship and the adoration offered to him "that sitteth on the throne". All this we find again in different variations both in the Old and in the New Testament. This holiness of God is not a "property" among other "properties". It is rather what might be called the divine atmosphere, the background that is always there—explicitly or implicitly—in all that the Bible has to say about God.

When we come from the Old to the New Testament we notice two things. First, the word "holy" has a much wider use than previously. Not only is God the Holy One, but Christ is "the Holy One of God" (John 6.69, RSV): there is the holy Spirit, the holy Church; "the holy ones [saints]" is the technical term for the Christians, the new people of God: this is "an holy priesthood" (1 Pet. 2.5). Secondly, God's being high and lifted up is no barrier to his being near, as it was in the later parts of the Old Testament, where angels and other intermediary beings are thought of as mediating between him and the world. Admittedly, even in the New Testament some intermediary beings of this kind are found. But they play a very subordinate part as compared with the direct relationship to God that comes about through Christ and the Holy Spirit. When the Christians are described as "holy" or as "saints", this is not due to their moral perfection, but is due to Christ who "has sanctified himself for their sakes" (John 17.19), "dwells" in their hearts (Eph. 3.17), or to their being "sanctified by the Holy Ghost" (Rom. 15.16). At the same time we find a constant requirement of a life lived in purity and blamelessness. To take one example: "I beseech you therefore, brethren, by the mercies of God, that ye present your bodies a living sacrifice, holy, acceptable unto God, which is your reasonable service" (Rom. 12.1). Holiness includes opposition to sin and all evil, but it is never reduced to being just "a moral quality"—either when the word is used about God or in other contexts.

Before we leave this review of the symbols which the Bible uses about God, something must be said about the phrase, God's "personality". The word "person" is not used about God in the New Testament. It may say that God is "a spirit" (John 4.24), but it never says that God is a "person". Strictly speaking, therefore, we should have no reason to comment on this expression. But in view of the frequent use of this word later, what needs now to be stressed is that the phrase "person"—a word taken from the world of human life—is also a symbol word, though this has sometimes been overlooked when people have referred to God as a person, and then to "theism" in contrast to "pantheism". To use "person" as an "adequate" concept would immediately result in humanizing God, an inappropriate anthropomorphism, for God would then be regarded as a sort of human or, rather, superhuman, person, a person of higher dignity than man. If a word like this is to be used about God at all, it is important to retain its character as a symbol. But as a symbol it can serve a useful purpose, in so far as it guards against any tendency to talk of God in a "natural" way as some obscure, undefined force, and so long as it is used to bring out the character of an active being with a will of its own that we find in the Bible image of the living, active God.

THE IMAGERY OF JESUS

The symbols of God that we have mentioned so far are taken from the Old and New Testament books of the Bible. Recent research has been increasingly directed to analysing the imagery of the Bible. Symptomatic of this is the fact that the article on imagery, which in the first 1948 edition of the *Swedish Bible Encyclopedia* covered two columns, in the second 1962 edition had increased to thirty-eight columns and was one of the longest articles in that edition. There is every reason to suppose that research will continue with this energy. It is only natural that Bible images appear in varying guises in the different books. The images of the Psalter have a character of their own, so have those in the chapters of Isaiah, of Jeremiah, and of Ezekiel and the other prophets. In the New Testament the images of the synoptic Gospels are distinctly different from those of the Johannine writings. At the same time, in the Bible as a whole, there is a certain constant and recurring imagery—Ivan Engnell has rightly pointed to this as one criterion of the unity of the Bible. Many of the images used in the New Testament have been at the heart of the Old Testament and are therefore full of associations when they appear in the New. Unless attention is paid to these associations, it is impossible to understand fully what these images meant to those who listened to Jesus and the apostles as they used them.

In speaking now of the images of Jesus, we are not going to deal with the whole wide range that the Gospels present, but just to illustrate the image of God that is reflected in some of the parables and the actions of Jesus. We find in John 1.18: "he hath declared him". This declaring was not done through regular theoretical instruction. It is only in exceptional cases that there are direct statements about God as, for instance, in the Sermon on the Mount: "thy Father, which is in secret". Jesus makes no statements about God's "being" or "qualities". He develops no teaching about "God's person and work"—to use a traditional theological formula. Still less do we find any cosmological speculations or proofs of God's existence. John's expression that he has declared what God is like means something very different, that his words and actions reflect "what God is" and how he acts. Words and actions with Jesus are inseparably combined. When he chooses to speak in parables, they are directly related to what he was doing.

We shall have a look at four of the parables in the synoptic Gospels: the lost sheep (Luke 15.1–7 and Matt. 18.12–14), the prodigal son (Luke 15.11–32), the labourers in the vineyard (Matt. 20.1–16), the invitation to the wedding feast (Matt. 22.1–14 and Luke 14.16–24). All these parables are aimed at "the lawyers and the Pharisees", that is to say those who claimed to be the foremost representatives of Israel, to be "the holy remnant". They are also, all four of them, a defence of the way Jesus acted, and of his keeping company with publicans and sinners that so shocked the lawyers and Pharisees.

Like all the parables of Jesus, they are connected with conditions in the Palestine of his day. But the behaviour they describe is by no means the normal behaviour of their time. The way the central figure behaves is always irrational and shocking to the normal way of looking at things. The shepherd leaves the ninety-nine sheep to look after themselves, and instead goes looking for the one that has gone astray. The prodigal son, wastrel and debauched, is welcomed by his father as if returning triumphant. The workers in the vineyard are paid on a system that from an economic point of veiw is quite absurd. His hearers must have thought all this was quite ridiculous. The Pharisees and the lawyers must have been doubly offended by the criticism of them that it implied. Jesus contrasts their murmuring with the joy of heaven, with God's joy: "joy shall be in heaven over one sinner that repenteth, more than over ninety and nine just persons, which need no repentance." The parable of the prodigal son culminates in a description of the elder brother's criticism and the father's combination of reproach and appeal to him. As Joachim Jeremias pointed out in his book on the parables of Jesus, this is an appeal to the elder

brother to reconsider his attitude. The murmuring labourers in
the vineyard hear the question: "Is thine eye evil because I am
good?" In the parable of the wedding feast, as it is told in Matthew's
Gospel, the Pharisees and the lawyers have excluded themselves
from the celebrations by answering No to the invitation.

Like many others, all these parables are a defence by Jesus of
the way he acted. So far as he was concerned the defence was
attended by very real risks: the cross is casting its shadow across
his path. To the religious leaders who felt themselves severely
criticized, the course of action defended in the parables was
clearly a breach of God's law and order, indeed sheer blasphemy
in cases where Jesus dispensed forgiveness of sins, thus usurping
God's powers.

But the parables were not only a defence of Jesus' actions. They
were at the same time an illustration, a revelation, of how God
acts. In the minds of those who heard the parables the images must
have awakened many associations with which they were familiar.
The Scriptures had often spoken of a shepherd: "The Lord is my
shepherd" (Ps. 23). The prophet Ezekiel has painted a picture of a
shepherd of the people who would "seek the lost". The image
of the vineyard had long been associated with the people of
Israel, and the prophet Isaiah (25.6–8) had spoken of a feast that
God would one day make on Mount Zion. The image of God's love
that is reflected in the parables is the love that seeks the lost,
rejoices at the finding of one gone astray, that welcomes with
unlimited forgiveness and with a generous goodness beyond all
understanding. It is undoubtedly a very different image of God
from that held by the religious leaders of the time. In their eyes
there was no room for such extravagant generosity: "Is thine eye
evil because I am good?" Naturally these religious leaders too
could talk about God's grace and mercy—but it was grace that was
given to those who were properly qualified, a grace on the basis of
fulfilling the law. In his book Joachim Jeremias has quoted a
rabbinic parable formed very much like the story of the labourers
in the vineyard. But there is a profound difference. The rabbinical
parable also tells of labourers with different numbers of hours of
work in the vineyard. The last to come were a couple who had
worked only two hours and yet got the same wages as the others.
But then the reason is given: these two had both done more
in two hours than the others had done in the whole day.

And that gave a sound reason for the wages they were given.

What happens in Jesus' parables—and in his actions—might be called a derationalizing and demoralizing of the image of God held by the Pharisees and the lawyers. Moralism and rationalizing belong together. Relationship to God is based on performance and calculation. God's grace is explained by, and adjusted to, what the law and commandments require. From this point of view it is entirely appropriate and entirely reasonable that God shall pay due attention to the qualifications displayed, be well pleased with them, and reward them with his grace. In his story of the Pharisee and the publican in the temple Jesus gave a sharply etched picture of this kind of relationship to God.

The image of God that is sketched in the parables of Jesus is in sharp contrast to this kind of religious attitude. To him there is no question of suitable qualifications nor that God's way of behaving should match what people might expect and reckon with. On the contrary it is in fundamental and shocking contrast with the reasons approved by moralism. From the point of view of moralism this way of behaving is unquestionably offensive, unreasonable, absurd. But just when it appears most unreasonable, just when the way God acts seems utterly different from all that human beings would expect, it is there that perspectives open of a depth and a width one would never have guessed at.

Of course it would open the way to complete misunderstanding if one started from moralist reasoning and interpreted these actions as indifference and passivity in face of "sin" and evil generally. Jesus' parables are battle parables, not just in the sense that they battle against contemporary moral attitudes, but also in the sense that the battle for humanity is here joined at a far deeper level than was ever possible for moralism. The divine love here reflected is worlds away from indulgence and leniency. Battle is the word; love is in action to free men from bondage to the violence of hostile powers.

The contrast to the moralistic reasoning of contemporary Judaism is clear enough. But its relationship to the Old Testament is a different question. It is with good reason that we have to remember the wide range of Old Testament associations in the parables of Jesus and how much life and content they contributed to the images Jesus used. We have still more reason to remember how Jesus unreservedly spoke of God as the God of Abraham,

Isaac, and Jacob. He aims his shafts at the religious leaders of his time, but not at the Old Testament. This is not to say that the image of God of the parables and of Jesus himself can be immediately referred back to Old Testament types. When the Gospel of John can formulate it as: "the law was given by Moses, but grace and truth came by Jesus Christ", it is clear that the view of the Gospel is that something new had come with Christ.

Certainly even in the Old Testament God is a God of love and mercy. Even there he is a God who forgives sins. God's loving care reveals itself primarily in his choosing and bringing up Israel. His choosing of Israel is not conditioned by any special qualifications that they had. It is an entirely unmotivated act of God's goodness. At the same time the "covenant" that God made with Israel is a covenant based on law. This did not mean—or did not necessarily mean—that relationship to God had to have a moral character, in the way that it undoubtedly had in the Judaism that faced the wrathful criticism of Jesus. We have to note that in the Old Testament the law is readily thought of as one of God's gifts, as a result of the love that exposes, judges, and challenges. In the religious attitude of the Pharisees that Jesus attacked, on the other hand, there was a refinement of those tendencies in Old Testament tradition which in the process of refinement had necessarily to lead to a thorough-going moralism and therefore to that self-righteousness which looked down with scorn on "this people who knoweth not the law" (John 7.49). Jesus turns to these despised people. And when he does so, he does not stop at talking about a God who can forgive, but he absolves them, he gives them forgiveness of sins, direct. In other words, he acts on behalf of God, in a way which had no precedent. Jesus demonstrates in action what he had talked about in the parables, and the parables defend what he had demonstrated in action.

The Old Testament was Jesus' Bible and he treated it as such. He directed his criticism at the Judaism of his times, both the Pharisees and the Sadducees. His conflicts with the scribes and Pharisees were fierce: they had "omitted the weightier matters of the law, judgment, mercy, and faith" (Matt. 23.23). But Jesus' attitude to the Old Testament was entirely positive. He did not declare any "other God" than the God of the Old Testament. What he learned from these writings determined his view of his task in life. What was new and revolutionary was the sovereign authority with which he spoke and acted on God's behalf. The result of this was that his attitude to the Old Testament—like that of the New Testament later—was dialectic, marked both by continuity and by the replacement of the old covenant by the new covenant. This is what is expressed in the Johannine words of how "grace and truth" came by Jesus Christ.

These words from St John have as their background the whole completed life work of Jesus. The New Testament has many statements of this kind. There is another of them directly referring to the image of God: "Hereby perceive we the love of God because he laid down his life for us" (1 John 3.16). The love here spoken of is nothing but God's own love. The relationship between, on the one hand, the words and actions of Jesus and, on the other hand, the apostles' account of the significance of his completed life's work is a question we shall deal with later. Here we shall only make the preliminary point that the apostles' account is linked with, and based on, the imagery of Jesus as we find it in the first three Gospels, in the parables and actions. Here we find the "new wine", the "new bottles", the "new garment" and—with eschatological perspective—the "new age". Among the actions of Jesus we think first of the symbol action of the last evening; the "new covenant" which replaces the old is not based on the law as the old had been. It is based on the victory of self-giving, sacrificing love.

Talking about God

We have had a look at a number of the symbols to which the Bible has recourse when it has something to say about God, and we have also considered some of the parables in which Jesus defends his way of working and at the same time attacks a view of God which he condemns as distorted and false. The picture this has given us of how the Bible talks about God powerfully supports our thesis that symbol language is the mother tongue of faith.

Our next question is how this symbol language functions, and what are its potentialities. This leads us into a number of problems which have recently been attracting increasing interest and giving rise to a growing body of writing: the question of the use of symbol language and how far it can be used in religious contexts.

These problems include questions of the theory of knowledge, of linguistics, of psychology. We cannot deal with all of them, so we shall limit ourselves to trying to illustrate the function and potentialities of symbol language.

Just symbols? Yes, unquestionably, so long as we are within the area of the life of faith, so long as we are dealing with what faith has to say. Just as when the Bible has something to say about the way God works, how he "speaks", it always uses symbols, so it is whenever Christians talk about God. The Bible symbols—at least the most important of them—will always be our main guide when Christians talk about God. This does not mean that no symbols other than those which we find in the Bible are to be used among Christians—to limit ourselves to those would mean that God had ceased to function. Of course we can well create new symbols. Just as the Bible symbols were often directly linked with daily life and thought in those times, so it is to be desired that nowadays we should create symbols directly linked to life in our time. For Christian preaching this is a task of great importance. And we look especially to our Christian writers for new creation of this kind.

Yet through all this the language of faith remains the language of symbols. God is not an object to be analysed, defined and determined like objects in the world of sense. He is not an "object" at all. To want to define what God is "in himself" is beyond all human abilities and from the point of view of faith is an act of arrogance with no respect for mystery. It was not without good reason that Luther in his time advised against all speculation on "God's high and holy majesty". Over against those who suppose it is possible to know God in this way the Bible stands guard with such passages as these: the Father dwells in secret, no man hath seen God, God dwells in light which no man can approach, his ways are past finding out. Above all, we have to remember that the Bible is constantly asserting that there is a contrast between "this age" and "the age to come" when we shall "see God face to face". Because God is *different* from this world, and yet all the words we can find to use are taken from this world, whatever we say about God must be said in the form of symbols. It is with the help of symbols that the man of faith speaks of the God with whom he knows that he is involved, the God upon whom he is dependent and in whom he puts all his trust. It is through symbols that we

illustrate and make real the image of the God who makes relationship to God into what it is. The whole time what we are dealing
with is relationship to God or God as he makes himself felt in that
relationship. On the other hand, for this it is an entirely foreign
idea to attempt to give any abstract definition of what God is "in
himself", in formulas like "Being itself" or "the absolute Subject".
We look in vain in the Bible for definitions of this kind. Fundamentally there is no room for any definition except the purely
tautological: God is God. But the relation of this God to man and
the world is made real and illustrated through symbols that comple-
ment one another and limit one another.

To turn now to the potentialities of symbol language. This
language is used not only in the world of religion; it is used in
many connections. In scientific work it is used in such "strict"
sciences as modern mathematics and physics. But interesting as
this use of symbols in science is, we are more concerned to think
of the wide use of them in poetry and other writing and in creative
art. We might here propound the thesis: the deeper the dimension
to be illustrated, the more symbols appear as a necessary form of
expression. There are dimensions, there are spiritual realities
which cannot be referred to and explained except through symbols.
Their potential is greater than that of any other form of expression.

Why are symbols used? Why are parables used? Not only
because they are the only possible things to use but also because
symbol language provides a wide range of expressions for the
essentials of religion. This is shown by what we learn from the
parables and actions of Jesus. They are not tame accounts that say
nothing. They have a power to unveil truth in the sharpness of the
shock they give. They are loaded with explosive. They present
their message with a direct appeal and an inescapable challenge.
Indeed all the symbols of God that we have earlier referred to,
each in its own way, proclaim a God who is at work.

If we are now to consider the part that symbols play, the function
they have, there are two limitations to be borne in mind: they may
be undervalued and looked down on, or, on the other hand, they
may wrongly be regarded as "adequate" definitions.

In the first case, people may try to play off "reality" against
symbols. They say they are "only symbols", not reality, not about
God himself. This is misleading. Symbols, as we have seen earlier,
are not "only symbols", they are not something which could only

be loosely connected with what is the highest reality for faith, with God. Contrasting symbols with reality empties symbols of their meaning. It underestimates the function they actually perform. Admittedly symbols are primarily what one might call a witness to something else. They show how people have in various ways become involved with God. But that is not the sum total of their task. Their decisive and essential function is that they are the means in which and through which God reveals himself to faith— and God "making himself known" is not just the communication of theoretical insights but first and foremost God coming in contact with man, "speaking" to him and "dealing" with him. Here it makes sense to talk about God's *word* directed to man, awakening him, revealing, challenging, giving. A symbol is not something that stands between man and a supposedly distant God, but it is a means that carries a message not only about God, but from God.

Yet, on the other hand, symbols cannot be treated as adequate definitions. There is hardly likely to be any risk of this so long as images are taken from the world of nature. To speak of God as "a rock" or as "a fountain" is very expressive symbolism. Nobody would think of identifying God with a rock or a fountain. If we read "God is light", it does not lead to anyone reversing the proposition and saying "Light is God". But the danger is very different with symbols taken from the world of human life. It becomes very easy to formulate what is said about God in terms of human behaviour, for instance to describe God's "love" and "wrath" from human patterns. The history of theology shows that the great danger is that these definitions are adapted and humanized so that they can be fitted into and serve to support previously constructed theological arguments. "Love" is one of the symbols that has been treated in this way. In this case there is a special danger of identification. Does not the Bible itself say: "God is love"? Yes, it says it and repeats it. It is one of the very few places in the Bible where there is a direct statement of this kind. It is not there by chance. And we must beware of trying to reduce its importance. The Epistle is clearly trying to say that there is nothing in the things God does that is in conflict with his being "Love". But naturally this does not mean that we here have an "adequate concept" with a clear meaning, or that the sentence can be reversed as "Love is God". The word "love" is a word of many meanings and shades. God's love, his *agapē*, is not any kind of love. This is no isolated word with self-evident meaning, but it is a symbol that reveals its nature and its meaning through the contexts in which love in action is described.

The reason why symbols have to be used has been answered. The language of symbols is the mother tongue of faith. When the Christian faith naturally and almost automatically moves in the world of symbols, it finds available a language which has exceptional possibilities of sketching the meaning of relationship to God. We might follow up the question why symbols are used with another question. Why do we have to have theology? Why not stop at having symbols? If the language of symbols is the mother tongue of faith, theology and its language is almost like translating it all into a foreign language—and all translations from one language to another have their difficulties. Is translation of this kind desirable? Is it necessary?

We started this chapter with a look at Emil Brunner's view of the task of theology. We might now take a closer look at his argument, which actually deals with the relationship between the immediate language of faith and theology. The message of the Bible, says Brunner, comes to us in "a poetic and childish, unreflected form". The task of theology is to present it in a form that is in accordance with reason and is scientific. But the more "scientifically" this is done, the more theology departs from "the original truth of faith", from which it advances (whither? one might ask) and to which it must at the same time refer back. We are struck here not only by the rather supercilious words about its being childish and unreflected, which obviously refer to the use of picture words, but even more by the remarkable statement that the more scientific theology is, the more it departs from what Brunner calls the original truth of faith. If this were a necessary consequence of scientific theological work, we might well dismiss it. A "scientific" work which instead of analysing the object of its study only departs from it and busies itself with something else, would hardly have any purpose in existing.

Of course Brunner did not really mean anything as bad as this, and it would not be right to say that his own work followed such a strange course. But what we are interested in is not Brunner's theology, but the ideas that lie behind his theological programme. Some of these ideas are of a considerable age, particularly the idea of a contradiction between a lower level of faith and a supposedly

ID

higher insight of theology, a higher "gnosis". It would then be the task of theology, as it were, to lift faith to a higher dignity, to change the primitive ideas of faith to a higher gnosis—as, for instance, when some nineteenth-century theologians wanted to translate faith into Hegelian speculation. But it can hardly be any part of scientific study to get involved in dubious experiments of this kind. It cannot reasonably be claimed to be a task for theology to remodel faith in God into something other than what it really is. Nor can it be the task of theology rationally to demonstrate "the truth of faith"—for this too would be to make of faith something different from what it is. If theology is study, its primary task must be to analyse and elucidate the object of its study, Christian faith in God.

When we have defined—and limited—the task of theology in this way, the relationship of theology to the symbol world of faith must be very different from what it is in Brunner's programme. No one can deny that the Bible contains the basic and decisive material of Christian faith. This faith makes its immediate impact on us, clothed in the language of symbols. It is therefore impossible for theology to talk slightingly of this impact. It is unthinkable that theology could do its work by withdrawing from what is here given. On the contrary, one of its main tasks must be to analyse symbols in order to clarify their meaning. It must interpret them, not reinterpret them. It is not a matter of saying something different from what the symbols say, but to understand what they are trying to say, to listen to and to determine the religious meaning of symbols.

One of the chief tasks of theology must therefore be to elucidate the meaning of symbols. To start with the Bible symbols, they must be studied historically and analytically. Symbol language is expressive, and many of the Bible symbols speak to us immediately in a way that time cannot dim. But we cannot shut our eyes to the fact that many of these symbols are taken from conditions which no longer exist, and have become wholly unfamiliar to people of today. And New Testament symbols and parables are linked with a great many Old Testament associations which were well understood by people in those days and which gave rich and meaningful content to what was said. But these associations and contexts are not immediately understood nowadays. Study of the parables has shown that, when insufficient attention has been paid to the original context of the story, interpretation has digressed into vague allegories, the point of the parable has been lost in a variety of speculations or in trivial exegesis where the religious meaning has disappeared. We must not forget that there are also parables which the Gospels have intentionally shrouded in a veil of secrecy, especially the "messianic" parables or those illustrating Jesus' sense of vocation, because the meaning of these could not be rightly understood until Jesus' life's work had been completed.

We find the same sort of secrecy in the symbolic actions of Jesus, as told in the Gospels. Their meaning is hidden so long as they are regarded as bare actions without regard to their symbolic significance. Take, for instance, the Johannine story of the wedding at Cana or the story of the barren fig tree in Matthew's and Mark's Gospel. The miracle may appear as rather banal conjuring so long as people do not realize what the symbol means. The action is really illustrating "the new wine", the richness and joy of the new covenant, and referring to the Lord's Supper as the seal of this new covenant. The curse on the fig tree that withered is a meaningless absurdity until it is understood that what was being condemned was the religious leaders of the Israel of those days who had sealed their doom by rejecting both the gospel's new message and its messenger. All this helps to show the necessity and significance of Bible study directed at elucidating the meaning of the symbols.

But theological work on the symbols cannot stop here. If we are to define the image of God sketched in these symbols, we cannot stop at analysing a number of isolated symbols. Two questions arise. The first is the relationship between the symbols, the links or the tensions or even the contradictions between them. The second question is the changes which may have taken place in the image of God during the long period of time in which the books of the Bible were being written. Are there symbols that have been eliminated or whose meaning has been altered by being set in a different context or for other reasons? In both cases what is at stake is preserving the original image of God.

These questions will not be answered here for they come up later. Here we only try to make the problem concrete.

In the relationship between different symbols of God, we might distinguish three sets of symbols. One of these illustrates the sovereignty of God, symbols such as power, Lord, King. We find a second set in such symbols as goodness, love, mercy, long-suffering. Finally, a third set speak of the wrath of God, God as judging and punishing. These groups are not wholly exclusive. And there are some symbols that refer, not to one of these groups, but to some intermediate concept. When the image of "shepherd" is used about God, it may be linked both with the first and the second set of ideas. Still more so, righteousness is related both to the second and the third group. When God's righteousness is rather one-sidedly taken as an expression of his radical opposition to, and condemnation of, evil, this does not tally either with the Old Testament or the New Testament use of this word in, for instance: "God may be trusted, in his righteousness, to forgive our sins" (1 John 1.9, Twentieth-Century New Testament). Actually the relationship between these three sets of symbols has been one of the main themes in the history of theology, in which there have been widely differing interpretations, varying between tensions, direct contradictions, and all kinds of attempts to reconcile them.

To turn now to the second group of questions; this brings to a head the relation between the Old Testament image of God and that of the New Testament. Three points are to be noted. First, the God of the New Testament is the same as the God of the Old Testament: the God of Creation, the God of Abraham, Isaac, and Jacob, the God who deals with Israel and has entered into a covenant with his people. God is the unchanging, who is the same at all times, through all generations and to eternity. But, secondly, this does not mean that the New Testament image of God is necessarily and at all points identical with that of the Old Testament. There can be, and undoubtedly there is, a change of slant, so that some symbols are stressed more heavily than they were earlier. Not only this; there are also changes in the interpretation of the meaning of some symbols. This is particularly true of some of the power symbols. Whereas in the Old Testament there are cases where the power symbols have been taken to mean that not only goodness but also evil have their origin in the divine will, in the New Testament God's power is set in radical opposition to every kind of evil—and evil is linked with a power that is at an enmity with God. Above all—and this is our third point—the New Testament throughout regards what God has done through Christ as unique and of decisive significance. This means that the relationship between the two Testaments becomes dialectic, marked at the same time by continuity and by contrast. It means too that no image of God can claim to be fully Christian unless it is supported by the evidence of what Christ did. To put it in other words, what Christ did must act as a compass when we interpret the meaning of symbols.

I should like to conclude this section by delineating three *wrong images* of the God of Christian faith.[1]

1. The God of Fate—god as a demon

The element that is characteristic of this caricature of God is that people try to find God's sovereignty, his almightiness, in everything that happens. His almightiness is taken as meaning all-causality. The difference from the Christian image does not lie in this talking about God's almightiness or sovereignty. Christian faith admittedly does this too. But the difference is that when almightiness is taken as being all-causality, the drama disappears from the image: people argue as if we were already living in a world of perfection. When the image of God is rationalized in this way, God ceases to be the power of love. He is no longer "an ever-flowing spring, overflowing with goodness and from which all that is good emanates" as Luther wrote in the *Large Catechism*. It is not only what is good but also what is evil, indeed the whole nameless suffering of all creation that is then derived from God as the cause of all. The result is that god becomes amoral, a god of fate, a god of naked power, as it were. Not only this; the god who is the source of good and evil without distinction must be described as a cruel god, a god who has become a demon. To use an image: divine and demonic intermingle in a stream of turbid water.

2. The God of Vengeance—god as a moralist

This wrong image is more insidious. Unlike the caricature we have just been describing, people try emphatically to stress God's radical opposition to, and condemnation of, all that is evil—which is an essential part of Christian faith. But whereas the false image of the god of fate sees everything in the perspective of unqualified

---

[1] The following pages, 123–5, form a supplement specially written by the author for the English edition.

power, here everything is seen from the aspect of what is right. God's righteousness, his "right", has been infringed by human sin and his demands for justice are then satisfied by Christ, through the restitution made by what he did. The dramatic perspective is not eliminated, but it is thrust into a narrow legal or quasi-legal framework. There is then of course no room for the spontaneity and self-giving which is typical of God's *agapē*, of God's love. When theological thinking of this kind appears in popularized and crude form—as often happens—God will be taken as being a niggardly god, asserting his rights, a moralist. This is expressed particularly in the law of God being regarded moralistically, almost as a catalogue of what is forbidden or permitted. The result is a wrong image of the law which is always and everywhere described as a law of love.

3. The God of Inoffensiveness—
the god of dedramatized and depleted love

This false image is incomparably the most insidious. For here it is possible to talk and talk about what is at the heart of the image of God, its alpha and omega, while what is being talked about is a love that has lost its power. Of the harsh conditions in which Love has to live in this world of ours, this view seems to know nothing—the drama has gone out of it. It knows nothing of the Love that unmasks, disturbs, and judges, and nothing of the Love that gives life. It becomes a love along the lines of Voltaire's famous remark about forgiveness as God's profession: "c'est son métier". Love becomes a pillow on which to go to sleep, not a rousing, creative, life-giving power. The only thing it has in common with the *agapē* of the Bible is its name.

In view of wrong images of this kind one can at a pinch understand the reactions found in the diffuse theology of our day that proclaims "the death of God". There are undoubtedly some images of God and concepts of God for which it would be highly desirable to be able to issue a death certificate, especially so if it were to take effect. This is true not only with the naively anthropomorphic god above the clouds or with abstract concepts of god that people suppose they can prove, but still more so with caricatures of the kind we have mentioned—the nightmare god of fate, the tyrannical god of moralism, the caricature of the god of love which has nothing but the name. Much of the "God-is-dead" theology is really gunning for these wrong images: the monism that finds expression in the all-causality god of fate, the moralist god who regards man as not yet come of age. But this is one thing. It is a very different thing to replace the monism of a god of fate with a wholly this-worldly monism and to publish this, humanity alone in a world without God, as if it were a gospel of freedom. Whatever may be said about a theology of this kind, we have to realize that to solve the problem in this way is to treat too lightly, too unrealistically, the whole problem of the destructive forces in the world. Besides which, this theology is so busy with the wrong images that it has no eyes for the God of whom the gospel really speaks, the *agapē* which is so far from treating man as if he were not come of age that on the contrary it sets him free and makes him a fellow-worker in the work of creation and redemption.

To believe in God, in the Christian sense, is to believe in the power of his love, his *agapē*: the love that has created and is still creating, that is at war with everything that is evil and destructive in our world, that enters into the depths of suffering and shares them, that unmasks and judges, yet at the same time raises up and sets free—the invincible might of life-giving, victorious love. There is nothing else in which we can believe. Of course it may be objected that after all this is only a belief, but not that it is blind belief or random belief. For the power that we are talking about has not left itself without witness. Anything that Christian faith can speak of is nothing but variations of this single great main theme. Anything that does not fit in with that theme has no connection with Christian faith. There is nothing else to believe in except this alone.

Demythologizing?

Recent decades have witnessed a vigorous discussion in theology on "demythologizing". The man to whom was due the flaring up of this discussion and its spread around the world was the German New Testament scholar, Rudolf Bultmann. The programme which he propounded, calling for theological demythologizing, has been variously interpreted. This is due not only to the difficulties inherent in the subject, but also to the fact that from the start Bultmann's programme contained a certain inner contradiction. The principal term, demythologizing—*Entmythologisierung* —indicates a purely negative attitude to the "myths" of the Bible, and this negative tendency is strongly marked in the course of the programme. At the same time, however, there is a more positive intention to preserve in some form the religious content of the myth, attempting to do so with the help of existential philosophy. Among the questions this raises are two: whether, in accordance with the principal term, the negative aspect is not the preponderant one; and whether the new framework of existential philosophy does not actually mean that *one* mythological background has been replaced by *another* more modern mythology.

It is not possible, nor for our purposes necessary, to go into the details of the voluminous and chequered discussion on demythologizing. We shall return to what is the most critical point so far as Bultmann himself is concerned in our next chapter dealing with the Christ drama. Of demythologization as a general programme, we may say: If the choice is to lie between, on the one hand, "demythologizing" in the proper meaning of the word, freeing theology from all connection with the Bible myths, and, on the other hand, trying to understand and make clear what lies hidden behind the mythological dress, there can be no doubt about which choice to make. After all that we have said about symbols and symbol language, the only possibility is the second alternative.

There is of course plenty of mythological material in the Bible. Symbol and myth are not to be identified, just like that. Symbol expressions about God—rock, shepherd, father—are not themselves myths. But like other symbols they can appear in a mythological context. And mythological descriptions and stories have always the character of symbols. This is so with what the Bible has to say about "the beginning" and "the end of all things", the accounts of creation and the eschatological pictures in the Book of the Revelation and elsewhere in the New Testament. This is also true of the mythological elements and passages which occur frequently through all the Bible history, the whole story of how God deals with man. The Christ drama is no exception—we have only to point to the story of Christ's ascension.

It is obvious that descriptions of this kind with their mythological colouring as a rule have their background in the ancient view of the world, a view that has long been part of an irrevocable past.

The complex of problems that Bultmann has in mind when he talks of demythologizing is not a new issue in our days. It is a problem theology has long been working on. Problems of this kind can be solved neither by trying to preserve as much as possible of the ancient view of the world nor by writing off "the mythological element" as meaningless or irrelevant. What has to be done is to try to unmask and reveal the religious content which lies hidden behind the mythological dress. It is quite clear that much of the criticism levelled in the last centuries against such beliefs as that in creation on the basis of its cosmology, has been caused by the idea that here was a theory of the origin of the world which was in competition with scientific theories or with a scientific view of the world, so far as we may speak of one. So long as views of this kind were prevalent, a conflict between theology and science was inevitable as we see clearly from the situation in the nineteenth century. The conflict had to continue so long as theology was regarded as a kind of quasi-scientific science of a metaphysical character—and so long as science aimed at being more than pure science, for instance being metaphysics with a negative key signature. Science is absolutely right to be against this kind of quasi-scientific theology. But, on the other hand, it has no authority, as science, to make statements about areas that are not part of science. It is quite a different matter that scientists such as Einstein and many others can make religious statements and that these statements may have scientific study as their background; but, even if they have this kind of background, they are making not scientific but religious statements.

What is of fundamental importance here is that all statements of religious character must be understood and judged in their own context, with their own perspective—just as ethical and aesthetic statements must be understood in their own context. If we transfer a religious statement—let us say, about God as creator —over to a scientific or any purely theoretical context, it loses its character and becomes quite meaningless. But it retains its meaning and validity when it is taken religiously and in its own context. In that case it is a matter of complete indifference whether we reckon with a few thousand years, as the ancient view of the world did, or with billions of years; the question is not whether one or other theory of the origin and development of the world is right. What is essential for belief in creation is that this is giving expression to a certain form of relationship with God, and—let me add—to a relationship with God which makes itself felt at the present time. Belief in God as creator would lose its meaning if there were only an act of creation which was carried out once a long time ago. We are not attempting here to elucidate in detail the exact meaning of Christian belief in creation but only to stress how this belief is inseparably linked with, and is an expression of, relationship with God. As we have earlier said, belief in creation gives expression to that relationship with God which is given *in and with life itself*. So it is a relationship which encompasses the whole of life. It is another matter that this relationship can take different forms and be viewed in different perspectives. What is important, however, is that a statement about God as creator is always a statement about *a relationship to God*. Belief in creation cannot be altered into a metaphysical statement divorced from, and independent of, relationship to God. If this is done, it means that the symbol language of the Bible has been misinterpreted; if so, belief in creation loses its religious meaning and is changed into a quasi-science or quasi-history. The Bible language of myths and symbols is the guardian power, protecting the religious meaning from being infringed.

The same is true of the mythological descriptions in the Bible of the "consummation of all things". What is said here about Christian hope is wholly anchored in relationship to God as it makes itself felt now. Hope springs from faith, it is indeed one side of faith, of relationship to God. The religious meaning of the symbols is concerned with this relationship and with nothing else. If it is taken out of this context, it is altered into independent concepts, supposed to relate to the future, thus losing its meaning. Symbols that represent eternal life or the consummation of all things as a victory over evil are meaningful because they say something about the nature of relationship to God—and only for that reason.

What is true of the individual symbol terms is also true of descriptions in mythological dress: in both cases it is a matter of understanding what is the essential from a religious point of view. The term "demythologization" is at this point misleading because basically it presupposes a negative attitude. It is quite a different matter that concentrating on what from a religious point of view is essential at the same time involves being set free from the possibility of being limited to the world-view of ancient times. We find a particularly clear instance of this in the story of the ascension of Christ. A present-day reader of this story may find the mythological form of the description so closely linked with the ancient view of the world that the whole thing becomes meaningless, absurd. Yet it is more than doubtful whether the early Christians and the Bible authors themselves—in this case Luke— thought of this description in a material way and in a literal sense. It would appear that actually they did not do so. Bible statements of this kind tend to shift their character. It is not always easy to decide whether and to what extent what they say is thought of as literal or symbolic. However that may be, what is far more important in our context is what the Bible itself has to say about this "thing", this "exaltation" which Luke has clothed in mythological dress. It is often spoken of in other parts of the New Testament writings. The symbol of "the ascension into heaven" as H. Riesenfeld says, "even in the days of primitive Christianity was by no means regarded in a material and literal sense". The theme that recurs in different forms is this: God has highly exalted Christ, he has "given him a name which is above every name" (Phil. 2.9); Christ has been exalted above all the bounds of time and space, and has thereby been given the power to complete his work through all ages and generations. So the ascension does not mean a removal, nor being enclosed in a local heaven, but instead a being present "alway, even unto the end of the world" (Matt. 28. 20).

We can now leave the subject of demythologizing. This programme as presented nowadays has caused a good many difficulties for what is in other ways a most interesting discussion. In so far as what they were trying to do was to set the idea free from the link with the ancient view of the world, this development is self-evident. In so far as there was an attempt to draw a line through everything that was mythological, it meant that they had failed to understand the language of faith. In so far, finally, as they were trying to put the essence of Christianity into an existential frame, any attempt to fit it into this philosophical mould has very dubious consequences.

So the programme of demythologizing has to be written off as being ambiguous and therefore misleading. The really important question, as we have stressed, is the question of religious content, the religious *meaning* which lies hidden behind the mythological dress. But we must add that this question applies not only to mythological descriptions but to symbol language in general. If we tackle the problem in this wider aspect, we are confronted by two main questions. One is how to retain the religious perspective unimpaired. The other is the context of meaning in the symbol language of the Christian faith.

Derationalizing

It is of course very instructive to survey how in the course of time theology has treated the Christian symbols. We shall deal here with one aspect of this—the relationship between faith and *ratio*. Two opposed points of view call for our attention. On the one hand, through the ages there have been many theological statements reinterpreting the religious content of the Christian symbols by rationalizing of one kind or another. On the other hand, we find theological tendencies in reaction against this, ending up in what we might call irrationalism. We find then a theology where paradox, which has an undoubted place in the world of faith, is transformed into logical contradiction and where as a result *ratio* is disconnected from the theological analysis of symbols. Here too we have tendencies which have appeared through the centuries. The watchword *credo quia absurdum*—I believe because it is absurd—is of ancient date. None of these points of view does justice to the task of theology. Theology fails in its task if the Christian symbols are made the object of rationalizing reinterpretation. If their meaning is to be rightly understood, some derationalizing may be necessary. But this kind of derationalizing does not mean that *ratio* is disconnected. If theology is study, analysis of some definite object, it must work with *ratio* just like any other study, with the implements of logic. A theology which finishes up in logical contradiction condemns itself. So we shall now see what is meant by the term derationalizing and then deal with the context of meaning in the language of Christian symbols.

Rationalization of the Christian faith is by no means limited to what is often called the age of rationalism. It is much more widely spread and appears in very different connections. All scholastic theology, both medieval and post-Reformation, shows the marks of far-reaching rationalizing, the after-effects of which are still felt today. The process of rationalizing has two main causes. One is that the purely religious content of the symbols has been linked with statements of a rational and metaphysical character. The other is that the symbols are no longer clearly recognized as symbols but that instead they are treated as if they were adequate concepts. This involves advanced anthropomorphizing. When people have been talking, for instance, about love and righteousness as divine "properties", these are thought of in more or less human terms, and then the problem arises how they are to be linked and fitted in with one another. Here are some examples of how these types of rationalizing are formed. The first type we illustrate by starting from the concept of omnipotence regarded from a rationalizing and metaphysical point of view, the other type by observing how in the doctrine of atonement people try to make a rational adjustment between God's love and his righteousness.

In the first instance, the problem is how, in view of the actual nature of our existence, it is possible to link the idea of omnipotence with the idea of a loving God. The task of theology comes to be to try to produce a defence for God, a theodicy. Attempts at giving a rational explanation of God's relationship to the world and all the evil that is in it take many and varied forms. People try either to minimize the reality of evil, or to find some kind of *modus vivendi* in the idea that God does not will evil but yet "consents" to it. But whatever explanations people turn to, they are all compromises, and must continue to be so, as long as omnipotence is thought of as God's all-causality, that is as long as all that happens is thought of as being derived from God's omnipotence. In these circumstances we shall never progress beyond *attempts* to reach a rational explanation, attempts that must inevitably run aground on the intractable rocks of the material.

In the second instance, rationalizing succeeds—apparently—better in the whole problem of the relation between God's righteousness and his love, of how reconciliation and salvation are possible. The main thought, of which we find many variations, is that the divine righteousness must have its due, must be properly satisfied before the divine love can be effected. This requires some adjustment between righteousness and love, and the instrument, the fateful term used to effect this adjustment is the idea of "merit". Medieval scholasticism spoke of merit in two senses: the merit that

Christ effected by his sacrifice, and human merit. God is reconciled, his exacting righteousness is satisfied by the merit earned by the sacrificial death of Christ. This gives God's righteousness the compensation, the satisfaction, that was required because of human sin, and that made it possible for his love to function effectively. But over and above this satisfaction, a "merit" was required from the side of man, of higher or lower dignity, for salvation to be realized. The Reformation with its watchword "by faith alone" swept away all thought of any human merit of this kind. But post-Reformation scholasticism preserved most of the medieval doctrine of atonement, the idea that the demands of God's righteousness had obtained their due satisfaction through the sacrifice of Christ. This gave a rational explanation of how God could now meet man with his forgiveness, his "grace".

It might now be asked: But is not this perspective of the death of Jesus, as given both by earlier and by later scholasticism, in complete agreement with what the New Testament itself says? The answer is that the death of Jesus is often spoken of here as a *sacrifice*, and that this is undoubtedly to be regarded as a main New Testament theme, an image which has something of essential importance to say about the significance of the cross. At the same time we have to notice that the Bible also uses a number of other images for the same purpose, and that each of these images gives its own special aspect. It speaks of the death of Jesus as a bearing of the punishment that was involved in sin, of the death as a ransom paid, as a victory over the devil and the powers of destruction, as an abolition of the enmity which separated God and man, as a setting up of "the new covenant". What happened in scholasticism was that *one* or two of these images were taken out of their religious context and set in an unfamiliar, rational context dealing with concepts so foreign to Bible thought as merit and satisfaction. The result of these manipulations was not only alien to the gospel message, the radical gospel, it was directly contrary to it. The whole point of the message was lost, that God's forgiving and liberating love is *not* something that can be rationally calculated, motivated, and explained, but is instead something that defies rational explanation; a love that "passeth all understanding", is wholly undeserved and in that sense is "paradoxical". The logical consequence of the scholastic doctrine of atonement was drawn by a nineteenth-century theologian called Philippi, who

pointed out that now that God had got his satisfaction, we had the
right to demand a share of his grace. This was a caricature of what
the schoolmen had intended. But here, as often, the caricature is
revealing. To sum up: *sacrificium vicarium* is no doubt a key word
in the New Testament, but you will search there in vain for *satis-
factio vicaria*.

We have now given a couple of examples of how rationalizing
theology looks, how it argues. Many examples could be given, but
these are enough to illustrate its character. Any attempt to
defend God, any kind of theodicy is wholly alien to Christian
faith; a god whom man has to try to defend is no longer God.
Equally alien is trying to give a rational explanation of the possibility of salvation, of what God can, or cannot, do here: the
divine love that is then spoken of is wholly different from the
radical *agapē* of which Christ and the Gospels speak. In both cases
the characteristically religious perspective gets lost A rationalizing
theology is a theology of over-curious presumption. It asks wry
questions and gives wry answers. And, besides, it imagines it can
give answers to questions that have no answer.

This should be sufficient to show why theological derationalizing is required. A theology of this type misinterprets the meaning
of Christian faith. Further, the interpretations, or rather the misinterpretations of rationalizing theology have proved very tena-
cious. If we look at present-day discussion of Christian faith, we find
that it is often confused through the continuing influence of
rationalizing theology. It is not the task of theology to conduct
apologetics. It is a different matter that elucidation of the content
of faith is obviously linked with criticism of misinterpretations.

"Derationalizing"—religious statements of a paradoxical nature:
Does this mean that we are abolishing reason in theological discussion? And does this lead to branding theology as inferior or
pointless? Or to our having to come to a halt with varying, disparate, and more or less contradictory religious propositions or
statements?

Some people might think so. But only as long as they had not
seen clearly what is the task of theology. Theological derationalizing does not in any way mean that reason is to be disconnected
from the activities of theology. Theological study has to work under
the same basic conditions as any other study. The point of urging
derationalization is not of course to exclude reason, but that analysis

working with rational and logical means shall be done in such
a way that justice is done to the nature of the material that is being
studied. Like other sciences, theology has to work with the method
or methods that best serve the purpose, which is to *understand*
Christian faith.

The main reason for the uncertainty that marked, and still
marks, the attitude to theology—and sometimes too theological
work itself—is a traditional and still prevalent confusion of religion
with theology. People seem to imagine that theology is to function
in the same way as religion, that it is to produce dogmas. Confusion of this kind has fateful results both for theology and for
religion. Theology is given tasks that do not belong to it and cannot
be carried out, and belief is rationalized with the result that its
proper nature is obscured. Theology does not set forth any
doctrines of its own, nor does it transpose faith to any higher kind
of insight or knowledge. It is not so presumptuous as to attempt to
be a "knowledge about God". It is belief which is its object. What
it is trying to do is to use all available means to analyse what belief
as relationship to God signifies. For this purpose theology seeks
the help of many special sciences, history of religion, philology,
psychology, sociology, etc., not forgetting philosophy. But in all
this, theology still has its own function to fulfil: it is to analyse the
content of faith and to do it in such a way that this content is made
clear, not reinterpreted and altered into something different from
what it is.

Something needs to be said about the relation of theology to
philosophy. Right from the days of the early Church, theology has
had manifold and intimate relations with philosophy. For theology
these have sometimes involved dependence, sometimes a never-
ceasing struggle. This double-sidedness is understandable.
Theology does not do its work in a vacuum. It has to enter into
dialogue with contemporary thought. But if this dialogue helps
theology—and there is no doubt that it does—this relation to
philosophy also has its obvious risks. For philosophy has presented
itself as a way of looking at life with a more or less religious character. Dependence on a philosophy of this kind, whether in Platonic,
Aristotelian, Kantian, Hegelian, existentialist, or other form, could
never be limited to a merely formal plane. It subjected theology's
treatment of Christian faith to pressures in one way or another,
with reinterpretation of the faith as a result. It was obvious that

this would lead to ruptures or wrestlings between theology and philosophy, to attempts by theology to break free from the hard bonds of philosophy. The whole of this encounter makes the most exciting history of ideas, full of variations between dependence and movements of revolt—though this applies not only to theology. There have been times when philosophy has been dependent on theology, or perhaps more properly on the Church.

It lies outside the scope of this book to describe all the fluctuations in this history. But there is good reason to say something about the present situation. The advances made both within theology and philosophy have opened new possibilities of fruitful association between the two sciences. Conflict between them is inevitable so long as theology is confused with religion and so long as philosophy behaves as a rival attitude to life, a religion or metaphysics with positive or negative key signature.

The present situation is dominated by two main theological streams. One, existentialist philosophy, is mainly to be found on the continent of Europe. A good deal of continental theology has associated itself with this. We find here the same mixture of dependence and tension which has often appeared in earlier times. We do not attempt to deny that existentialist philosophy's analysis of the present situation and its complications has been instructive and has made possible a dialogue between theology and modern thought. But, on the other hand, it is obvious that attempts to put theology in a framework of existentialist philosophy has created difficulties for an impartial analysis of the content of Christian faith, and has introduced reinterpretings of it.

The other main stream of present-day philosophy is the purely analytical philosophy which is principally based in the Anglo-Saxon countries and in Scandinavia. This philosophy on principle avoids propounding any attitude to life. From that point of view it seeks to be neutral. It tries to be a "linguistic" philosophy aiming primarily at investigating what is meaningful and what is not. In so far as this philosophy keeps strictly to this line and does not limit its analysis to what is empirically possible to verify, does not end up in metaphysics with a negative key-signature, entirely new possibilities open up here for relationship between theology and philosophy. There is an instructive illustration of this by Anders Nygren in an article on changes in Wittgenstein's philosophy with the significant title *From Atomism to Contexts of Meaning in*

KD

Philosophy. The investigations of formally orientated philosophy have implications for all kinds of study, and must have special interest for the theology that is aiming at analysis of religious language and its meaning. That this kind of philosophy presents theology with some difficult problems is not to be denied. But this is in no way something to be regretted. On the contrary, it is quite in order, it is desirable, and it is something that in any case *can* contribute to giving additional clarity to theological propositions.

Context of Meaning

Symbols, as we have seen, cannot be dismissed as being "only symbols". On the contrary they have something of essential importance to tell us about the God to whom faith is related. But at the same time the language of symbols does not tolerate statements of faith being rationalized. Behind what is revealed and can be put into words there is always the thing that is hidden, unfathomable. The words of Isaiah have abiding validity for the Christian faith: "For my thoughts are not your thoughts, neither are your ways my ways, saith the Lord. For as the heavens are higher than the earth, so are my ways higher than your ways, and my thoughts than your thoughts" (55.8–9). This means that God cannot be made an object to be investigated and explored like an empirical object. It means that the image of God cannot be measured in human terms or sketched with human patterns. The language of symbols stands on guard uncompromisingly against any rationalizing or anthropomorphizing of this kind—the two are inclined to go together. In the world of faith God is not made in the image of man. On the contrary, man is created to be "in the image of God". Man is urged to be perfect as God is perfect, to forgive as God forgives—the fifth petition in the Lord's Prayer by no means reverses this relationship. The fatherhood of God is not drawn on the pattern of human fatherhood—he is the Father above every kind of fatherhood.

After this introduction, we can now define the difference between a statement of faith and a reinterpretation that rationalizes it. The rationalizing reinterpretation changes the religious symbol into an adequate theoretical definition, which would be valid in any context. But a religious proposition is not an adequate theoretical definition of this kind at all. Its meaning is entirely dependent on the context in which it belongs. If it is transferred into a context where it does not belong, it loses its meaning.

A few examples will make this distinction clear. We can start with the example given above, a rationalizing when speaking of God's relation to evil and to the sacrifice of the death of Christ. It cannot be denied that the New Testament links the suffering and death of Jesus with the will of God. God "gave his only-begotten Son" (John 3.16), he "was delivered for our offences" (Rom. 4.25). Such texts as these have a perfectly clear meaning in the context where they belong. But they lose their meaning if they are transferred to a different context and used to answer questions for which they were not meant. The thing that is in agreement with the will of God is, in the words of Paul, that Christ was "obedient unto death, even the death of the cross". This is the religious significance of God's "giving the Son". But this religious perspective cannot be changed into a general theoretic proposition about God's attitude to evil. From one proposition, meaningful in a religious sense, one cannot draw the conclusion that God would have willed the treachery of Judas, or the maltreatment of Jesus by the Roman soldiery—nor can one take it in the modified form that God would have "consented" to it. Conclusions of this kind disconnect the religious statement from the context where it belongs and put it in an alien context where it is not only meaningless but even directly misleading.

We can take another instance. It is perfectly clear that when the New Testament speaks of man's "salvation" it regards this as wholly a work of God, a gift of God's undeserved grace. When it is said here that salvation is received in faith, this faith is regarded not as a human achievement deserving merit, but as something that is wholly the work of God. That salvation is received "in faith" does not imply any limitation of its being "the work of God." A religious statement of this kind has a clear meaning. It gives clear expression to the character of relationship to God. God is always the one who is giving. Any saving oneself is precluded. But this wholly religious perspective would lose its meaning if it were detached from the context of relationship to God and turned into a theoretical proposition from which all kinds of conclusions might be drawn about the attitude of God or man to all that happens. One rationalizing conclusion which might be drawn could be that salvation presupposed that God in his arbitrary will has predestined some to salvation and others to perdition. A rational conclusion then about man's situation might be that there is no point in human activity—indeed one writer drawing rational consequences in post-Reformation theology did actually declare that, as salvation was a work of God, it could only mean that man should keep himself as passive as "stock or stone".

In opposition to that kind of teaching, the New Testament speaks frankly about human activity: we are to pray, to seek, and to knock, to seek first the righteousness of God, to turn and become like children. These exhortations are followed by promises that we shall find, shall receive, that it will be opened. It is clear that the Bible has no inhibitions about urging courses like this on man—it abounds in them. On the other hand, in post-Reformation theology and preaching we find a certain anxious consideration and restraint. And why? Clearly because people were afraid that rational motives would come to be attached to salvation, by dividing it up into what God does and what man does. That would make salvation depend not entirely on God's giving and doing, but partly on man's merits and performance. This means that the Bible admonitions would be put into a context where they do not belong. If we keep to the words of Jesus quoted above, it is clear that the promises that we shall find, or get, or that it will be opened, everywhere refer to something that will be given; it is God who allows us to find, who gives, who opens. But the admonition and the gift go together. They belong together because faith, relationship to God is—as we have said—involvement. The significance of admonitions is not to give a rational explanation of the possibility of salvation. If they are misinterpreted like that, the result immediately is a division between what God does and what man does, and what man does is at once regarded as a deserving, meritorious achievement. Paul's famous words in Philippians 2 point the religious aspect most clearly: "Work out your own salvation with fear and trembling, for it is God which worketh in you both to will and to do of his good pleasure."

What I have written above is meant to show that the meaning of a religious statement is dependent on the religious context in which it belongs, and that it cannot be taken out of this and turned into a general religious proposition without losing its meaning and leading to what are, from a religious point of view, quite incorrect conclusions. But this does not mean that we have finished with the question of the character of religious propositions nor with the question of the connection between various statements of faith.

As for the character of these statements of faith, we have to take notice of what meaning it can have—and not have—to speak of their being "paradoxical". To illustrate this, let us take again the example of the relationships of salvation. On the one hand, we found the doctrine that salvation is throughout a work of God, a gift of God's undeserved love, on the other hand, the unhesitating words of Jesus that we are to seek, to pray, to knock, to repent, or, as Paul puts it: Work out your own salvation with fear and trembling. These counsels present no difficulties to our thinking. Anthropologically and psychologically they are perfectly understandable—they are not a doctrine at all. But it is different with the first proposition. That defies all rationalizing. It states that the action of divine love is not based on any performance from the side of man, that this love accepts man, unworthy as he is and fundamentally wholly unacceptable. This would entirely lose its religious meaning if it were subjected to rationalizing interpretations, whether they attempted to discover some human qualifications or to develop the idea that through Christ God was given some compensation or satisfaction. In either case God's *agapē* would cease to be what it is for faith: wholly undeserved and therefore incomprehensible, a mystery. It is like this in the parables of Jesus and in his way of acting of which the cross is the final epitome and symbol.

It is in contexts of this kind that words like paradox and paradoxical crop up. These words are widely used in recent theology, thanks to the influence of Kierkegaard, who never tired of calling the Christian faith "paradoxical" through and through. The question now is what talk of this kind really means, with what right and in what sense the ideas of Christian faith can be said to be paradoxical. It can hardly be denied that the word is often used incautiously and disconcertingly. Semantic considerations can help us here to overcome the undeniable confusion attached to the word.

There is a certain ambiguity inherent in the word "paradoxical". It can be used in different senses, and it is not always made clear in which sense it is being used. *One* thing is that something being described is beyond our ability to express, and may therefore appear to be a mystery—a very different thing is that to illustrate this it seems necessary to use language which is logically contradictory. In the former instance it is the content of the doctrine which is paradoxical, in the latter it is the linguistic form. So the word has a very different meaning in the two senses in which it is used. Ambiguity arises because the word is used as if it were univocal, without paying attention to the different meanings. When used about the content of a doctrine, the word means that this content cannot be rationally explained, and that we have not the ability to interpret it and give an adequate description of it. But this does not necessarily mean that the linguistic form in which the doctrine is clothed need be paradoxical in the sense of being logically contradictory. So the word "paradox" occurs in two quite different senses, and it is the confusion of these two that gives it an ambiguous character. It is essential to keep the meaning aspect and the language aspect separate. An example will illustrate this. Take a proposition of this type: the more we comprehend the love of God, the more incomprehensible it becomes. As we see, the statement is logically contradictory, and therefore from a language point of view unsatisfactory. But the question is whether it would have been possible to express what people are trying to say through this awkward and unacceptable proposition without having to end up in this logical contradiction. What people are trying to express is not the unreasonableness that the comprehensible is incomprehensible, and becomes more incomprehensible the more we comprehend. It is rather a statement of faith that the love of God in accepting a person who knows himself to be quite unacceptable to God appears different from, and contrary to, everything that we might reckon with, expect, or imagine, in fact a mystery. Further: the more we comprehend the function and content of this love, the more unreasonable it becomes for us to look for rational *explanations* of it.[1]

Statements such as these, that the peace of God passeth understanding, or that the love of Christ passeth knowledge, are not meant to assert that we do not begin to comprehend this peace or this love, nor that their incomprehensibility increases with the ability to comprehend them, which would be meaningless. The meaning is different. The proposition about love is trying to say that

[1] Cf. Ben Kimpel, *Language and Religion* (1957), pp. 94–6.

our "knowledge" of this love in our earthly life is and remains "partial" and that it cannot be rationally explained without ceasing to be what it is. This is what is paradoxical in the statement—a very different paradoxicality from that which means logical contradiction.

This is always the case with the propositions that theology has incautiously clothed in language that is logically contradictory. Many examples could be given of how religious paradoxes become changed into logical ones. As long as the religious perspective is preserved intact, we have no occasion to formulate theological statements in a form that is logically contradictory. If people think it necessary to formulate them in this way, it is an indication that the thought has been taken out of its religious context and changed into a theoretical statement supposed to be valid independent of its context. If, for instance, someone says that evil must have its origin in the will of God, since he is "almighty", and at the same time that it must be in conflict with his will because he is "love", a statement which is so logically contradictory and therefore meaningless is primarily due to the word "almighty" being torn from its religious context and made into an abstract, rational concept. If the word "paradox" is to be allowed at all in a theological analysis of doctrine, it should never be used in the sense of being logically contradictory.

We turn now to the question of the connection between various doctrines and various symbol terms for God. The real problem here is the unity of the image of God, the inner connection between different symbol statements. In its analysis of Christian faith, theology is confronted with a number of different assertions about how God has acted and still acts, and the symbols associated with this. It is possible that these assertions are each religiously meaningful, but that one might contradict another. The question then is whether there is an inner connection between them or if they are conflicting and the image of God is therefore disconnected, made up of disparate images, disintegrating.

When we were talking of derationalizing, we found that rationalizing theology assumed a supposed contradiction between various divine attributes. The feat performed by theology was as far as possible to even out these contradictions. The fatal thing was that this evening out, this rational explanation of how one thing could be combined with another, constantly suppressed and altered points that were essential for faith itself. If the religious perspective is preserved intact, the situation is entirely different, as we shall see in the next chapter. There will be no more trying to balance between supposedly contradictory concepts, such as might, love, and anger. The image of God will not be divided up and classified first, and then put together. If it is understood in a religious sense, it resists any attempt to divide it up into sections. It demonstrates its own unity in the midst of all changes of relationship and all admitted tensions. If we think of the great Christian themes of God acting as Creator, Saviour, and Judge, it is a symptom of the inner connection between them, forming therefore part of the image of God, that all three can refer to one and the same action. The theology of the early Church fought vigorously against the idea that the God of creation was different from the God of salvation. Actually faith regards salvation as one expression—and not the only one—of God's ongoing work of creation: "if any one is in Christ, he is a new creation" (2 Cor. 5.17, RSV). It is hardly necessary to add that salvation also refers to God as judge—no judgement is more radical than the judgement that is connected with God's saving *agapē*. There are, of course, tensions in this relationship: God can hide himself, he can keep silence, he can make men feel his wrath. But all this does not mean that the image of God is divided up into "wills" in conflict with one another. That kind of image of God would be no Christian image of God —it would be entirely different from the image that appears in the context of action centred on, and verified by, Christ—who "has made God known" and who "reflects the glory of God and bears the very stamp of his nature".

In this chapter we have repeatedly touched on the question of the task of theology. One final word. If the task is to analyse the content of *Christian* faith, this analysis must obviously be anchored in the Bible writings. But it cannot be limited to a purely historical analysis. It is not only exegesis and "Bible theology". Christian faith in God has two thousand years of history behind it, and at the same time it is a living reality today. Theology has to enter into dialogue with earlier interpretations, not only because they are of historical interest, but also and more importantly because they still more or less determine the modern attitude to Christian faith. But theology also has to conduct dialogue with contemporary thinking, whether this adopts a positive, or undecided, or negative attitude to Christian faith. It may not always be necessary to account in detail for this kind of dialogue. But it must always be there as a background to the theological presentation of the content of faith in God, if this presentation is to be both illuminating and available. Without dialogue of this kind, theology would be up in the clouds and would cut off all its potential contacts.

4 THE DRAMA

The word drama has occurred often in this book. It forms the title
of this final chapter because of the decisive part played by the
dramatic perspective in the context of the Bible. What the Bible
describes is a universal drama. The God to whom it bears witness
is a living and active God, a God ever at work. This action of God,
his "mighty deeds", we find described as action at war with opposition, at war with all that is anti-God and destructive of his creation.
Action versus opposition equals drama. What we find here is an
all-embracing drama, reaching from "the beginning" in the first
book of the Bible, to the final act, "the end", which the last book
in the Bible, the Revelation, foretells. Within the framework of
this universal drama there is a special, more limited, drama, that
of the history of the election of the covenant people, Israel. This
special drama issues in, is concentrated upon, and is brought to a
head in, the drama of Christ. But at the same time this central
drama of the Bible is focused within the universal perspective: the
Christ of the Bible belongs both to "the beginning" and to "the end".

In the universal drama of the Bible, Christ has the key role. The
work he accomplishes is the turning-point of the drama and determines the course of the drama as a whole. Here is revealed the
meaning of the drama, the aim of the battle. By this the Christian
image of God is inseparably linked with, and qualitatively determined by, the drama of Christ. This does not mean that God's
action is limited to what he does in and through Christ. But it
means that God's ultimate aim is none other than what is revealed
in the drama of Christ and that no other image can claim to be
Christian than the image reflected here at the climax of the drama.
So the main theme of this chapter is the image of God in the drama
of Christ.

The Son of Man

The drama of Christ as sketched in the New Testament has the
character of a confession of faith, of belief in Jesus as Christ and

Lord, as Kyrios. This is true not only of the Epistles, but also of the Gospels. These contain a collection of stories about the earthly life of Jesus, most fully described when it comes to the drama of the Passion. But the four Gospels are not written as a biography in the usual sense of the word. When the Gospel of John in the last verse of chapter 20 states that this has been written "that ye might believe that Jesus is the Christ, the Son of God: and that believing ye might have life through his name", this aspect is equally applicable to the other three, the synoptic Gospels—Mark begins his Gospel with the words: "The beginning of the gospel of Jesus Christ, the Son of God."

We run at once into a problem with a wide scope: the relation between the New Testament witness and Jesus himself, "the historical Jesus". The problem was raised as soon as the Bible became the object of historical and critical study, and has never ceased to be important. If from time to time it gets eclipsed, it invariably comes out again with renewed intensity as we see from the present situation in exegesis and study. The nature of our sources presents historical study with a number of difficulties, some of them insuperable. If by a solution of the problem we mean the possibility of drawing up a clear and definite line between the things that go back to Jesus himself and the things that have been more or less coloured by, or that spring from, the interpretation of the faith by the apostles or the primitive Church, then the problem is admittedly insoluble. But this does not mean that scholarship has to stop short at pure scepticism about the historical credibility of what we are told of what Jesus did and preached.

So for the time being we shall pay attention only to what must be regarded as the main question here: the relation between Jesus' own consciousness, or rather his witness to himself, on the one hand, and, on the other, the witness of the apostles to him. There was a time when New Testament scholarship, or at least a major part of it, thought that there was a fundamental contrast here, that the statements made by Jesus about himself according to the Gospels, particularly those about the Son of Man, did not really come from him himself, but from the apostles' interpretation of him. They thought that Jesus spoke as a rabbi, and that it was the apostles who by their interpretation turned him into the Son of Man and the Messiah. But this interpretation has not been accepted. Later research has shown that this theory is by no means

based on unprejudiced analysis of the material, but on the scholars'
preconceived ideas of what Jesus could or could not have thought
about himself and his task.

What is the background and what is the meaning of the title,
Son of Man, so often used in the Gospels? There was a time when
it was usual to interpret "Son of Man" in the Gospels as being
synonymous with "man". People thought that, when Jesus used
this name about himself, he was meaning to speak about himself as
an ordinary man among men, and that this name did not involve
any special claims. But this is as wrong as it could be. Study of the
history of the term has shown beyond question that Son of Man is a
name that makes great claims. It has its ancient roots in the Old
Testament where we find it as a title of the King Messiah alongside other titles such as "Son of God" and "Servant of the Lord".
In later times, in the Book of Daniel, Son of Man appears as the
title of the saviour figure of the heavenly Messiah who was to come
and to introduce the messianic age. An important document in
this connection is the Ethiopian Book of Enoch in which the Son
of Man has some features that remind us of the suffering Servant
of the Lord in Isaiah, but where it is also expected that he will
appear as the final judge of the world and its redeemer.

Now it is this title with all its meaning and associations that in
the Gospels Jesus seems to have often used about himself. On the
other hand, he is most chary of using the title Messiah, probably
because he was inclined to reject the political and nationalist
messianic ideals of his time. In the image of the Son of Man which
the evangelists sketch, his "heavenly" origin emerges. But during
the days of his earthly life he appears as one who is hidden and
lowly. He suffers and dies, but he is to be exalted and finally on the
last day he will be revealed in glory. It is understandable that from
a modern point of view people have tried to deny that Jesus used
the title Son of Man about himself; the ideas associated with it
seemed entirely foreign, fantastic, mythological, and unreasonable.
What people did when they attempted to dissociate Jesus from
"the Son of Man" may be described as an attempt to demytholo-
gize the gospel image of Jesus. We shall return to this problem of
mythology later. For the moment we shall merely make the point
that the attempt to dissociate what Jesus said about himself from
the title "Son of Man" not only has no support from the Gospels
but is also disproved by the fact that the title "Son of Man" does

not appear a single time in the Epistles, which use quite different names to honour "Jesus Christ", particularly Lord, Kyrios. So *if* it seems difficult to deny that Jesus saw himself and his work in the light of his being "Son of Man", this means that there is also a clear inner connection between what Jesus said about himself and what the apostles said about him as Christ and Kyrios. In fact a connection of this kind is shown by the very way in which Jesus acted on God's behalf, dispensing forgiveness of sins.

The essential element in the apostles' confession of Christ is really to be found in what Jesus said about himself as Son of Man. The perspective here is primarily that of the election and its history. The Son of Man is the promised one, "he that should come", he who was to fulfil the promises of God, the saviour figure who was to establish the messianic kingdom. But there is also a universal perspective: the Son of Man has his origin in heaven and his function is linked not only with his work on earth but also with the final "completion". Both these points of view on the drama of Christ—that of the elect people and that of the universal—appear with variations in the apostolic preaching where the work of Jesus on earth is seen throughout in the light of Easter and Whitsun. As an example of the primitive Christian confession of Christ, let us take the one we find in Philippians 2—regarded by many present-day scholars as a confession of faith in the liturgy of the primitive Church, included by Paul in his epistle. In the *New English Bible* it reads:

The divine nature was his from the first; yet he did not think to snatch at equality with God, but made himself nothing, assuming the nature of a slave. Bearing the human likeness, revealed in human shape, he humbled himself, and in obedience accepted even death—death on a cross. Therefore God raised him to the heights and bestowed on him the name above all names, that at the name of Jesus every knee should bow—in heaven, on earth, and in the depths—and every tongue confess, "Jesus Christ is Lord", to the glory of God the Father.

The Christ drama is described here in terms of being made destitute and being exalted. The condition for exaltation is obedience in earthly life even unto death. To this there are many parallels in the New Testament, expressing in different ways the universal perspective. Christ is God's only-begotten Son (John

1.18). He is "the first-born of all creation" (Col. 1.15, RSV). He is the Word that "was in the beginning with God" and that "was made flesh, and dwelt among us" (John 1.2 and 14). He was at work in creation: "All things were made by him; and without him was not anything made that was made" (John 1.3); by Christ "were all things created, that are in heaven, and that are in earth, visible and invisible" (Col. 1.16; cf. Heb. 1.2). His humiliation is described both as Christ's own action and as God's action. Christ has "humbled himself", "come down from heaven", God has "sent him", "given him". His exaltation, on the other hand, is always described as the work of God. God has raised him from the dead. Christ has been "carried up into heaven" (Luke 24.51) and so has "ascended up" there (John 6.62). God has "set him at his own right hand" (Eph. 1.20, etc.), "far above all principality, and power, and might, and dominion, and every name that is named, not only in this world, but also in that which is to come" (Eph. 1.21; cf. 1 Pet. 3.22, etc.). As the Exalted one, he reigns "till he hath put all his enemies under his feet", and "when all things shall be subdued unto him, then shall the Son also himself be subject unto him that put all things under him, that God may be all in all" (1 Cor. 15.25–8).

These New Testament passages, and many similar passages, give a clear picture of how the Christ drama is viewed from an all-embracing, universal perspective. But at the same time this universal perspective is inseparably linked with the perspective of the chosen people; the work of Christ and all that happens with him involves a fulfilment of God's promises to the fathers—everything happens, as it says repeatedly, "according to the Scriptures", in conformity with what had been promised "in the law and the prophets". The New Testament is full of references to the Old Testament, to demonstrate and to substantiate the correspondence between what had been promised and what had come about.

These New Testament statements about Christ are the point of departure and the basis for the "doctrine of Christ" that later developed in the Christian Church. The *aim* of this "Christology" of the Church has only been to safeguard the New Testament witness to Christ. As a matter of fact, the Church's Christology has not intended to state anything except what was already stated in the New Testament. It is quite a different matter that the terminology which this Christology uses has been different from that of the New Testament, and that this terminology, taken from Greek thought, was sometimes more or less suitable for the purpose—less suitable when the philosophical terms did not correspond with the Bible symbols. But it is outside the scope of this book to attempt to deal with post-biblical Christology. Our main interest is the relation between the image of God and the Christ drama as it is traced in the New Testament. The main questions are: How is God thought of as taking part in this drama, and how does this reflect on the image of God?

But first we must say something about the "mythological" element in the New Testament description of the Christ drama. This has been touched on already in the chapter about symbols, where we discussed Bultmann's demands for "demythologizing" which have led to one of the liveliest theological discussions of our day. We found that there is nothing new in this programme. There was a "demythologizing" —and a very radical one at that— in the theology of the age of Enlightenment in the eighteenth century. There was actually a more radical demythologizing here than in any later theology inasmuch as all that was essential was regarded as being given in "natural theology", the religion which people thought could be reached on purely rational premises; to this Christ had basically nothing to add. Again the liberal theology of the end of the nineteenth century and the turn of the century was extremely "demythologizing". The whole emphasis here was on Jesus' preaching of God as the loving Father.

The latest phase of demythologizing, principally represented by Rudolf Bultmann, differs from earlier liberalism in that the emphasis no longer is laid on the historical Jesus and his preaching, but on the "kerygma". The shift in emphasis is due, largely but not exclusively, to Bultmann's scepticism whether it is possible to arrive at any reliable knowledge of "the historical Jesus". When the emphasis is laid on the message, the kerygma of the crucified and risen Jesus, it might seem that Bultmann was on the same line as the apostles', especially Paul's, preaching, and also as the characteristic theological interpretation through the centuries. But this is not so. The kerygma is to be interpreted "existentially"—an interpretation of this kind leads man to an understanding of his own existence and to "authenticity". What is important here is not the historical data—the resurrection and all the New Testament statements about Christ belong to the world of "myth". The

existential question that modern preaching of the kerygma puts
to us is how we understand our existence. It is a question of decision and surrender. Believing in the cross of Christ is making his
cross our own, being crucified with him. The resurrection of Jesus
is an "eschatological event". What is important for us is to rise
again with Christ today, in our daily life to share in his resurrection.
Faith means a surrender in obedience to the God who acts in the
kerygma preached about Jesus Christ.[1] This faith confronts us with
the unseen reality which is Love, it involves release from the world,
and, as forgiveness, release from our own past; it opens up a future
for us and signifies not death but life. In faith, man is given an
"eschatological existence".

It is clear that Bultmann's theological interpretation lays the
decisive emphasis on what is happening at the present moment,
whether this is thought of as being an act of God through the
instrumentality of the kerygma preached or as man's decision and
surrender, his "crucifixion" and "resurrection". It is difficult to
decide exactly the part played by "what happened", the Christ
drama, in this existentialistically orientated theory of salvation—
but that we are here dealing with an advanced attempt to cut the
Christian faith loose from its anchorage in history to which the
New Testament bears witness, is incontrovertible.

The term "demythologization", as we have already seen, can be
understood in two senses: either as a rejection of the mythological,
pure and simple, or as an attempt to discover and lay bare the
religious meaning which lies concealed within the mythological
clothing. It is to the first sense, to rejection, that Bultmann refers
everything said in the New Testament about the humiliation and
exaltation of Christ—with one exception. And that is the resurrection. Admittedly even the resurrection is regarded as a myth. But
this myth is given an existentialist interpretation. The cross of
Christ represents man's "dying" and all the negative side, whereas
his resurrection represents the positive side of man's release into an
authentic and "eschatological" existence.

The question of the resurrection and the part it plays for Christian faith is a separate matter to which we shall return later. But
when Bultmann finds himself compelled firmly to cut out everything that the New Testament has to say about the humiliation

[1] *Kerygma and Myth*, ed. H. W. Bartsch (S.P.C.K. 1964), pp. 38–43 (The
Theology of Rudolf Bultmann).

and exaltation of Christ, this is evidence that he has failed to understand the symbol language of faith. If we are going to understand such expressions as "came down from heaven", "ascended into heaven", "sitting at God's right hand" in a quite literal and indeed local sense, then of course they have to be discarded together with the whole ancient world-view with which they are associated. From a contemporary point of view they would appear quite imaginary and meaningless myths. Bultmann is not alone in regarding New Testament statements in this light. Robinson's book, *Honest to God*, and its successful sales, have shown how widespread this view is, and also that people feel relief when the Christian faith is released from all this heavy mythological ballast.

I am not going here to inquire into how a situation of this kind has arisen. One thing is certain: all this makes definite demands not only upon theology, but even more so on preaching and teaching. To regard what the Bible says about heaven—God "who is in heaven", Christ "sitting at the right hand of God"—as just nothing but meaningless mythology, reveals the same high degree of incomprehension of the mother tongue of faith, symbol language, as trying to take these expressions in a literal and localized sense. That the terminology of the New Testament writers is linked with the cosmology of their times with its three tiers of heaven, earth, and hell, really goes without saying. Even if terms like this may seem to be terms of locality, this does not mean that God was regarded as localized at a fixed place in heaven, on his throne. God is also in "hell", no one can get away from him. Still less are the expressions that God is in heaven and Christ is on his right hand only intended to localize God and Christ; the essential point is that these symbol terms reveal the greatness, the power, and the glory of God and Christ. They are symbols and their meaning is wholly misunderstood so long as they are taken only in a literal sense.

The same is true of anthropomorphic symbols, such as calling Christ "the only-begotten Son of God". This expression cannot reasonably be taken literally. To do so would be the grossest kind of anthropomorphism—making God into the human father of a child. It is perfectly obvious that this is a symbol, and that its purpose is to emphasize the unique nature of the relation of Christ to God. The symbol, "the only-begotten Son of God", like the symbol expressions of the heavenly origin of Christ, and his exaltation to

LD

heaven all belong to the universal perspective in which the New
Testament views the Christ drama. We shall return to this at the
end of this chapter after we have considered how the image of God
is reflected in this drama. For this we shall look at what the
Gospels tell of the earthly life of Jesus, and what the New Testament has to say about him crucified and risen.

The Radical Gospel

It has often happened that theology has not paid much attention to
what the Gospels tell of the earthly life of Jesus. It has concentrated
exclusively on his passion and death on the cross. This has been
particularly characteristic of one main stream of Western theology,
both Roman Catholic and post-Reformation. For the doctrine of
atonement worked out by medieval scholasticism, primarily by
Anselm of Canterbury, the only factor of importance was the
satisfaction which by his sufferings and death Christ was thought to
have given God on behalf of mankind as an atoning sacrifice for
its sins. We find the same main theme, though in a modified form,
in post-Reformation scholasticism and in the theology of pietism.
A strong emphasis on the suffering and the cross is in itself in
complete agreement with what we find in the New Testament. All
the four evangelists describe the story of the passion in great
detail, and regard this as not only the end of the earthly life of
Jesus, but also as its climax. The interpretation in the Epistles of
what Christ did is also focused on the cross. But here, in the New
Testament, there is no question of isolating the suffering and the
cross. These are regarded—in contrast to what we so often find in
Western theology—as inseparably linked both with what came
before, the work and preaching of Jesus during his earthly life,
and with what followed after, with Easter and Whitsun. And it is
this context which throws light on the meaning of the passion and the
cross. When the liberal theology of the nineteenth century emphasized the earthly life of Jesus, particularly his preaching, this is to
be regarded as a healthy reaction against the one-sidedness of
earlier theology; a theme that had been neglected is brought
forward once again into notice. But at the same time we find another
sort of isolation: the preaching of Jesus is now taken out of the
dramatic context of the New Testament. The perspective of

battle disappears. The fatherly love of God, which is now put forward as the central theme of the preaching, is dedramatized and glossed over. The hard conditions in which the love of God has to work and suffer in our world are more or less lost sight of. And incidentally the radical gospel is also lost sight of.

The Creed speaks of Jesus Christ as "true God" and "true man". The double aspect which theology intended to preserve has not always been kept. Sometimes one aspect has suppressed the other, sometimes the double aspect has been turned into a division so that people have tried to separate what Christ did "as God" from what he did "as man". Theological manipulations of this kind never correspond to the image which the New Testament conveys. When we consider what the Gospels have to say about the earthly life of Jesus, we have to recognize first that it is not always that theology talks as frankly and realistically about the humanity of Jesus as the Bible does. People have not wanted to think that Jesus was really tempted or have tried to suggest—as Thomas Aquinas did—that his suffering affected only a lower stratum in the soul of Jesus. Docetic ideas of this kind, allowing Jesus' relationship to God to suppress his real humanity, are quite foreign to the Gospels.

The picture drawn here is a picture of a man battling under difficult conditions to fulfil in unswerving obedience to his "heavenly Father" the task for which he knows he is sent and called. The thing that lies hidden behind the stories of how Jesus was "tempted by the devil" was certainly not mere sham, but was grim and bitter spiritual reality, all the more so because temptations to make use of various kinds of demonic powers were very relevant to the fulfilment of the great task of his life: the way of obedience in contrast to the by-ways of demonic powers. Among the very human features is all that is told of Jesus as a man of prayer, all that is told of his grievous suffering. His life was a life borne up by constant prayer to the heavenly Father. His suffering was certainly not limited to any "lower strata of the soul". Suggestions of this kind are sheer misinterpretation, when we hear him say: "My soul is exceeding sorowful, even unto death" (Matt. 26.38) or when his suffering culminates in the cry of desolation from the cross. The Epistle to the Hebrews reflects these very human features in the Gospels when it says: "We have not an high priest which cannot be touched with the feeling of our infirmities; but was in all points tempted like as we are, yet without sin" (Heb. 4.15); again: "Who in the days of his flesh, when he had offered up prayers and supplications with strong crying and tears unto him that was able to save him from death" (Heb. 5.7).

The Gospels are all written to tell of Jesus as the Son. Yet they have preserved sayings of Jesus that witness not only to his true humanity but also to the limitations which go with being human. On several occasions in the Gospel, Jesus speaks of the world to come, the end of this age, when the kingdom of God will come in power. The Gospels include a saying of Jesus when he says that he does not know when this will be: "Of that day and that hour knoweth no man, no, not the angels which are in heaven, neither the Son, but the Father" (Mark 13.32). But they also include the saying when Jesus is talking about the end as being near: "Verily I say unto you, That there be some of them that stand here, which shall not taste of death, till they have seen the kingdom of God come with power" (Mark 9.1; Matt. 16.28; Luke 9.27). Similarly in Mark 13.30: "This generation shall not pass, till all these things be done." Prophetic utterances of this kind have not been fulfilled, at any rate not literally. They are evidence that "not even the Son" knew, evidence that true humanity involves human limitations.

So if the Gospels plainly paint a picture of the "true humanity" of Jesus, they also witness clearly to his unique relationship to God. This is true not only of the Gospel of John, where this theme is most fully developed, but also of the other three, the synoptic Gospels. We shall not here deal with this theme to its full extent. We shall restrict ourselves to determining a few of the main features in what the first three Gospels have to state, and then later come back and examine the New Testament witness as a whole. The image which these Gospels give of Jesus' relationship to God is marked first by his acting and speaking by divine commission and with divine authority. We think here of his "mighty works", his battle with demonic powers, his dispensing forgiveness of sins; he behaves as the bearer and steward of the radical gospel, and links the break-through of the kingdom of God with his own person.

There is a certain ambiguity in what is told about his mighty deeds. On the one hand, they are presented as being part and parcel of the work Jesus was given to do. When John the Baptist asks Jesus if he is "he that should come", he is referred to what has been done in agreement with what prophecy foretold of the expected and promised Messiah (Matt. 11.2–6). On the other hand, Jesus will have nothing to do with those who ask for "a sign" to prove the rightness of his claims: "There shall no sign be given unto this generation" (Mark 8.12). He does no signs to demonstrate his power, only to help people in need and in suffering. What the Gospels declare with one voice is that he cared not only for the needs and sufferings of their souls but also of their bodies.

A theme that constantly recurs in the Gospels is Jesus' battle with demonic powers, for which we find different expressions: devil, Satan, Beelzebub, evil spirits. The passage in 1 John 3.8: "For this purpose the Son of God was manifested, that he might destroy the works of the devil", is a telling description of one of the main themes of the Gospels. The significance that Jesus himself according to the Gospels attached to this battle against the evil spirits is shown in Luke 11.20: "If I with the finger of God cast out devils, no doubt the kingdom of God is come upon you."

This whole set of ideas has an unquestionably mythological formulation. To talk of driving out evil spirits, of Beelzebub as the prince of devils, of Jesus' struggle with the devil, or of seeing Satan fall as lightening from heaven (Luke 10.18) is to move in a world of mythology, quite foreign to modern thought. Medical science uses quite different categories when speaking of sicknesses that in the Bible were said to have been cured by driving out evil spirits. The idea of a "personal" devil, we might continue, is not only of a mythical figure—it has also in the course of time been linked with ideas of fright and dread, fraught with fateful consequences. The conclusion might be drawn that all these ideas of demons, of the work of the devil and evil spirits is due for demythologization in the sense of being entirely written off—after all, fifty years ago in a famous newspaper discussion in Sweden the devil was formally "abolished". But just to write him off in this way would be to write off something that is unquestionably an important theme in the Bible. The important thing is to find out what is concealed in this mythological clothing.

This question cannot be answered by discussing whether there is a personal devil or not. This kind of discussion would serve no useful purpose, and would only lead us away from the essential point. "The devil" is an expression for the concerted powers of evil. One has only to use the allied words demonic and demonism for realism to break through the mythological veil. What the Bible's drastic language is trying to say about these things is simply the antagonism, the struggle that rages between the power of God and the hostile power complex, whether described in the singular or the plural. In my book *Christus Victor* I have analysed the treatment of the Bible theme of struggle in theology and tried to indicate the reality which is concealed behind the Bible language about evil spirits. In his extensive review of the philosophy of religion, *Twentieth Century Religious Thought*, John Macquarrie referred to this book, saying that its presentation of Christianity is obviously relevant to an age like our own which has to struggle with "vast forces that threaten to enslave or even to engulf mankind".[1]

The ultimate question here is of something that lies at the root of all biblical and Christian preaching: God versus the demonic and destructive forces in existence. One of our Swedish hymns says:

> *Two mighty ones battle to capture man's soul,*
> *To win it into their obedience whole.*

This puts in a pregnant form the gist of the Bible theme—the decisive point is the struggle that goes on in man's world between the power of God and the anti-God power or powers. Two destructive powers are singled out in the Bible: Sin and Death. What is characteristic is that Sin is not regarded only as transgression of certain commandments, that is, that Sin is not seen in moral terms, but as a destructive force, holding mankind imprisoned, in thrall. On the same analogy Death is regarded as a destructive force, an enemy holding mankind captive in a grip of iron.

People have sometimes thought that this Bible perspective would lead to man's being regarded only as an object over which the struggle raged, as if man would not be affected by the struggle over him, and would have a kind of depersonalized view of what was going on. But this indicates a complete lack of understanding. The struggle for mankind is not like a struggle for territory between two hostile armies fighting one another. It is not the kind of struggle where man is just the object being fought over, uninvolved in what is going on. The struggle for mankind is fought out within man—

[1] Op. cit., p. 329.

between an involvement which enslaves him and an involvement which sets him free.

Against this background *the radical gospel* is drawn, which Jesus not only proclaims but also puts into effect. What is this radical gospel? To answer that question we start from the New Testament account of Jesus' dealings with the representatives of the Jewish religion of his day, "the scribes and Pharisees". The reason for these conflicts is described by the evangelists in the same terms. Jesus gave offence by associating with "sinners and publicans": "How is it that he eateth and drinketh with publicans and sinners?" (Mark 2.16). There were constant complaints of this kind about the behaviour of Jesus. The offence which people took culminates when he administered "forgiveness of sins". In the account of how Jesus cured the lame man (Matt. 9.2–8; Mark 2.4–12) Jesus says to him: "Son, thy sins be forgiven thee." The scribes' reaction is: "Why doth this man thus speak blasphemies? Who can forgive sins but God only?" But this criticism does not lead to any retreat on the part of Jesus. Nor does he deny that it is God's business to forgive sins. He makes the curing of the lame man a demonstration that "the Son of man hath power on earth to forgive sins". The forgiveness which he thus grants on God's behalf is a completely spontaneous action on his part. It is not dependent on any special qualifications on the part of those who sought his help. The only qualification is simply that they sought his help with expectancy. It is this that the account calls their faith: "when Jesus saw their faith", he acted.

We shall now illustrate how the radical gospel is reflected in Jesus' struggle with the scribes and Pharisees. We have already mentioned it in Chapter 3, where we were dealing with the parables of the lost sheep, the prodigal son, the labourers in the vineyard, and the invitation to the wedding feast. In them Jesus defends his behaviour and attacks a religious attitude based on morality and rationalism, which he brands as a perverted image of man's relationship to God and of God's relationship to man.

Attacks of this kind, however, appear not only in the form of parables. The Gospels also give a number of direct castigations with angry words and biting severity. We read: "Woe unto you, scribes and Pharisees, hypocrites! for ye pay tithe of mint and anise and cummin, and have omitted the weightier matters of the law, judgment, mercy and faith" (Matt. 23.23). If this verse brings out Jesus' criticism of the religious leaders' attitude to "the law", the story of the Pharisee and the publican in the temple (Luke 18.9–14) is a typical example of what Jesus regarded as being wrong with their religious life: the list of merits in the prayer— "not as other men are, extortioners, unjust, adulterers, or even as this publican". The Pharisee begins: "God, I thank thee." There is no reason for thinking that his thankfulness was not sincere, or that Jesus wanted to brand him as a hypocrite. What Jesus is branding is not hypocrisy but the kind of religious devotion that marked the Pharisees' way of life. It is this that gives the words of Jesus their sharp and cutting edge. It is aimed at the religious attitude that is bound with the bonds of self-righteousness. When Paul in his Epistles keeps on returning to the point that no one is "justified by the works of the law", this is only what Jesus himself had been saying in this story and often elsewhere, most of all in his way of acting through which he was manifesting the radical gospel. Though we have been speaking of a criticism along moral lines and a criticism along religious lines, these are not basically different things. The criticism is really aimed at a single thing, a moralistic and legalistic religious attitude, which is also orientated on rationalism. By referring to appropriate achievements, it tries to give a rational explanation of how it is possible to come to a right relationship with God. This also gives it an egocentric focus; at the heart of it is the Self and its qualifications.

When Jesus settles accounts with the Pharisees in this way, it is not to be read only as an historical document of interest for the history of religion, nor as an exhaustive description of Pharisaism, which it is certainly not. His criticism has an abiding significance for the Christian Church, where the moral type of religious conviction appears in many different forms. How insidiously this attitude can drape itself and disguise itself is shown by the fact that the publican in the temple, wrongly interpreted, has been able to appear as a model, to vouch for a rational and egocentric attitude—a thing that usually happens when penitence, confession, and doing penance are made the achievements required for man to qualify for the forgiveness of sins and the grace of God. The meaning of Jesus' criticism is seen more clearly when we see how Jesus proclaims and administers the radical gospel. First, then, let us see how this radical gospel is inseparably linked with *the radical law*.

Jesus, we read, has not come to destroy the law or the prophets (Matt. 5.17). Instead, he has come to fulfil. These words appear as an introduction to the interpretation of the law given by Jesus in the Sermon on the Mount. "Fulfilment" may be taken in a double sense. It may be taken as an expression of Jesus' own fulfilling of the law—by his obedience unto death. But, in the context we have been referring to, it means almost that he has laid bare the deepest meaning of the law, that he has revealed the law at its most radical. When we read further in the sermon on the Mount that "one tittle shall in no wise pass from the law", it does not mean that Jesus sanctions all the injunctions of many kinds in the books of the Old Testament, still less all the interpretations of the law that were current in his day. A classic instance to the contrary is the story of the conflict between Jesus and the Pharisees about the keeping of the Sabbath (Matt. 12.1–14 and Mark 2.23—3.6). Jesus heals a sick man on the sabbath day while people were watching him to find something of which they could accuse him. He carried out his act of loving care, claiming that it was "lawful to do good on the sabbath day" and looking on those who opposed him "with anger, being grieved for the hardness of their hearts". What happened here was an evaluation and a grading of the various commandments, issuing in the command to love being set over, determining, and regulating all the other commandments. This aspect of the law is formulated expressly by Jesus when in answer to a question as to which is the "great" commandment in the law, he replied with the double commandment: love of the Lord thy God is the first and great commandment, and after that comes one that is "like unto it": the commandment to love one's neighbour (Matt. 22.36–9).

So the law does not consist of a series of commands, fixed down to the last detail, commands that can be kept meticulously. It is reduced—or rather widened—to a single inclusive commandment. This commandment has no limits. The interpretation of the law that we find in the Sermon on the Mount does not mean that a number of new commandments are added to the old ones, to what "was said by them of old time", nor may Jesus' directions be regarded as fixed requirements about what is always to be done under all circumstances. His interpretation instead gives an example of what the all-embracing command to love *can* require, it is an illustration of the outreach of the commandment, of just how radical it is. How limitless this is cannot be more clearly indicated than when Jesus draws into the picture the behaviour of "the heavenly Father", and concludes: "be the children of your Father which is in heaven: for he maketh his sun to rise on the evil and on the good, and sendeth rain on the just and on the unjust. . . . Be ye therefore perfect, even as your Father which is in heaven is perfect" (Matt. 5.45 and 48). What Jesus demands here is that our behaviour shall be a reflection of God's own profuse love.

The command to love is a double command, both to love God and to love one's neighbour. In his book, *Den kristna kärlekstanken*, Anders Nygren has emphasized that, if they are to be interpreted in accordance with the Gospels, these two commandments must neither be isolated from one another, nor confused. As an example of confusing them he mentions the theory that love of one's neighbour is to be directed not really towards that neighbour as such but towards "God in one's neighbour". In this connection we ought to draw attention to two features characteristic of the Gospels. There is no competition between the two commandments, in such a way that it might be possible to show love for God while neglecting the requirements of love for one's neighbour. Whoever comes "to the altar" with a gift and is not reconciled with his brother must first be reconciled with his brother and then come and offer his gift (Matt. 5.23–4). Nor is it possible to evade one's obligations to father and mother by saying: "What you would have gained from me is Corban (that is, given to God)" (Mark 7.11, RSV)—that would be setting aside God's commands for human regulations. What is here condemned is really the same moralistic and egocentric religious attitude in favour of achievement supposed to provide merit as those we have already heard Jesus condemn as an abomination to God and man.

The relation of love to God to love to one's neighbour has a shaft of bright light thrown on it in the pericope on the last judgement (Matt. 25.31–46) where the theme is: "Inasmuch as ye have done it unto one of the least of these my brethren, ye have done it unto me." That is to say, whatever has been done to a neighbour has been done directly in the service of God. Here there is none of the confusion of which Nygren was speaking. What has been done has been done with the neighbour in mind, in simple, matter-of-fact care of him, without any sidelong glances. Just because of this, it has been something done in the service of God, service to him who identified himself with all human need. This strong emphasis on what the commandment means in terms of practical care for one's neighbour is to be noted all the more carefully, seeing that the perspective of the Gospels is pervaded with the idea of the imminence of the end. The short eschatological perspective is found to be linked with a down-to-earth, concrete view of the meaning of the command to love.

Finally, it is worth noting that Jesus does not put himself forward as a legislator, still less that he brought forward a law that was different from, or on a different line from, that of "the old covenant" or different from the law of creation. The law, God's law, in its aim and direction remains unaltered. What is new is the revelation of how radical it is. The First Epistle of John (2.7–8) rightly expresses what has happened when it speaks of "an old commandment which ye had from the beginning" and at the same time "a new commandment"—new because the old commandment has been made concrete in the preaching and actions of Jesus. So it is perfectly consistent when both the Gospels and the Epistles make the commandment issue in a demand to follow Jesus—which may also be called to follow God: "Be ye therefore followers of God, as dear children" (Eph. 5.1).

Jesus reveals just how radical the law is. He also reveals in his preaching and actions just how radical the gospel is. He acts in the power of that undeserved and unfathomable love, which does not depend on human merits and which in this sense is "unwarranted", by virtue of God's sovereign *agapē*. These two, the radical law and the radical gospel go together. Without this link love would lose its quality and be reduced to flabby leniency, losing all its power to create. We find all through the gospel how the whole of Jesus' work is born up by, and stamped with, this undeserved and unwarranted love. Well-known passages support this view: "I came not to call the righteous [who think themselves righteous], but sinners to repentance" (Mark 2.17); "the Son of man is come to seek and save that which is lost" (Luke 19.10). The radical law and the radical gospel—both are summed up in that Jesus came to put into effect the sovereignty of *agapē*, and this is identical with the sovereignty of God, the kingdom of God. He came to reveal "the mystery of the kingdom of God" and to make men "the children of the kingdom".

It is here that we find the deepest contrast between Jesus, on the one side, and the scribes and Pharisees, on the other. This was over the Pharisees' safeguarding of the tradition they had inherited and especially of the law of God—a safeguarding that they took very seriously—and the way in which they carried this out. They regarded the way in which Jesus acted as infringing the majesty of the law and of God. It is not difficult to understand their attitude to him. When he acted in the power of God's sovereign *agapē*, this involved a radical upheaval for them. Admittedly the covenant that God had established with the people of Israel had never been represented as being based on any special qualifications that made this people meritorious—it had always been based on God's unwarranted goodness. But the covenant as such rested on the foundation of the law, and, however much was said later in the Psalms and other Old Testament writings about the love of God, his forgiveness and his grace, it was always presumed explicitly or implicitly that this attitude of his depended on man's fulfilling the law, fearing God, and, when necessary, returning in penitence and confession of sin from the path of transgression to the path of obedience to the law. In view of this established and, it could only be thought, reasonable arrangement, the radical gospel of Jesus appeared not only unreasonable, but also a direct infringement of God's majesty. Fellowship with God, forgiveness, having a part in "the kingdom" were no longer based on obedience to the law, nor on any human qualifications or merits. They were based only on God's unwarranted *agapē*.

Here we are facing what is unquestionably the heart of the gospel which Jesus preaches and puts into effect. From all that the Gospels say about this, let us look at the passage in Matthew's Gospel where Jesus says that no one knows the Son except the Father and that "neither knoweth any man the Father, save the Son, and he to whomsoever the Son will reveal him". This exclusive saying finishes up with another of universal application. "Come unto me, all ye that labour and are heavy laden, and I will give you rest." Somewhere in the background lies the fundamental opposition between Jesus and the scribes; he praises his heavenly Father that he has "hid these things from the wise and prudent and has revealed them unto babes". The Father whom the Son makes known is he who in and through the Son deals with people in undeserved *agapē*. The passage finishes with the words: "Take my yoke upon you and learn of me . . . for my yoke is easy, and my burden is light" (Matt. 11.25-30). What Jesus says here—as is fully shown by other things he said—does not give any assurance that life will be "easy" in the sense of having no difficulties and trials. But the words are clearly in contrast to what Jesus had said about how the Pharisees "bind heavy burdens and grievous to be borne, and lay them on men's shoulders". The contrast is a contrast between moralism and the radical gospel.

If the radical gospel is the very centre and focus of the preaching and actions of Jesus, it must be a matter of prime importance to preserve it intact. It is therefore important that we do not impose any qualifying conditions that would prevent the gospel from having its full effect or break into its radical inclusiveness. It is not for us to change the free gospel of God's undeserved love into a conditional gospel. No one can claim that the Christian Church has always safeguarded it in this way. On the contrary, the history of Christianity shows in how many ways people have tried to surround the gospel with what they thought to be provisions that would ensure its security. There is no reason for picking on any particular Church in this connection, as being more guilty than others. Rather every Church should examine its own conscience on this. It is not only the Pharisees who have been shocked at Jesus' way of keeping company with and "receiving sinners". The risk of shock is never far from us. It is natural for us always to look for a rational explanation of what seems, and must always seem, irrational, to try to rationalize the gospel and to find some way of explaining how God's *agapē* can be accounted for.

We are not going here to catalogue and register all the various ways men have tried through the ages when they have de-radicalized and rationalized the gospel. We shall limit ourselves to three types of this. The first type is when people try to determine the degree of "faith" that must be professed for a person to be accepted. This means that "faith" is intellectualized and the acceptance of a certain form of profession, such as the use of a particular dogmatic formula about the person of Christ, is made the condition for being acceptable. There is no parallel to this in any of the Gospels. Jesus never required any profession of faith of this kind from anyone who sought his help. The "faith" that was meant was the actual seeking of help as such—whether this faith was "great" as in the case of the Roman centurion (Matt. 8.10) or

doubting and hesitant as in the case of the man who came to Jesus
with his sick son: "I believe: help thou mine unbelief" (Mark
9.24).

The other type that we have in mind is the one that makes
confession of sin the qualification that makes possible and explains
forgiveness. God can forgive *because* man has qualified himself by
sorrow for sin, penitence, and confession. By this the sinner has
become acceptable. Penitence and confession can be fitted into a
definite schedule, into a fixed economy of grace, where one stage
follows another, each being a prerequisite and condition for the
next. But this kind of schedule and qualifications is wholly alien
to all that the Gospels tell us. We read there of spontaneous confession—as when Peter at his meeting with Jesus says: "Depart
from me; for I am a sinful man, O Lord" (Luke 5.8), or the publican's cry for mercy in the Temple. But there are plenty of instances
of how Jesus receives and accepts people into his fellowship without any confession of this kind. One of the disciples whom he calls,
Nathanael, is given this good character: "Behold an Israelite
indeed, in whom is no guile." There are even instances of Jesus
giving forgiveness of sins without anything being said about sins
having been confessed—in the story of the lame man who was
cured on the sabbath day, to the indignation of the Pharisees. The
point of what the Gospels tell us about Jesus and forgiveness is
that it is not given to those who have made themselves acceptable,
but to the sinful person in spite of his sin, the person who is not
acceptable.

A third type rationalized the radical gospel like this. It is of
course true, they say, that *agapē* goes out to meet and deal with
unworthy people. The way love works does not have to be justified
by what people are like or how they have acted, but rather by the
idea of what they could become and what they could do, by the
change that will come to them and their actions, the service they
can render. But explanations of this kind are once again quite alien
to, and indeed contrary to, the outgoing love and its spontaneity,
which is the mark of the way Jesus acts in the Gospels.

It is easy to misunderstand this idea of love and its relation to
man. In all three types most important things are at stake. Confession of faith, confession of sin, sanctification, and "shewing
one's faith by one's deeds" are all things of great importance in our
relationship to God. Nothing is more apparent than that in his

dealings with men Jesus both makes very definite demands on them, and has a clear purpose; he knows that he is come to effect the sovereignty of *agapē*. The same idea is present in the Bible words that he is come "to save", words that unfortunately nowadays have become so worn and emptied of meaning that they have lost much of the scope and quality they have in the Bible.

As a result it might appear that this examination and analysis of these types of rationalization are little more than splitting hairs, and of no real importance. But this would be a grave misunderstanding. We have, I imagine, only to put these types of rationalization into question form for it to become crystal clear how important it is to preserve the radical gospel intact. These questions would be: How much do I have to believe to become acceptable? How can I be sure that my confession of sin is full enough and radical enough to pass muster? When have I become changed enough and sanctified enough or rendered enough service to become "a child of the Kingdom"? Questions like this are not unknown. They become inevitable, and impossible to answer, as soon as the radical gospel is rationalized and moralized. This brings out the meaning of this gospel in a flash. The questions reveal how essential it is that the gospel is not based on, not justified by, human qualifications and merits, that the gospel is for the unworthy—though, as we saw on page 139 above, this does not mean that the gospel rules out any human activity. There is no question of this, nor of reducing the significance of confession of faith, confession of sin, sanctification, and a life of service.

The watchword of the radical gospel is: "Come as you are". The background to this is the actual situation of all human life, all the need and distress that is part of it. In other words, the background is the fact that human life is lived in conditions of sin and suffering and death, in a world where the forces of evil carry on their work, but where the law of creation is ceaselessly in function, attacking all that is destructive, advancing all that is constructive. Both law and gospel are in the service of, and are instruments of, the struggle waged by the love of God against the forces of destruction. In the words of the famous Definition of Chalcedon, they are united "unconfusedly, unchangeably, indivisibly and inseparably". Law and gospel are both expressions of God's relation to the world—even if, so far as the law is concerned, this relationship may be unseen, as it is when people carry out the demands of the law without confessing the name of God. They both serve the divine love, and both are expressions of its radical, militant opposition to all that is evil. This is also true, wholly and unconditionally, of the law and is not nullified when this radical opposition also expresses itself in the form of "wrath" and "punishment".

But law is law and gospel is gospel; they are so "unconfusedly and unchangeably". The radical gospel has a function of its own, a function very different from that of the law. It consists of making relationship to God into fellowship with God. Here law has to relinquish its claims. *Fellowship* with God does not rest on the basis of the law, but on God's undeserved love. However, this does not imply any indifference in relation to anti-God evil. On the contrary: no demands of the law reveal this as radically and decisively as the radical gospel.

A distorted image of the relation between law and gospel arises if—as has often happened—the Jesus of the Gospels is contrasted with the image of God. There has been a tendency to represent Jesus as the bearer of love, while God is represented as holy, strict, wrathful, punishing, condemning. But it is on principle impossible to make a division of this kind if it is true that Jesus in word and deed has "made God known". Besides, this is a caricature of the Old Testament image of God. Admittedly it is true that all these features are emphasized when describing God's reactions to the disobedience and unfaithfulness of the chosen people. But God's love, on which the election was based, is never questioned, still less eliminated. The Old Testament abounds in stories of God's grace and mercy, that grace of which Psalm 103 (RSV) says: "as the heavens are high above the earth, so great is his steadfast love toward those who fear him: as far as the east is from the west, so far does he remove our transgressions from us."

In addition, the image of Jesus that is contrasted with the image of God is a caricature, sentimentalized and made effeminate. It is a very different image from the one we find in the Gospels, where Jesus is anything but the "sweet" Jesus people sometimes try to turn him into. In the Gospels there is no lack of incisiveness in his behaviour. He speaks in anger and sternly, he unmasks, rebukes, warns, and condemns in words of biting severity. The gospel is full of statements of this kind. *His* salt had certainly not lost its savour. All this is inseparably linked with the radical gospel he preaches and puts into effect. It is, with all its tensions, the other side of the coin of *agapē*.

The God of the Old Testament is the God of Jesus. He proclaims no other God. Yet the Old Testament image of God has to be adjusted to the image of God seen in the life and work of Jesus. He stands closer to God than anyone before him. Therefore he "knows" more about him, and therefore, in the words of St John's Gospel he "has made him known" by word and deed. This is what is happening when with authority he reveals the law in all its radical strength and when in action he puts into effect the radical gospel. The same thing may be expressed by saying that, through the one he sent, God has gone into hand-to-hand battle with the anti-God powers of destruction. We shall return to this when we come to the climax of the Christ drama.

The Symbol of the Cross

In a Good Friday article in a Swedish church newspaper in 1964, the author wrote that there is too much "preaching of a spiritualized, sublime and elegant cross of which we have no need" of the kind that "we can see over many an altar". Our motive for these may be that we want "to spare the congregation" but perhaps "we ought to consider making a change the next time the church is restored". For "the congregation has a right to have the truth and nothing but the truth before their eyes". No objection can be made to this last statement, but the rest of it raises some deep problems. We need not discuss the doubtful wisdom of removing old works of art from our churches—what we are discussing is something very different. The author seems to think that in the interests of truth the Crucified must always be portrayed with brutal realism. This may agree well enough with some modern theological currents, based, as the article shows, in much of the deep and bitter sufferings of the present generation, for whom it has become the theme they wish to stress that "in the very depths of suffering, God is to be found".

Now undoubtedly the cross in all its brutality reflects the deepest human suffering, and undoubtedly Christian faith finds God at the very depths of that suffering. Yet at the same time, when we consider representations of the crucifixion, we have to remember that until the thirteenth century the Crucified was represented not only as a martyr, but as one who in his martyrdom had won the victory. In the later Middle Ages a change set in. People now enjoyed depicting suffering in all its cruelty and horror. Theologically the change was connected with the shift in the doctrine of atonement and with the passion mysticism that became such a feature of late medieval religion. The emphasis was placed on following Christ along the stages of his path of suffering, on sharing with Christ his pain and suffering. So the question really is: Which of these two lines of thought is best suited to bring home the Christian truth which a congregation has a right to have set before its eyes?

All four Gospels lead up to the story of the passion of Jesus, his crucifixion and resurrection. The other books of the New Testament in their interpretation of the Christ drama focus on the cross and the resurrection. We shall return to this, but first we should note that in the New Testament the cross and the resurrection always go together. They belong together, not just that one is added to the other on some sort of *a*-plus-*b* formula. They are one inseparable unit. When the New Testament Epistles speak of the cross and its significance, they include the resurrection; when they speak of the resurrection and its significance, they include the cross. One is nothing without the other.

If Paul says that, when he came to the Corinthians, he "determined not to know anything, save Jesus Christ and him crucified" (1 Cor. 2.2), this would have had no meaning for him at all unless the Crucified had also been the Risen Christ. When further on in the same Epistle he says: "if Christ be not risen, your faith is vain" (1 Cor. 15.14), this is not isolating the resurrection—the words are being used about the Crucified. When the celebration of the Last Supper is described: "as often as ye eat this bread and drink this cup, ye do shew the Lord's death, till he come" (1 Cor. 11.26), this does not mean that the Communion is to be celebrated as a requiem for the dead. Even the final words show that what was said was said with reference to the Risen Christ. In the Acts of the Apostles we read several times that the task of the apostles is to bear witness to the resurrection. In Acts 1.22, a new apostle is appointed "to be a witness with us of his resurrection"; "with great power gave the apostles witness of the resurrection of the Lord Jesus" (Acts 4.33; cf. 17.18). To be quite exact, the witness was to the Risen Christ, rather than to the resurrection, of which there were no witnesses. It is in character that Paul can just as well speak of the power of the cross of Christ, of the cross of Christ as "the power of God" (1 Cor. 1.17–18), as of knowing Christ "and the power of his resurrection" (Phil. 3.10). All this shows that the New Testament regards the cross and the resurrection as an inseparable unit with a single task. When we read in Romans 4.25 that Christ "was delivered for our offences and was raised again for our justification", this does not mean that his suffering and death had one purpose and his resurrection a quite different purpose; there is one single purpose in the whole. To bring this review to a conclusion with a text from St John that has two meanings, emphasizing the oneness of the death and the resurrection: "I, if I be lifted up from the earth, will draw all men unto me" (John 12.32). This clearly refers to something in the future, yet at the same time the cross is regarded as in itself a lifting up, a "being glorified", a victory.

All that the New Testament says about Christ shows that the cross and the resurrection are viewed together. This is of fundamental importance for the New Testament interpretation of the work of Christ, and of its view of the relation of God to the Christ drama and of the image of God as a whole. But whereas the New Testament saw these as one, this has not always been the case in later theology, and this has had profound effects, expressed in different ways. Actually the whole history of theology might be written from the point of view of the problems involved in the cross and the resurrection. Here is a perspective that could be most fruitful and be very informative. This could be illustrated by some indication of different positions affecting the problem and they would also show how wide is the scope of the problems involved.

It is the dramatic aspect that constitutes the New Testament view; the unit of the cross and resurrection is seen to be the climax of the drama. This means that God's relation to the world is also seen from the same angle of drama. In that drama which here reaches its highest tension and at the same time its solution, Christ goes the sacrificial path of obedience to death. His obedience to God is at the same time an action performed in solidarity with mankind. This self-sacrificing action can be described in the New Testament as substitutionary, a ransom, an atonement. But from whatever aspect it is seen, it is established that it not only led on to victory, but, in the light of Easter, *was* a victory—a victory that was Christ's *own* victory and at the same time God's victory over the anti-God powers. His victory in the completion of his task here on earth gave him a position of power, thanks to which his life's work could be continued and completed in new forms. Easter and Whitsun mark the transition to this continuation which the New Testament describes both as a work of the "exalted" Lord, the Kyrios, and as a work of the Spirit who is both the Spirit of Christ and God's own Spirit.

This perspective of drama with the cross and the exaltation viewed together was retained for the most part in the early Church and is still preserved in Orthodox Christianity. But it was not so in medieval scholasticism. Here the New Testament balance was gradually lost, and the whole emphasis was laid on suffering and the cross, while the resurrection was squeezed out. It was still found in the Creed of course. But in scholasticism it no longer plays a real part. Everything now depends on the "satisfaction" that Christ brings to God through his sacrifice. It is this that gives the scholastic doctrine of atonement its characteristic *structure*. God's demand for compensation has been met, his wrath has been averted, he has been propitiated by the compensation for man's sin contained in the satisfaction. We see here how separating the view of the cross from the view of the resurrection has at once altered the image of God. The whole theme becomes quite different from the New Testament theme that finds its classical expression in the words of Paul: "God was in Christ, reconciling the world unto himself" (2 Cor. 5.19). The scholastic type of doctrine of atonement has been a most influential factor in the history of Christianity. Even Luther could use the traditional scholastic language. But at the same time the primitive Christian perspective of the early Church comes out in him. And with a genius of his calibre it is right to pay more attention to the new lines in the spirit of the Bible than to the old ones taken on from the current tradition. But in orthodox post-Reformation theology the atonement doctrines of medieval scholasticism recovered their predominance, albeit in modified form.

We mentioned earlier medieval passion mysticism. In its powerful emphasis on the suffering Christ, the stress is laid on his suffering unto death upon the cross. Like the scholastic doctrine

of atonement, passion mysticism allowed paintings and representations of the Crucified to be centred on his martyrdom, to present
the cruel nature of his sufferings with the greatest possible realism.
But passion mysticism represents a type different from that of
scholasticism. Scholasticism has undoubtedly a certain intellectual
coolness. So far as man is concerned, it involves assenting to the
transaction between God and Christ. Passion mysticism deals
in more "personal" categories. For man it is first of all a sharing of
life with the suffering Christ. But this relation to him is given
the character of an emotional sharing in the sufferings of Christ
in his pain. This brings in a very different perspective from what
we find in the New Testament writings. Admittedly we often
read there of suffering with Christ, of sharing in his suffering.
But there is never any question of suffering that people seek
voluntarily and aspire to, nor of any emotional sharing in suffering,
but of the kind of suffering that can befall man when he is serving
Christ. Above all, when the New Testament speaks of sharing in
Christ's sufferings, it speaks at the same time of sharing in "the
power of his resurrection" and in his "glory": "That I may know
him, and the power of his resurrection, and the fellowship of his
sufferings" (Phil. 3.10); "as the sufferings of Christ abound in us,
so our consolation also aboundeth by Christ" (2 Cor. 1.5).

The Reformation is a reaction against passion mysticism. We
can read of the nature of this reaction in some sober words,
leading in a very different direction, taken from a Good Friday
sermon by Olavus Petri. The remembrance of "the hard death
and pain" of Jesus Christ has often been celebrated "with sorrow-
ful gestures and ceremonies, which, as people commonly opine,
are held to the end that we shall be sorrowing and weeping with
Christ who this day hath suffered pain and death, and that we shall
bewail him that hath been treated so atrociously upon this day".
According to Olavus Petri, sorrow should be differently directed:
"We should indeed sorrow, not therefore that he hath suffered
such pains, but therefore that we have brought it about that he
must suffer." Olavus, we might say, expounds the words of Jesus
on the road to Calvary: "Weep not for me, but weep for yourselves"
(Luke 23.28). The Reformation reaction did not prevent influences
from medieval passion mysticism making themselves felt in various
ways and in various forms in post-Reformation theology and
devotion, not least in some pietist currents. We have one example

in the hymn that was used as a gradual at mass on Good Friday, no. 92 in the Swedish hymnal. After the first verse bidding "tears to flow, laments to sound", there follows a drastic description of the physical suffering Jesus had to undergo, and the first four verses end with the questionable statement: "Through such pains did Jesus go. No one ever suffered so."

We have considered two concepts where the Bible way of viewing the cross and the resurrection together has been discarded and replaced by a theology of the cross in isolation. At the beginning of modern times we find in the Enlightenment theology a view for which the element which in the Bible is the climax of the drama now has no part to play. This view is undoubtedly developed as a reaction to the orthodox view with its doctrine of atonement in terms of a judicial settlement between God and Christ. In contrast to this the fatherly love of God is proclaimed—a fatherly love in which there are no problems and no drama, basically self-evident. The whole emphasis is placed on the teaching given by Jesus as teacher or rabbi about God as "Father". This teaching is thought of as being in complete agreement with what can be reached along the path of reason. In these circumstances there is no place for cross or resurrection. The cross only comes into the picture from a more or less Stoic aspect.

There is an echo of this kind of Stoicism, typically mixed with some sentimentality when Wallin writes in one of the Passiontide hymns: "Yet moved with pity for our woes, you hardly felt your pains."[1] The rest of the hymn is in a different strain. The fact that the resurrection plays such an unimportant part in the theology of Enlightenment is due to the idea that the immortality of the soul is taken as self-evident. This type of theology, like the orthodox doctrine of atonement, had powerful after-effects during the nineteenth century, both in the popular interpretation of Christianity and in the theological. Adolf Harnack's book *What is Christianity?* (1900), much discussed in its day, may be regarded as a document which—if in modified form—gives an elegant review in popular form of the basic view that sprang from Enlightenment theology.

If I describe Harnack's book as a document that closed a chapter, this is because since then the optimistic atmosphere has vanished, the optimism that formed the background of the idea of the un-

[1] Swedish hymn no. 86, verse 2.

problematic and self-evident nature of God's fatherly love. The change in climate, linked with the great world wars and their consequences, makes itself felt at many points of twentieth-century theology. Two Swedish theologians illustrate this point. One is Nathan Söderblom, a most sensitive barometer of changes in spiritual atmosphere. Just after the end of the First World War he published two small documents. In one of them, *The way of the people of Christ in this age—new old-fashioned preaching*, we find the idea that "God has a share in our suffering". Söderblom seems to shrink back from this idea, yet it seems inevitable:

For me, this kind of groping and unsteadying idea of God himself actually suffering and battling in world developments comes close to the strange and tragic circumstances of life in our world; and the real nature of Christianity is not a homily fitting God and world events into a patent harmony where everything goes well from start to finish.

In the second document, *Are we moving towards a renewal of religion?*, the cross is presented as "the climax of revelation":

The only religion that is worth the name is a new irresistible preaching of the Cross, a fresh convincing experience of the mystery of salvation, revealed in the Saviour's sacrifice of himself in life and death. I am not pleading for any impious doctrine about some change in the nature of God nor for any pagan theory of sacrifice. But for what has been the very heart of Christianity, ever since the time of Paul an offence to godly and ungodly rationalists.

The other Swedish theologian of whom I think is Einar Billing with his book *Reconciliation* (1908), a work of deep-going theology which, had it been published in any of the great world languages would have won international attention. It may well be said that Billing here heralds and represents the new orientation so eloquently expressed by Söderblom. Billing's perspective has a strong note of drama. It focuses on the drama of the history of the election, the centre point of which is the life of Jesus, his death and resurrection. What is particularly noticeable in relation to contemporary theology is the strong emphasis on the resurrection and the work of Christ that continues from that starting-point.

There is no question of charting all the various contemporary theological attitudes to, and interpretations of, the Christ drama, which in the New Testament has its climax in his death and resurrection. We shall touch on only two lines of thought: (*a*) the interpretation of theology from an existentialist viewpoint as we find it in Bultmann, and (*b*) the frequent present-day talk of a suffering God. If we choose these two, the reason is that they are both particularly suited for illustrating the problems involved in present-day interpretation of the Christ drama.

(*a*) To the presentation already given of Bultmann's demythologizing interpretation of salvation in the light of the cross and resurrection, we shall now add some reflections on the relation to the Christ drama of this existentialist doctrine of salvation. It is not an easy question to deal with, and interpretations of Bultmann's theology are often accused of having been guilty of misunderstanding it. If we regard Bultmann's relation to the Christ drama from a wide historical perspective, it might well appear that he belongs to the theological stream that one-sidedly emphasizes the cross. Admittedly he speaks of the resurrection, but it is no longer the resurrection of Christ that he means. To some extent one might say that there is a kind of kinship between Bultmann's theology of the cross and a theology of the passion mysticism type—in any case the stress on *imitatio Christi* is common to both. Yet naturally there is a great difference between them. There is nothing of the traditional theology of the cross. We might formulate it tentatively by saying: *If* there is anything in the Christ drama that is significant for Bultmann's theology of salvation, it is the cross. Of this significance he himself can write:

The historical (*historisch*) event of the cross has, in the significance peculiar to it, created a new historic (*geschichtlich*) situation. The preaching of the cross as the event of redemption (*Ereignis*) challenges all who hear it to appropriate this significance for themselves, to be willing to be crucified with Christ.[1]

The significance that the cross has as a fact of history is that it serves as an example to follow, as an inspiration calculated to call forth the decision which implies transition from unauthentic to authentic existence.

The resurrection too has to be understood existentially if its real meaning is to be revealed. But whereas referring to the cross was referring to an historical fact, this is not true of the resurrection. The resurrection of which Bultmann is speaking he describes

---

[1] *Kerygma and Myth*, ed. H. W. Bartsch (1964), p. 37.

as "an eschatological fact" which takes place in the lives of men. The significance of the resurrection is symbolized by baptism—Bultmann is able here to refer to Romans 6, which speaks of baptism as death and resurrection. The resurrection is the transition to the new, authentic life, which must then express itself in a battle for liberation and cleansing from sin. In other words, resurrection is the resurrection of a fighting faith—this is the existential significance of the message of Easter, which basically is identical with that of the cross. Bultmann's interpretation of the Christ drama is, as we see, markedly directed to the individual—all the time it is a matter of what happens to the individual person. The significance of the crucifixion of Christ is that it illustrates the decision, the "death" which means the transition to an authentic, existential life, and the resurrection illustrates—with a different set of words—the same transition and its consequences. Relationship to Christ or rather to what is proclaimed about him in the Christian Church bears throughout the character of imitation of him. However, when Bultmann wants to speak of God's forgiveness in connection with the cross of Christ, this has no significance except that the *impulse* to make the decision does not come from within man but—via proclamation of the kerygma—from the historical example that is to be followed. To this extent there is just a touch of the gospel in the picture.

(*b*) If we now take up the theme of "the suffering God", the purpose of this is to establish which problems are brought into focus by this theme which appears so often at the present time. Recently we mentioned Söderblom's speaking of God's suffering. He shrank from the thought but found it impossible to escape from it. But let us note that the formula he used was "God, suffering and fighting". The word "fighting" is not unimportant—it gives special colour to what he had to say. It would not be difficult to find many statements on this theme in the theology of this century. Here I shall quote only three. First, one from William Temple, who later became Archbishop of Canterbury. As early as 1910 Temple writes:

When Reason says, "It is God who made all the world; He is therefore responsible; it is He who should suffer", we answer, "Yes, of course; He does suffer; look at the Cross." And when Reason cries, "If God were the loving Father of whom you speak, He could not endure the misery of his children; His heart would break", we answer, "Yes, of course; it does break; look at the Cross."[1]

Secondly, in meditations on *The Suffering God* (1921), Erling Eidem, who later became Archbishop in Sweden, writes: "Jesus' suffering to death on Calvary is the culmination of God's own suffering and thus the source of all forgiveness of sin." The third quotation is from Bonhoeffer's *Letters and Papers from Prison*, where he says: to participate in the life of Jesus is to suffer with him, to watch with him in Gethsemane. What distinguishes Christians from the heathen is that Christians range themselves with God "in his suffering" and "participate in the sufferings of God at the hands of a godless world".[2]

It is by no means the first time in the history of Christianity that we find ideas of this kind. At any rate, the idea of God "taking part in" human suffering is not foreign to Christian faith or to Old Testament faith. So far, so good. But it is quite a different matter to couple Christ's suffering and death on the cross with God's own suffering, and to do so as convincedly as is done here. Is there Christian justification for this image of God? Yes, unquestionably this line of thought has something important to say about God's relationship to the Christ drama. It claims that God has not only "sent his Son" into the world, and then has stood back, as it were, to watch what happens. On the contrary, he is actively involved in what is going on, he acts in it, not least at the deepest point of suffering, in the martyrdom of Christ. In other words, the cross reveals the love of God as *a suffering love*. This kind of interpretation is entirely in agreement with, and is indeed included in, Paul's statement: "God was in Christ, reconciling the world unto himself." But the significance of these words is not exhausted by the mere idea of how God suffers in the martyrdom of Christ. To stop short at this point, at the martyrdom of Crucified Love, would not lead to any reconciliation. It would mean that the last word would go to tragedy, to the meaninglessness of life. So it is not surprising if the idea of God suffering is regarded as a dangerous idea. It is still more dangerous if it is isolated. It was not without good reason that, when Söderblom spoke of God

[1] William Temple, *The Faith and Modern Thought*, p. 168.
[2] From the Swedish translation of *Widerstand und Ergebung* (E.T. *Letters and Papers from Prison* (1967)).

as suffering, he coupled with it the word "fighting". That makes it clear that it was not only a passive, enduring suffering, but an active, purposeful suffering. Suffering is part of, is a form of, the battle of God's love against all that is anti-God and destructive.

But in Christian perspective, this battle of suffering is not without its results. The cross is victory. God's suffering love is a victorious love. Whether it is possible to go all the way with Erik Gustaf Geijer in his poem:

> Nothing is left unwon,
> By Love that suffers.

is not for us to say. But even if the question remains unanswered, there is no doubt that for Christian faith the suffering of God's love is not just impotent but is victorious. There is no doubt about that in the authors we have quoted.

On this point it is interesting to read Bonhoeffer who paints in such strong colours the powerlessness of God reflected in the suffering and crucifixion of his love. It is in this powerlessness that the hidden power is revealed. The God of the Bible is "the God who conquers power and space in the world by his weakness". "God allows himself to be edged out of the world and up on to the cross, God is powerless and weak in the world, and only in this way is he with us, to help us." This, of course, does not mean that in himself God is powerless—the suffering of self-giving love is a self-assumed weakness. Bonhoeffer's criticism is directed, he says, against a "metaphysical" and an "individualistic" interpretation of the Bible message: "Neither of these is relevant to the Bible message or to the man of today." The point of these remarks is directed against an abstract metaphysical view of God's omnipotence. To think in this way, deriving all that happens from God's omnipotence and attributing to that its cause, can only give a wrong image of the real nature of God's power.

This is enough to make it clear that it is not Bonhoeffer's intention to consider Christ as powerless. For him Christ is Kyrios, the Lord who has the right to make, and indeed actually makes, demands on what Bonhoeffer calls "the world come of age". This means that the cross and the resurrection are inseparably linked with one another. To have a share in the suffering of Christ is at the same time to have a share in his resurrection. But this sharing is in no sense an escape from the deep "this-worldliness" of Christianity. On the contrary: the this-worldliness for which Bonhoeffer pleads is "the deep earthiness, which is full of discipline and is lived face to face with death and resurrection". The The art of dying, *ars moriendi*, man can possibly learn. "But to overcome death is resurrection. It is not from *ars moriendi* but only from the resurrection of Christ that a new cleansing wind can blow into this world." "Christ, our Hope—this is the formula which is the power in our lives."

I have referred to these words of Bonhoeffer about the resurrection, not only because his image of "the God who suffers" would be distorted if they were omitted, but also because they lead on to a theme which, in the present situation must necessarily be dealt with—the whole problem of the resurrection. We have already seen how Bultmann laboured with this theme and how his solution was that "the Resurrection" was to be regarded not as an historical fact but as an "eschatological" fact in the life of the individual human being, involving his transition to an authentic life with all the consequences this implies. In Bonhoeffer the problem is vital. But the *Letters from Prison* do not go beyond seeking a new theological treatment of the problems of the resurrection. This is interesting because of the criticism made by Bonhoeffer in two directions. On the one hand, he is against a "positivist doctrine of revelation" of which—rightly or wrongly—he makes Barth the representative. This basically denies that any problem exists. There is a given doctrine which "has to be swallowed as a whole or not at all". On the other hand, he is against Bultmann, who is admittedly given credit for not avoiding the problem, but at the same time is criticized for the "reduction process" by which the "mythological" elements of Christianity are dropped and Christianity is reduced to its "essence".

I am of the view [he says] that the full content, including the mythological contents, must be maintained. The New Testament is not a mythological garbing of the universal truth; this mythology (the Resurrection and so on) is the thing itself.

So it is this "thing itself" that the theology he asks for would need to elucidate.

We have seen, then, that in the New Testament cross and

resurrection form one indivisible whole. It now remains to analyse
their meaning.

The first thing that needs to be said—and it is obvious—is
that what happened to the disciples at Easter involved a radical
change. We could express this in the words of one of our Easter
hymns

... to men of the earth
with heavenly hope, faith is given new birth.

The cross and the suffering had proved a catastrophe for the faith
of the disciples. The situation is realistically described by the two
disciples on the road to Emmaus: "We trusted that it had been
he which should have redeemed Israel" (Luke 24.21)—we trusted,
but we trust no longer. The treachery of Judas and Peter's denial
tell the story of how their faith and hope vanished. Through what
happened at Easter, the disciples, whose faith had been shattered
by the catastrophe, were turned into apostles with the confidence
and courage to bear witness to the resurrection; for them, the
catastrophe of the cross had been turned into victory. The reason
for this change is everywhere said to be their meeting with their
Risen Master. Similarly the basis of their apostolic mission is
everywhere said to be that this Risen Master himself sent them
out to preach. The constant theme in the stories of the resurrection
is: Go and say, "As the Father hath sent me, even so send I you"—
a call that culminates in the words in St Matthew's Gospel:
"Go therefore and make disciples of all nations".

One thing is clearly established: without what happened at
Easter, there would never have been any proclaiming of Jesus as
the Christ. The apostles would not have had anything to preach.
It would not have been reasonable to expect them to go out and
tell men how their hopes had been dashed by the catastrophe of the
crucifixion. We may well ask if we should ever have heard of Jesus
of Nazareth. If we had, it would only have been a note about
someone claiming to be a messiah, put to death like so many others,
in this case during the Roman occupation of Palestine. No Gospels
would have been written, no *ecclesia* would have come into being.

We have been using the formula "the thing that happened at
Easter". What was it that happened? The answer given by the
New Testament is: the resurrection of Christ—God has "raised"

him from the dead. The apostles are called "witnesses of the resurrection". This expression does not mean that the apostles, or the women mentioned in the story, witnessed the actual resurrection. No one saw that. No one witnessed that. But the apostles and the women mentioned in the story are presented as witnesses of the Risen Jesus.

How did the "witnesses of the resurrection" regard the relationship between the Risen Christ and the master with whom they had walked? Undoubtedly to them the Risen Christ was none other than he who had been crucified. But, at the same time, they do not seem to have imagined that the dead body of Jesus had been given new life—even if there are things in the story that point in that direction. There are unquestionably some details in the accounts of the resurrection which indicate that the tradition grew and was to some extent altered during the period between Easter and the final editing of the text of the Gospels some half a century later. At the same time, in the accounts of the resurrection there are some elements that indicate that they did not look at things in the way we have described—particularly in the repeated statements that they did not at first recognize him. Mary of Magdala did not, nor did the two on the road to Emmaus, nor those who were fishing on the Sea of Gennesareth. The Risen One had to give some help to those who saw him, for them to recognize him—by words or actions that reminded them of what had happened during his earthly life, demonstrating the continuity with the past.

The Jesus of whom we read in the accounts of the resurrection is transformed, changed. This is in full agreement with the oldest account of the resurrection in the New Testament as a changing of the "vile body" into a "glorious body" (Phil. 3.21; cf. 1 Cor. 15). What is essential for the primitive Christian belief in the resurrection of Christ, the thing that makes it unique, is *not* that a body which had been dead has been brought to life again—the Gospels tell of that kind of thing happening on several occasions, not only when they describe how Jesus raised dead people but also elsewhere (compare the mythological account in Matthew 27.52 of what happened at the crucifixion: "the graves were opened: and many bodies of the saints which slept arose", etc.). Instead, what for primitive Christian faith was unique in the mystery of the resurrection of Christ was that an act of God had taken place that was creative, revolutionary, transforming. Through this Christ had appeared, in the words of Paul, as "the firstborn from the dead" (Col. 1.18).

It would actually be in complete agreement with the first disciples' and with Paul's view of what happened to describe this with the term Bultmann used: an eschatological fact. But this would give the expression an entirely different sense from that in which he uses it. It is now no longer *only* a question of change on the purely subjective level, a change which unquestionably takes place in the disciples, but primarily of what happened to Christ, the thing that the New Testament writings express as: God has raised him. Before we consider what resurrection as an eschatological fact means for Christian faith, something needs to be said about the attitude of historical research to the resurrection narratives.

First, scientific research—exegetics as an historical science— is unable to study the historicity of the resurrection. It can only establish the fact that the early Christians believed in the resurrection, with the result that the Christian Church came into being and spread explosively in the ancient world. There are no incontestable proofs that the resurrection was an historical fact. Not even the accounts of the empty grave can be regarded as proof. These accounts are certainly a regular element of the earliest Christian tradition. But this is not incontestable proof—other explanations of that might be possible. Actually the early Church did not base its belief in the resurrection on the empty tomb, however important that might be. It was well realized that the empty tomb— as the evangelists tell us—could face attempts to explain it away, "painfully concrete explanations" as Gustaf Wingren puts it. Neither for the first disciples nor for Paul was the early belief in the resurrection a belief that the tomb was empty, nor merely a belief that a dead man had become alive again. There was no contradiction of either point, but neither expresses what was the essence of the early faith. For that lay not in the naked idea that a dead person had become living, but in the conviction that Christ as the Living One had taken up again and was continuing his unique life's work. The emphasis lies on what he is doing, what he is giving; on the fact that he acts as the Risen Lord endowed with power; on the task of mission that he commits to the disciples, to Peter after his restoration through forgiveness; on his promise to be with his own alway, even unto the end of the world; on the Spirit that he imparts to them. And it makes very little difference whether that imparting took place, as St John's Gospel says, at Easter, or, as we find in the Acts of the Apostles, at the Pentecost which followed.

The resurrection, as we see, is not regarded as one isolated happening, nor as one object of belief along with others. Instead, the resurrection, as we find it, expresses its meaning by linking what happened in the earthly life of Jesus with what is happening now and what will happen in the future through the continuing activity of Christ. When the New Testament speaks of this continuing activity, it paints pictures of how Christ acts as the One Exalted by God—resurrection and exaltation are inseparably linked in the New Testament. God has "highly exalted him, and given him a name which is above every name" (Phil. 2.9). God "raised him from the dead, and set him at his own right hand in the heavenly places, far above all principality, and power, and might, and dominion, and every name that is named, not only in this world, but also in that which is to come" (Eph. 1.20–1). We read of how Christ went up to heaven, in Luke 24 and Acts 1. The Epistle to the Hebrews describes him as the heavenly High Priest: "We have such an high priest, who is set on the right hand of the throne of the majesty in the heavens" (8.1.) We have already seen something of this image language in the chapter on symbols, the language of faith.

It would be a grievous misunderstanding to take these expressions literally as meaning that Christ was sitting at some definite spot in heaven. There can be no doubt about what is meant by the symbol expressions such as "ascension", "sitting at God's right hand". It is not meant to localize Christ and fix him at some definite place. On the contrary, it is to do away with all fixation of time and place. During the days of his earthly life he did his work within a limited area and during a very limited period of time. But the work he does as the Exalted One, he does freed from all the limitations of time and space. There are no limits of time; the promise of his presence is every day to the end of time. There are no limits of place. This is expressed, in accordance with the three-decker view of those days, in the Letter to the Philippians as "at the name of Jesus every knee should bow, of things in heaven, and things in earth, and things under the earth".

Martin Luther commented on the Bible's image of exaltation to God's right hand with the explanation: "God's right hand is everywhere."

If exaltation lifts Christ above all the limitations of time and space, his enthronement in the heavenly world implies dominion and rule of a universal nature. Christ, we read, has been set above everything that can be named, not only in this world, but also in that which is to come. It would be hard to express universality more powerfully. The Epistle to the Ephesians clinches its point with a quotation from the Old Testament: "He [God] hath put all things under his [Christ's] feet." No area is exempted from the dominion of Christ. The whole world is included in it. But it is primarily in the Church that Christ exerts his power. It is characteristic that immediately after the powerful words about the unlimited power of Christ, the Epistle to the Ephesians goes on to mention the Church: "He [God] gave him [Christ] to be the head over all things to the church, which is his body, the fulness of him that filleth all in all."

"All in all"—this is the phrase which shows how universal Christ's power is. "The new covenant" realized in the Church finally brings to an end the limitation in "the old covenant". "The middle wall of partition" has been broken down—"There is neither Jew nor Greek, . . . ye are all one in Christ Jesus" (Gal. 3.28). *Ecclesia* is what it is, but it is *ecclesia* only because it is here that Christ exercises his power, only through fellowship with Christ. Two things must, however, be noted. First, the exercise of Christ's power is not limited exclusively to the sphere of the Church. Christ exercises his power even outside the boundaries of the Church. Secondly, the boundaries of the Church are not static, but dynamic. The Church acts as an instrument for the outreach of Christ's power. It is given the same commission as was originally given to the apostles.

The image of Christ's dominion and power given in the New Testament writings might be thought to lead to two conclusions: first, that his power was divine, and secondly, that the Christ drama was now completed. The first conclusion may be said to be inevitable. A power which is described as a power "over every name that is named" cannot be anything but God's power. It can only mean that Christ shares in the power of God. But the other conclusion would be utterly wrong. It would mean that the work of

N<small>D</small>

Christ was finished. But actually what is said about Christ's power is exactly the opposite; through the victory which he won on the cross by his "obedience unto death", he has been granted power to continue and complete the work which he was doing during his years on earth—at war with the anti-God forces which he himself had overcome. His victory did not mean that these forces had ceased to exist and to pursue their evil purposes. The position of power which Christ has won by his victory does not mean that his power is at work and is reflected in everything that happens. To interpret it like that would be to repeat the same wrong interpretation that followed with disastrous consequences when God's omnipotence was understood as all-causality. But the victory he won means that he *is* the more powerful, the Stronger One, in the warfare which in the world of time he never ceases to wage against the destructive forces of evil. There are some words in the translation of Luther's hymn, "A safe stronghold our God is still . . .", which can easily be misunderstood. When it says: "He harms us not a whit; For why? his doom is writ", the latter statement is true enough. But it would be quite unrealistic to interpret the first line as meaning that "the prince of ill" has no power to harm us. It would be perfectly right if it were interpreted to mean that in face of Christ he has lost that power, and that the power he possesses is brought to naught where Christ wins power and "reigns" in the world of human life. This is in entire agreement with Paul's remark that Christ "must reign, till he hath put all his enemies under his feet" (1 Cor. 15.25). This opens an eschatological perspective. Paul looks forward to the consummation where the Christ drama is finally completed.

Under the Law of the Spirit

We have been discussing the Christ drama as it is unfolded in the earthly life of Jesus, in his suffering, his death upon the cross, and his exaltation. We might speak of three acts in this drama. We find the first in the picture drawn by the evangelists of the earthly life of Jesus, and we have written of it in this book under the title "The Radical Gospel". The second we find in his suffering and death upon the cross, the third in his exaltation and in the continuation of his work. One of the main points of view in this treatment has been all the way through to emphasize as strongly as possible that all this is one indivisible whole, where one part cannot be separated from the others—this is true not only of the second and third acts, but equally of both in their relation to the first. Our question therefore now becomes: Why this strong emphasis on the different acts of the Christ drama being one indivisible whole? What is the significance of this for faith in Christ, or, in other words, for that faith in God which at the same time is faith in Christ?

We have already touched on this theme, but we now need to go more deeply into it. Exclusive emphasis on the first act of the drama turned out to lead to dedramatization. What is emphasized is the doctrine of God's fatherly love proclaimed by Jesus. So "faith" comes to be regarded as being assent to this doctrine, in an intellectual way. The weakness of this conception is not that God's fatherly love is brought out into the foreground—there would be no grounds for objecting to that—but that sight has been lost of the harsh conditions in which this love has to fight its battle, and consequently also of its radical opposition to evil, to the destructive forces in creation—it is this that gives rise to the dedramatization. The background to this is an idealization of life to which there is nothing to correspond in the real world. It assumes an optimistic view of evolution and existence as a whole. If this system is broken up, the whole concept and its basis in reason loses its firm footing—it becomes like the house which, in the parable of Jesus, was built on the sand, and fell when "the rain descended, and the floods came, and the winds blew, and beat upon that house".

These concepts, in various ways placing the whole emphasis on the second act of the drama, the suffering and the cross, share in common a more realistic view of the nature of the universe. The medieval doctrine of the atonement, the doctrine of satisfaction, in all its variations sees clearly God's radical opposition to, and condemnation of, evil as it expresses itself in human sin and guilt. But when the suffering and death of Christ has been onesidedly regarded as a satisfaction given to God, a recompense for the wrong man has done by his sin, a satisfaction which appeases the demands of God's "righteousness" and thereby makes it possible for God's love to find fulfilment, this whole concept involves a deradicalizing of the radical gospel. The one-sidedness consists in having no clear view of how the love of God functions in the sacrifice which Christ makes in solidarity with both God and men. The secret of reconciliation—that Paul describes in his words about God being in Christ reconciling the world to himself—has been rationalized. This concept too is bogged down in the intellectual system of thought. Faith almost becomes a matter of accepting the doctrine that God forgives man's sin on the basis of having received satisfaction for it.

The concept that is associated with the theme of a suffering God does not have the same firm structure as the two interpretations we have already mentioned. To begin with, it is clear that there are no illusions about the conditions in which we live. Eyes are focused on all the suffering there is, all that comes from sin and guilt, from human wickedness and hardness, from demonic injections and pestilences such as Nazism, racism, etc., bearing in mind that life is lived in a passing, fleeting world, surrounded by accidents, catastrophes, and other unpleasantnesses. The emphasis now falls on God's not being unfamiliar with all this, nor standing aloof from it, but, on the contrary, sharing in the suffering, right to the depths; the cross is the authoritative witness to his sharing in it, proving that his love has trodden the path of suffering to the uttermost. The God whom the cross of Christ reveals is "the God who suffers". Seen from this perspective, the mark of Christian faith is that it is linked with Christ in his suffering, and, secondly, that it expresses this in its relation to others.

In this interpretation the intellectual systematization which weighed heavily on both the earlier concepts has clearly been broken. But there is still a risk that victory over intellectualism can be bought at too high a price. What is said here about God having a share in suffering, about his love being revealed in the sufferings of Christ, about involvement with Christ in his suffering, and the consequences of this for our relationship to our neighbour is all deeply anchored in the gospel—provided that the cross is something more than merely a cross of martyrdom.

The lack of clarity, the ambiguity that attaches to the theme of the God who suffers on the cross is bound up with people's not always having realized under what conditions talk of this kind is meaningful. This applies both to what happened on the cross and to the actual image of God. The cross *is* a cross of martyrdom. It undeniably faces us with a very moving human martyrdom. From this point of view, what happens is but one of many pieces of evidence of how unrighteousness comes out victorious. The condemnation to death is judicial murder. Behind it there is a combination of casual administration of the Roman law of the times, and human brutality steeled by religious fanaticism (though naturally this does not mean that "the Jewish people" may be accused of being guilty of the death of Christ). This is not the only time where a religiosity, hidebound with tradition, has found itself at war with a revolutionary religion—with fatal consequences. From the aspect of martyrdom the Crucified appears as an idealist who, fully conscious of the risk, is faithful to his ideals to the bitter end. His ideals *may* then also be described as due to over-tension, in something of the way in which Pär Lagerkvist does this in his book on the death of Ahasuerus, with the natural result that it produces a sense of sympathy with the tragedy of the situation. But when the suffering of God is mentioned in connection with the cross of Christ, it is assumed that the cross was *not* merely a cross of martyrdom. It is essential that this is made clear and that it is expressly stated.

The image of God also comes into the danger zone here. The risk of the theme of the suffering God is that the image of God becomes imprisoned in past happenings, or, in other words, that one is dealing with a purely immanent image of God. The corrective of this is not to add transcendence to immanence. The Bible image of God does not deal in these categories. It neither speaks of God as an extra-mundane transcendent being nor as one immanent in all that happens in the world. What it does say is that God is engaged in what is going on, actively engaged in it and yet in his action not ceasing to be the Sovereign One who acts in power. It is also stated that this power can reveal itself in sharing in the deepest suffering, the deepest powerlessness. But suffering in itself has no power to "save". Admittedly people have sometimes tried to present it in that light. People have imagined that suffering as such can serve "salvation". But this is to confuse two points of view that need to be kept apart. Human suffering as such can just as well make life bitter as make life better. If anything is gained, this is due not to the fact *that* man suffers, but to *the way in which* he suffers. The gain comes when God is involved in the suffering and "takes charge" of it. The same is true of the suffering of Christ. When Christian faith speaks of its saving power, this depends not on the fact of Christ's suffering, but on the manner of his suffering, that his suffering was a sacrifice of self-giving, and that the power of the love of God was involved in the sacrifice. Just as what is said about the cross becomes meaningful only if the cross is not merely a cross of martyrdom, so the theme of the God who suffers becomes meaningful only if God is not merely a God who suffers. A God who merely suffers would be no God. It is important that this is clearly stated.

For Christian faith, what happened on the cross was not just a tragedy. Admittedly it was a tragedy inasmuch as the depth of human sin and depravity was here manifested. But what links Christian faith to the cross is not that a martyr died there, but the assurance that Christ's death was his victory—and God's victory. Without this perspective darkness would still hang over Calvary as thickly as in the Gospel narrative it did at the moment of Jesus' death, and as it did for the disciples who saw their hopes crushed there. When these very disciples later went out as apostles to proclaim "the gospel of the cross", they did this because the cross had for them become changed into a sign of victory. Their preaching was certainly—to use a sometimes misused term—a *theologia crucis*. But it was a *theologia gloriae crucis*.

All this means that the first and second act in the Christ drama is inseparably linked with the third, the exaltation and the continuation of the action of the Exalted. Without what happened after the cross, all that happened in the first and second acts would definitely belong to the past. The expression "what happened after the cross" has been chosen, because it refers not only to the exaltation to which the apostles bear witness, but also to all that happened through the ages and that is still happening among us. Two expressions from St John's Gospel illustrate its meaning. One is the saying about the corn of wheat: "Except a corn of wheat fall into the ground and die, it abideth alone: but if it die, it bringeth forth much fruit" (John 12.24). The other is the phrase with double meaning, characteristic of St John's Gospel: "I, if I be lifted up from the earth, will draw all men unto me" (John 12.32).

The first thing that happened afterwards was the growth of the Church of Jesus Christ. The Church took form as the fellowship, the *koinōnia*, where Christ was the giver of life, the saviour, and, at the same time, "the head", the Lord, Kyrios. It was not as though his action and the exercise of his power were limited to the Church. As we have already said, it is foreign to Christian faith to try to draw fixed limits to his sphere of power. It is also apparent that his influence makes itself felt along hidden paths, even in those who do not acknowledge him, who—to use a phrase common to St Paul and to Pär Lagerkvist—do not "bow the knee" at the name of Jesus. His field of power is not limited to his Church. But this does not prevent our eyes turning first of all to his Church. For two reasons: partly because the Church is the obvious witness to how Christ "draws men to himself" and creates *koinōnia* with himself, and partly because it is directly in his service and acts as the instrument for this "drawing to himself".

Turning our eyes in the first place to the Church of Christ may seem shocking. In the Creed, the Church is described as "one, holy, catholic". Nothing is more apparent than the failure to realize these qualities; division instead of unity, sin and worldliness instead of holiness, and confinement, enclosedness, and condemnation instead of the open heart of catholicity. All this is something which is noticed not only by those who stand outside, criticizing and not understanding. It is actually something which those who live and work within the Church recognize very well. The many failings of the Church are painfully obvious. But this is not the whole truth about the Church. It is no mere chance that the words about the Church are in the article of the Creed about the Holy Spirit, "the Lord, the Giver of Life". If the Church is something different from, something more than a witness to human failings, a sickly human society, this is entirely due to the fact that the Holy Spirit, Christ and his Spirit—the two are linked in the New Testament—here carries out his life-giving work in battle with all that destroys and damages life. There is as much incontrovertible evidence of this as there is of the Church's many failings through the ages. The epithets that the Creed uses about the Church become meaningless if they are taken statically, as if they were possessions. But they become full of meaning if they are taken dynamically, as something which "comes from the Lord who is the Spirit" (2 Cor. 3.18, RSV).

Now at last we find the reason why the title for this section is "Under the Law of the Spirit". The active presence of Christ in his Church is a presence in and through the Spirit. If we listen to the New Testament, we are struck by the power with which this theme dominates everything, especially when we think how often the Spirit has become hidden away in the history of Christian thought. Here are a few of the things that the Bible says: "the Spirit is life" (Rom. 8.10); "it is the spirit that quickeneth" (John 6.63); "the Spirit giveth life" (2 Cor. 3.6); "As many as are led by the Spirit of God, they are the sons of God. . . . The Spirit itself beareth witness with our spirit, that we are the children of God" (Rom. 8.14 and 16). The Spirit, on whose life-giving activity all is dependent, is not just any undefined spiritual power. The Spirit is defined by his relation to Christ. The connection between them can amount to—apparent—identity: "the Lord is that Spirit" (2 Cor. 3.17). But actually the relationship is not regarded as one of identity. The Gospel of St John, like the rest of the New Testament, sees it from a double aspect. In the parting conversations, we read that Jesus still has much to say, that the disciples cannot yet bear: "when he, the Spirit of truth, is come, he will guide you into all truth." So the Spirit will say things that Jesus has not said yet. But this does not mean that the Spirit would act independently, without relation to Christ. On the contrary: "He shall glorify me: for he shall receive of mine, and shall shew it unto you" (John 16.12–14).

In the Johannine statements, flexibility and fixity are combined. The flexibility, the elasticity, consists in the Spirit having something new to say in every age—he never ceases to lead men "into all the truth". The fixity springs from the fact that "Jesus Christ is the same yesterday, and today, and for ever" (Heb. 13.8). And the message about him is the same, given once for all in the apostolic witness of the New Testament writings, and in the holy actions of the sacraments. In preaching and in sacrament, what happened in the past becomes a living reality in the present. The first and second acts of the Christ drama are included in the third. Both forms of proclamation—the Word and the Sacraments—are the instruments by which the Spirit builds up the Church of Christ. When in Christian terminology they are described as "the means of grace", this must mean that they function as bearers of the radical gospel.

There are good reasons for adding some comments on the preaching of the word, of the message of Christ. It is clear that this preaching has an essential and permanent function in the Church of Christ. Paul's words in the Epistle to the Romans are permanently valid: "how shall they believe in him of whom they

have not heard? and how shall they hear without a preacher?"
(Rom. 10.14). The question is unanswerable. But this does not
mean that preaching is only possible in the form of sermons
preached at services arranged by the Christian Church. There is no
question of this kind of exclusiveness. Even within the framework
of services, preaching of Christ can take place in other forms than
that of a sermon. But preaching of Christ functions in many other
variations: in personal encounter, in personal talks (whether in the
form of confession or not)—and not least in acts of service that
bear witness to, that proclaim the power of Christ. To return to
preaching in services, it cannot unfortunately always be claimed
that this is effective, an instrument for the Spirit. But viewing
preaching with no illusions in this way does not reduce its importance. Within the shifting wide extent of preaching, the sermon
retains its importance. The purpose of what has been said is to
emphasize the demands that must be made, fundamentally
emphasizing the greatness and the importance of the task. And in
this connection, a word needs to be said about the sacraments,
Baptism and Communion. In the course of time, they too have
been subject to risks that are inherent in human interpretation and
administration. But at the same time in their fixed structure they
possess a resistance which gives them exceptional powers to stand
sentinel over the radical gospel.

That function of the Spirit which St John's Gospel describes
with the words, "he shall glorify me", is fulfilled when the Spirit—
to use an expression of Martin Luther's—makes the word living,
that is to say, when the message about Christ shows its power to
involve. The "glorifying" consists in Christ's power being revealed
and functioning. This can also be described as: Christ works
through his Spirit. What happens is that he, the living Lord,
involves man, creates confidence, conquers man and wins him,
sets him in living fellowship with himself, which at the same time is
fellowship with God. In so doing, he continues and completes the
action which he once performed during the days of his earthly life,
and which now, as the Exalted One, he can fulfil without hindrance,
The emphasis here lies primarily on the fellowship, the *koinōnia*,
which comes into being. Through this he puts into practice the
radical gospel, now as then. It is in the very fact that he "draws
unto himself", links with himself, takes people and puts them in
fellowship with himself, that we meet the gospel in all its radical

force. For all this happens, not because of any merit or qualifications from man's side, but simply because of unearned and
undeserved *agapē*.

It is most important to keep the "now" and the "then" linked.
To put the emphasis on what Christ does now as the living Lord
does not reduce the significance of the picture drawn in the
Gospels. It is really the other way round: what happens today would
lose its meaning unless we keep our eyes on the picture of the
preaching and actions of Jesus as told in the Gospels. Without that,
the radical gospel would not remain intact, or be shielded from
adulteration. But, on the other hand, it is just as important that
what happened is continued in what is happening now. And this
for two reasons. First, because this makes it obvious that a relationship of faith is primarily involvement and *koinonia* with Christ, and
not primarily an acceptance of a number of doctrines as true.
"Doctrine" is fully justified in its place. Any relationship with God,
which is determined by relationship with Christ, has undoubtedly
affirmations to make both about God and about Christ—and about
man and about the world. But this "doctrine" is not—as it would
appear to intellectual thought—one of the objects of faith. It is a
manifestation of faith.

Secondly, what the New Testament calls salvation, *sōtēria*, is
given its character by being mediated and given by Christ, as the
living Lord, as he who belongs to the sphere of God. The emphasis
lies, as we have already said, on fellowship, *koinōnia*. Because the
gospel is radical and because admission to fellowship comes
without merit or qualification from man's side, it takes the form of
forgiveness of sins. But forgiveness of sins cannot then, as we find
so often in recent theology, be regarded only from a negative point
of view, as the remission of guilt. Nor is it merely acceptance of the
truth that Christ once in the past took away sin and guilt, but it is
an encounter with Christ who is *now* taking away sin and guilt.
Above all, the thing that gives to forgiveness of sins its deepest
and principal meaning is fellowship, sharing in the life that is
God's. "Truly", says 1 John 1.3, "our fellowship is with the
Father, and with his Son Jesus Christ." Martin Luther gives a
corresponding description of the meaning of *sōtēria* in his interpretation of the Lord's Supper when he writes that the gift here
given is "the forgiveness of sins, life and blessedness". *Sōtēria* has
an eschatological character, both through what happens at the

present time, and because the *koinōnia* of faith includes a hope which stretches out beyond the limits of time and mortality. It is in this sense that Paul writes: "I am persuaded that neither death, nor life . . . shall be able to separate us from the love of God, which is in Christ Jesus our Lord" (Rom. 8.38–9).

The time has now come to look more closely at what the radical gospel means—and what it does not mean. The radical gospel and the radical law go together. Christ has not only proclaimed the radical gospel, he has also put it into effect in action. In the same way he has not only proclaimed the radical law, but has also put it into effect, fulfilled it, by his obedience unto death upon the cross. Now it is possible to speak about the law—and many people have done so—in such a way that the radical nature of the gospel is destroyed. It is also possible to speak about the radical gospel as if it made the law of none effect. Let us look a little more closely at these two problems, beginning with some New Testament statements about the law. "Christ is the end of the law" (Rom. 10.4); to be "under grace" is the opposite of to be "under the law" (Rom. 6.14). "The law was given by Moses, but grace and truth came by Jesus Christ" (John 1.17). If quotations of this kind might lead us to believe that the law had become a thing of the past through Christ, we find, on the other hand, such expressions as "the law of Christ" (Gal. 6.2), "the law of the Spirit of life" (Rom. 8.2), "the perfect law of liberty" (James 1.25). The First Epistle of John speaks of an old commandment which at the same time is "a new commandment" (1 John 2.7–8).

There might be thought to be some contradiction between saying that the law has come to its end in Christ and yet speaking of a law of Christ. But the appearance of contradiction only lasts while it is unclear in what context Christ is spoken of as "the end of the law". It is clear that in the New Testament there is a context where the law has no longer any say, where it has been put out of action. This happens when the radical gospel is at work. It happens —both in the Gospels and in the Epistles—as soon as we are dealing with *sōtēria*, with the announcement of the forgiveness of sins, with grace, with justification, in fact with being brought into fellowship with God. This does not come about, to use Paul's term, through "the deeds of the law", nor by reason of qualifications earned by fulfilling the law. Here, in this context where the undeserved love of God reigns, the law has been taken off the order paper, it has no longer any say, it has no power to accuse or condemn.

Theological discussion of law and gospel has sometimes become —I might almost say degenerated into becoming—a discussion of the right order, as if it were a choice between the alternatives: first law and then gospel, or first gospel and then law. A system of this kind has obvious risks, primarily that Christian faith and Christian life are put in a strait-jacket which does not correspond to the real conditions of life.

The thesis that the law precedes the gospel may be formulated as meaning that the law must do its work first, complete its work, before the gospel can make its entry. If the gospel is to enter in and function, this can be only where the law has achieved a due and full measure of broken-hearted contrition, confession of sin, and penitence. Without achieving this, man would be excluded from the gospel. In support of this kind of view, it may be pointed out that in St Mark's Gospel Jesus begins his preaching of the kingdom and its near approach by saying: "repent ye, and believe the gospel", or that he repeatedly said he had not come to call the righteous, but sinners to repentance. But to interpret these sayings in these terms would be a grave misinterpretation. Jesus never investigates whether "the law" has effected the necessary degree of confession of sin, contrition, and penitence in the hearts of those he is helping. His very words that he has come to call sinners really points in the opposite direction. He is helping those who seek his help—and not only that: he looks for people to help. An invitation such as "Come unto me, all ye that labour and are heavy laden" is not an invitation with strings attached; it is an unconditional invitation to people to come as they are, to come with the difficulties and problems that weigh them down, of whatever kind they may be. There is a deep truth in some words that Bonhoeffer writes in his *Letters from Prison*: "Jesus did not make every man a sinner first." The expression "Come as you are" is fully justified. With his gospel, the radical gospel, Jesus accepts people as they are. But he does not let them remain as they are.

But how misleading the theory is that the law must first complete its work before the gospel can step in, is not fully realized until we view the matter from a different point of view. Conviction of sin and confession of sin and guilt is not something which, as it were, has to be performed before the attainment of fellowship with Christ which is created by the gospel. What really happens is the opposite, this conviction comes fully and clearly into focus and the confession deepens as we enjoy fellowship with Christ. It is only in that context that it becomes apparent what demands the law makes and how radical they are; how the law unmasks and condemns and puts to death. We are not dealing with something that is going gradually to disappear, but, on the contrary, with something that is going to increase more and more. It is only in this context that it becomes increasingly clear how all fellowship with God is based on the radical gospel, on God's undeserved *agapē*. It is here that we find the real meaning of words such as these: "If we confess our sins, he [God] is faithful and just to forgive us our sins, and to cleanse us from all unrighteousness" (1 John 1.9). Here there is no room for the idea that confession is an activity that earns merit. Confession is an elementary, unavoidable expression of the actual situation, and our eyes turn wholly to God's "faithfulness" which shows itself in his forgiving and cleansing us.

But just as it is impossible to fix law and gospel in a systematic order, first law, then gospel, so it is equally impossible to put them in the order, first gospel, then law. This formula has been receiving attention at the present time, not least because Karl Barth has championed this order. If this line of thought were consistently applied, it would make the law, and fulfilment of the law, a monopoly of Christians. This would involve a denial of the law of creation by which God restrains and blocks the destructive forces and encourages actions that serve creation, that is to say, serve the love of God. The law that Christ reveals in all its radical nature is no *other* law than this law of creation. God's law is one and the same, both when it is working through people who do not confess his name, and when it is working through people who have been incorporated by the radical gospel, by Christ, into the sphere of fellowship with God. The Christian has no monopoly either of the law or of fulfilment of the law. To say that there is no fulfilment of the will of God outside the area of Christian life, but that within it the law is fulfilled, is both misleading and is evidence of a false exclusiveness, an undervaluing of what God does through the law of creation, a sign of Christian arrogance.

Further, to be involved by Christ, to have *koinōnia* with him, means being immediately put into service. Fellowship with him expresses itself, and must express itself, in acts of service. It is not only the Epistle of James which makes it clear that faith without works is dead. We find the same thing, with all possible emphasis in that "apostle of faith", Paul: "though I have all faith, so that I could remove mountains, and have not charity, I am nothing" (1 Cor. 13.2). The New Testament loves to speak of Christ as our Example. This does not mean that we are to do exactly the same things as he did, not that kind of imitation, but it means that our service is to be of the same kind as his, an imitation in loving service. That is why the New Testament sums up all commandments as love to God and love to our neighbour. Love to God expresses itself in faith—trust—and obedience, love to our neighbour in realistic, serving care. The demands thus made are both unflinchingly firm and endlessly elastic. There is no catalogue of directions and patterns of behaviour, unaltering at all times—that would be to go back to the moralism of the Pharisees, which the radical gospel did away with. The broad lines are given, once and for all, but their application varies, and must vary, as times change.

It now become possible to determine what is meant by the contradiction "under grace—under the law". To be under grace does not mean that God's law is thrust aside or made of none effect. But it does mean a radical change in the attitude to the law. There is no longer any question of "bondage under the law". The radical gospel has set us free from all moralism of that kind. To be a servant of Christ is not bondage, it is a privilege, a gift. We encounter the law then as "the law of the Spirit of life", "the law of Christ". To serve him may involve painful difficulties and hardships. It may have something of the character of "suffering with Christ". But with all this, to serve him is still a privilege and a gift. And the words of Jesus retain their validity: "my yoke is easy, and my burden is light" (Matt. 11.30).

The Drama of Christ and the Image of God

In giving this final section the title of the Drama of Christ and the Image of God, we are not embarking on any new theme. The whole of this chapter has really been dealing with this subject. The connection between the drama of Christ and the image of God has been illustrated from different sides. So what follows is in essence a summary and a closer definition of what we have already written about.

In the New Testament Christ and his work are viewed from a double aspect. He is a man like us, living under the same conditions as all other men. He is a man battling with temptation, praying and suffering. During the course of time, some theological views have found it difficult to allow his "true humanity" its full expression. People have regarded his temptations as merely apparent, or—like Thomas Aquinas—have thought that his sufferings touched only a lower level in Christ's soul. But speculations of this kind are quite foreign to the New Testament. Here we find no kind of limitation of the "true humanity" of Christ. But at the same time we find acknowledgement of Christ as Lord, as Kyrios. That is to say, he is given the same titles of honour as the Old Testament uses about God. As Kyrios, Christ is the object of invocation and prayer. But this Kyrios is none other than the crucified Jesus of Nazareth. When in the early Christian congregations there began to appear "docetic" tendencies making the living Lord eclipse the real humanity of Jesus, the Bible authors—John and Paul—emphatically repudiated this: Christian orthodoxy is that "Jesus is Christ, come in the flesh" (1 John 4.2; cf. 1 Cor. 11.26).

In its Creeds—the Apostles' and the Nicene—the Christian Church has attempted to preserve this biblical double aspect of Christ's person and work. The Creeds have not attempted to say anything except what was already stated in the New Testament. The same intention is found in the Definition of Chalcedon, which has some right to be regarded as the climax of the early Church's work on "Christology". When that famous and much-discussed Definition states that the "two natures" of Christ are united "unconfusedly, unchangeably, indivisibly, inseparably", there is no biblical ring about the words. The terminology is quite foreign to the New Testament. Equally foreign is the whole question how "the two natures" are related to one another. And yet the intention is undeniably to stand sentinel over the Bible view of Christ, with its double aspect of the person of Christ, and at the same time of the unity and integrity of that person. Whether it succeeded, whether that standing sentinel was effective, is another matter. A glance at the later history of theology shows that it was not always effective, and that this ineffectiveness was to some extent connected with the unserviceable terminology with which it was working. The history of theology shows instances of both the "confusion" and the separation that Chalcedon was trying to avoid. The confusion took the form of "docetic" tendencies, which more or less regarded Christ as a disguised god wandering around on earth. The separation tried to distinguish between what Christ did "as God", *qua deus*, and what he did "as man", *qua homo*. We are not concerned here to analyse the Christology of the early Church or of later theology, but only to provide some background to the brief summary of the Christ drama that follows.

The main point of this is that we have here a unitary and indivisible life's work, and that this has to be seen from a double aspect: as a human work and as a divine work. It is not a work that can be divided up into being partly human and partly divine. From one side, the whole life's work is a human work, through and through, but, from the other side, it is a divine work, through and through.

The human work of Christ is a calling, fulfilled in conflict with the destructive powers, in unbroken obedience to God, and in unbroken solidarity with man.

If we say that Christ's work is characterized by obedience to God and by solidarity with man, this is not two different things, but one and the same thing seen from different points of view. Obedience to God would not be obedience unless it showed itself in a life of service, which solidarity with man demands: "The Son of Man came . . . to minister." Serving in solidarity with man meant that obedience to God came—necessarily—to take the form shown in the conclusion of that text: "to minister, and to give his life a ransom for many."

"Obedient unto death"—that is how the New Testament describes the human life of Jesus in relation to God. Obedience involves faithfulness to the call, the task, given to him and accepted by him. We have already seen how this faithfulness expressed itself in battle against, and victory over, the demonic temptations that tried to induce him to go a way different from the way the motto of which was "to minister". The picture which the Gospels draw here show that it was not just a matter of gaining a clear insight into the task to which he was called, and in being faithful to it, but that it was a test of obedience, made increasingly stringent right up to the final suffering and death. This test of obedience concerned both his relation to God and his own personal integrity.

This can also be viewed from another side. The test of obedience turns out to consist of taking the obvious risks involved in the call, to be the revealer and the executor of the radical law and the radical gospel, both indissolubly bound up with one another. The one was as challenging as the other: Jesus' behaviour was branded as dethroning the law and as being blasphemy against God. For instance, when he showed in action that the commandment about the sabbath was not allowed to stand in the way of the action which love demanded, this appeared to the religious leaders of his day to be an affront to the majesty of the law and an undermining of the firm foundation on which relationship to God was based. It appeared—necessarily from their point of view—as "the end of the law". And it was indeed the end of the law in the sense that what was abrogated was the moralistic understanding and interpretation of the law. What was superseded, what came to an end, was that interpretation of the law which made the law serve the cause of self-justification, which made the law the "way of salvation" by which man, through fulfilling the various commandments and regulations, could present himself as "righteous" before God, as if he could "save himself". Actually the way Jesus acted was not a dissolution of the law, but an establishing of God's law in all its radical fulness. The Greek word which the New Testament uses when it speaks of Christ as "the end of the law". the word *telos*, has a double meaning: it can mean "end" in the sense of putting an end to, but it can also mean "goal, fulfilment", and it is this second meaning which is fully justified in this context. The thing that is put an end to is the moralistic law, the thing that is established and fulfilled is the law of love in all its radical fulness. Therefore Jesus' carrying out of the radical law is indissolubly linked with his carrying out of the radical gospel, with his "seeking and saving that which was lost" (Luke 19.10) and with his sovereign administering of the forgiveness of sins—all of which necessarily appeared to the religious leaders of his time as usurping God's power, as blasphemy pure and simple. The risks that Jesus took in the fulfilment of his call were of such a kind that a life and death conflict was unavoidable.

The way that led to suffering and death was inescapable. The confrontation between, on the one hand, the radical nature of the law and the gospel, and, on the other hand, the actual human situation, made it inescapable. Jesus went the way of sacrificial suffering in obedience to God and in solidarity with man—in battle with the powers of destruction. In this his human life's work reached its fulfilment. This theme—the theme of sacrifice—is treated in the New Testament with a multitude of variations. To take but a few examples, it speaks of how he "died for our sins" (1 Cor. 15.3), of how he "gave himself for our sins" (Gal. 1.4), of how he was "offered to bear the sins of many" (Heb. 9.28), of Christ as "our passover . . . sacrificed for us" (1 Cor. 5.7), of Christ "being made a curse for us" (Gal. 3.13). In returning here to this biblical theme of sacrifice, we are illustrating the theme both from the aspect of human action and from that of divine action.

The sacrifice of Jesus, as a human action, is determined by obedience to God and by solidarity with man. From this point of view, these biblical quotations are full of meaning. In solidarity with mankind, Jesus submits to the conditions of sin and suffers its consequences right to the bitter end of being forsaken by God. He assents to and takes upon himself and endures the judgement— the judgement of wrath—that the radical law pronounces on human sin, he bears this burden and endures the consequences that this entails. He dies in the literal sense of the words "for our sins", he dies the death "of the curse" that crucifixion involves. All this is full of deep meaning, and reveals the secret of love that offers itself for others in the battle against evil—so long as all this is viewed from the point of view of solidarity with man and obedience to God. But it would lose its meaning and it would ruin the Christian image of God if we were to regard the sacrifice and suffering of Christ as a punishment which God laid upon the innocent, to be the equivalent of, and the compensation for, the punishment which mankind deserved to suffer. Jesus' following of the path of sacrifice unto death on the cross was done in obedience to God, that is to say, in accordance with his will. But this did not mean that the crucifixion was a punishment that God laid upon him and required of him. It was men who crucified him, not God. That he submitted to the judgement of God that falls on human sin did not mean that this judgement applied to him personally. It meant instead that the judgement fell on him in his solidarity with those who were under the power of sin. In this connection we have good reason to remember the prophetic words about the suffering servant of the Lord: "he hath borne our griefs, and carried our sorrows: yet we did esteem him stricken, smitten of God, and afflicted" (Isa. 53.4). The same mistake which "we" in the prophet's description made has since also been made by a good deal of theology.

The path of unimpaired obedience led to death, but a death that was a victory, victory over the power of sin and death. The work of Christ, seen as a human work, results in his appearing as the New Man, the man who inaugurates a new humanity. This theme is given its classical formulation in the Bible when in the Epistle to the Romans, Paul contrasts "Adam" and Christ. "Adam" is there regarded not as a single individual, who existed once at the beginning of history, but as a description of mankind under the power of sin and death. Adam is the man of disobedience, Christ the man of obedience, the man who by his very obedience won the victory over the power of sin and death, thus representing a turning-point in God's history with man, introducing a new age and becoming the head of a new humanity.

This interpretation of the human work of Jesus directs our eyes forward to his continuing work. The thing that made possible the continuation of this work, the thing that was its basis was that he retained his personal integrity, that he was not overcome by, but himself overcame, the anti-God powers. The victory was his own victory, but it was no victory that he kept for himself. We find the same attitude to the continuation of Christ's work in one of the most remarkable books of modern times about the Christ drama, Einar Billing's book about the atonement, *Försoning*, published in 1908. The main emphasis of this book is on an analysis of the work of forgiveness that Jesus carried out during his life on earth, not as an act of "fairness", but as inseparably linked with "righteousness" and radical judgement of sin. The temptation that he overcame in the face of suffering and death was to let judgement have its way and to give up the way of forgiveness. When he instead submitted to suffering and death, this happened because "only by going to his death could he retain his life as the Forgiver". "So as not to be compelled to judge and condemn, but to be able still to go to all these groping, fumbling, lost little people with his old gospel now and to the end of days—that is why he goes to his death."[1] It may be true that in Billing's investigations there are

[1] Einar Billing, *Försoning* (1908), pp. 71 and 86.

traces of psychological analysis beyond what is possible. But this does not diminish the value of the perspectives that Billing opens up, for his basic idea is that the significance of the cross cannot be understood if it is regarded as an isolated fact, but only if it is seen in connection both with what went before and what followed afterwards.

So the work of Christ is a human work through and through, but at the same time it is a divine work through and through. God is involved in everything that happens here. When Jesus acts in obedience to God and in solidarity with man, this is at the same time one of God's own acts. God's relation to the Christ drama does not merely consist of, is not limited to, his having "sent" Christ to the world with a special task to perform, and, when that task was performed, having "exalted" him. This kind of limitation of God's relation to the Christ drama, by which God would, as it were, have stood back waiting while Christ carried out his work on earth, does not correspond to the picture drawn in the New Testament. In that, God does not stand at a distance, waiting for the result. Instead, he is actively engaged in what is going on. He functions as the subject. When Jesus is victorious over the temptation that might have led him to depart from and fail in his appointed task, it is God's own victory. When Jesus reveals God's law, the law of creation in its full radical nature, it is God who is revealing the meaning of the law, positively as a demand, negatively as a judgement on sin. When Jesus acts as bearer and steward of the radical gospel, this is one of God's own actions, an action by which he reveals his "tender mercies". Jesus' battle against the powers of evil is God's own battle—God enters the hand-to-hand battle against them. When in the exercise of the radical gospel Jesus goes the way of sacrifice and suffering unto death, this is the way of sacrifice of God's own love, the hard way by which this love forces its way through to victory.

Everything that has here been briefly said about God's relation to the Christ drama may be summed up in the text which has often been quoted: "God was in Christ, reconciling the world unto himself". It cannot be more clearly stated that God acted, functioned, was the subject in the settlement that is here called the atonement. The same point of view recurs whenever the New Testament speaks of atonement and salvation. It never says that God has been reconciled, or that Christ has reconciled him. God is never regarded as the object of an act of reconciliation carried out towards him. Admittedly God has been "reconciled" but only by "reconciling himself with the world". This has happened in and through Christ. Christ is described as a means of "propitiation" (Rom. 3.25), that is to say, as the instrument by which the reconciliation was carried out. Christ has become the means of propitiation, the means of expiating sin, by being obedient unto death, by bearing the burden of sin and guilt in solidarity with man—bearing it without being overcome by the power of sin, bearing it as the victor. The thought behind it is not that Christ has "changed God's mind" or placated him. That would be making God the object of the act of reconciliation. But he is not its object, he is the subject. What happened, happened in agreement with, in fulfilment of, God's "counsel" (Acts 2.23). A main thought in the Epistles is that when God intervenes, steps in, and acts in the Christ drama, he fulfils what he has promised, thus showing himself to be truthful, faithful, and righteous. The claim is that God has fulfilled his plan and carried out what he promised. "It pleased the Father that in him [Christ] should all fulness dwell; and, having made peace through the blood of his cross, by him to reconcile all things unto himself" (Col. 1.19–20).

The work that God accomplished through the Christ drama was work of salvation and reconciliation. "For God sent not his son into the world to condemn the world; but that the world through him might be saved" (John 3.17). This does not mean that God's radical opposition to, and judgement on, evil was abrogated and had ceased to function. It is characteristic that the same Gospel of St John that says "not . . . to condemn" also says "For judgement I [Christ] am come into this world" (John 9.39). The apparent contradiction is not really a contradiction. The objective was salvation, not judgement. But salvation could not be put into effect without judgement. This has two aspects. First, the love that "offers itself" and "fulfils the law" unmasks and condemns the things that love is opposed to: "this is the condemnation, that light is come into the world, and men loved darkness rather than light, because their deeds were evil" (John 3.19). Secondly, the act of salvation was from one point of view an act of condemnation, a condemnation of the power of evil—the New Testament leaves us in no doubt about that. In the shadow of the cross we read: "Now is the judgement of this world: now shall the prince of this world be cast out" (John 12.31). The sacrifice that was completed on the cross was, at the heart of the apparent powerlessness, a definite victory.

Reconciliation means the restoration of a fellowship which has been broken. God's fellowship with the world had been broken, shattered. It is this fellowship with God that is now being restored in and through the Christ drama. It is restored through Christ's fellowship with God remaining unbroken. No anti-God power had been able to break it. The anti-God powers, the enemies, had been conquered. They had no power over him, they could not master him. In relation to him, their dominion was broken. And so God's reconciliation "with the world" was restored. It was a reconciliation in and through Christ, a reconciliation for his sake, but at the same time a reconciliation that God himself effected.

In the New Testament this reconciliation is seen from a double aspect. Seen from one side, it is a non-recurrent action. As such it is a reality, a fact. This can be put in many ways: for instance, Christ has inaugurated a new humanity; a new age has come; Christ has broken through the anti-God opposition; he has lived in, and suffered in, God's love in the world; through him fellowship with God has got a firm footing in the world.

But reconciliation is not merely something that happened once for all. It is at the same time something that is continuously going on. The reconciliation that has been effected through Christ does not in any way mean that the world is now living in full and unbroken fellowship with God, that the anti-God forces have ceased to function, and that there is no longer any opposition to God. Paul, in the same breath as he writes that God was in Christ reconciling the world unto himself, continues by talking about "ambassadors" to whom is committed "the word of reconciliation". And the whole passage leads up to the exhortation: "we pray you in Christ's stead, be ye reconciled to God" (2 Cor. 5.19–20). In and through this "word of reconciliation", Christ continues through the ages the work of reconciliation.

This continuing work of reconciliation and salvation is inseparably linked with the exaltation of Christ. Everything that is here said of Christ as the Risen and Living One, of his ascension into heaven, of his sitting at the right hand of the Father, and of the sending and "pouring out" of the Spirit, is all intended to illustrate how the work of reconciliation continues, how still, and to the end of time, in the "word of reconciliation" and the holy sacraments Christ through his Spirit is making effective the same radical gospel as he preached during the days of his earthly life. The victory was his own victory. But the exaltation that was linked with this victory does not mean that he retained it for himself "as a prize of war", enthroned in far-away exaltation. On the contrary, it means that he is constantly re-enacting his work of reconciliation, and thereby demonstrating that the reconciliation and the radical gospel really applied to "the world". What happens in this re-enacting is the thing that St John's Gospel describes in the simple and inexhaustible phrase: "as many as received him, to them gave he power to become the sons of God" (John 1.12). To be sons of God is to live in his fellowship under the shelter of the forgiveness of sins, sharing the life that belongs to God, "eternal life".

From this point of view, the full meaning of the relation of the image of God to the Christ drama stands revealed. In the Epistle to the Colossians Christ is described as "the image of the invisible God" (1.15). God is, and remains in the conditions of earthly life, the Invisible One, whom no man has seen or can see, "the Father in secret". But God's image is reflected, as the New Testament over and over again assures us, in Christ and what he did. The glory of God shines out "in the face of Jesus Christ" (2 Cor. 4.6), Christ is "the brightness of his [God's] glory, and the express image of his person" (Heb. 1.3). St John's Gospel puts it concretely: "he that hath seen me, hath seen the Father", and the reason given is that the words Christ speaks, he speaks not of himself, and the works he does, "the Father that dwelleth in me, he doeth the works" (John 14.9–10).

An image of the Invisible. What does the image show? First and foremost this: "Hereby perceive we the love of God, because he laid down his life for us" (1 John 3.16)—the love that is "the fulfilling of the law" and at the same time puts into effect the radical gospel. We read more of this in the Epistle to the Ephesians 3.16–19, where it speaks of being "able to comprehend" that "which passeth knowledge", being "able to comprehend . . . what is the breadth, and length, and depth, and height; and to know the love of Christ, which passeth knowledge, that ye might be filled with all the fulness of God".

The work of Christ is God's own work. From this point of view light is thrown over the Bible witness to Christ and over its *universal perspective.* "And the Word was made flesh, and dwelt among us, (and we beheld his glory, the glory as of the only begotten of the Father,) full of grace and truth" (John 1.14). The Word was made flesh. The Word that was made flesh, or to use the theological term, was incarnate, is God's Word of Creation. This "Word" is described in St John's Gospel both as being in relationship to God and as being identical with God: "In the beginning was the Word, and the Word was with God, and the Word was God." That sentence about the incarnation of the Word might well be described as a summary of the Bible witness to Christ. We have to look at it from a double point of view.

Let us first see what it means in regard to the earthly life of Christ. Sometimes in the history of theology the incarnation is linked only with the birth of Christ, the Christmas message. In that case the incarnation is regarded as a once-only event, separate from the work of salvation and reconciliation which was completed on the cross. But this kind of separation can only obscure the real meaning of the event. It does not reflect the meaning of St John's Gospel which in the same verse speaks of the incarnation of the Word and of beholding the glory of Christ. The incarnation is not something that *only* refers to Christ's entry into the world. That was the beginning of the incarnation. But it was put into effect in and through the work of salvation. It is put into effect by Christ's living God into the world, fighting God into the world, suffering and overcoming God into the world. The incarnation of God is completed when this life's work was completed.

But this "the Word was made flesh" is not related only to the earthly work of Christ. The incarnation opens up the universal perspective of faith in Christ to its full, unlimited extent. The Word that was made flesh was the Creative Word of God: "All things were made by him; and without him was not anything made that was made" (John 1.3). This view point is not unique in St John, we find it elsewhere in the New Testament. We read in Colossians 1.16, RV: "in him were all things created, in the heavens and upon the earth, things visible and things invisible... all things have been created through him, and unto him." Statements of this kind may appear to a modern reader to be abstract and unintelligible speculation. But actually they have deep meaning. Fundamentally they express the final word on the Christ drama and the image of God: that the God of creation and the God of salvation are one and the same. They tell us that the meaning and purpose of salvation cannot be understood unless they are seen from the perspective of creation, and that the meaning and purpose of creation can similarly not be understood unless they are seen from the perspective of salvation. The origin, meaning, and purpose of creation are revealed in the work of salvation that God effects in and through Christ. The words that everything is created in, through, and unto, correspond directly with the song of praise, the doxology at the end of Romans 11 that now must form the tail-piece of all that I have said of the Christ drama and the image of God:

O the depth of the riches both of the wisdom and knowledge of God! how unsearchable are his judgements, and his ways past tracing out! . . . For of him, and through him, and unto him, are all things: to him be the glory for ever. Amen.

GENERAL INDEX

BIBLE PASSAGES